LAUBACH WAY TO ENGLISH

TEACHER'S MANUAL FOR SKILL BOOK 2

LAUBACH WAY TO READING

Jeanette D. Macero
Martha A. Lane

New Readers Press
Publishing Division of
Laubach Literacy International

Materials needed for this level of the Laubach Way to English series:

For the teacher

- Laubach Way to English: *ESL Teacher's Manual for Skill Book 2*
- Laubach Way to English: *ESL Illustrations for Skill Book 2*

For the student

- Laubach Way to Reading: *Skill Book 2 Short Vowel Sounds*
- Laubach Way to Reading: *City Living*
- Laubach Way to Reading: *Checkups for Skill Book 2*

ISBN 0-88336-393-3

New Readers Press
Publishing Division of
Laubach Literacy International
Box 131, Syracuse, New York 13210

Printed in the United States of America

Designed by Kay Koschnick, Caris Lester, Jeanne Oates, Martha Parks

20 19 18 17 16 15 14 13 12 11
10 9 8 7 6 5 4 3 2

Table of Contents

Page

18 **Acknowledgments**

19 **About the Authors**

20 **Introduction: What Is the "Laubach Way to English"?**

22 **General Procedures**

23 **Lesson 1**

24 **I. Conversation Skills**

Dialog (Buying a gift)
Vocabulary: Review of Chart and Story Words
Vocabulary: *wear, put on, take off*
Vocabulary: Articles of Clothing and Jewelry
Vocabulary: Names of Colors with *light* and *dark*
Structure Focus: Two Modifiers
Structure Focus: Indirect Object with *to* (Review)
Structure Focus: Indirect Object with *for*
Structure Focus: Questions with *Who* in Subject Position
Structure Focus: Short Answers to *Who* Questions
Pronunciation: /ē/ and /i/
Pronunciation: /b/ and /v/
Oral Evaluation

36 **II. Reading**

Chart 1: Page 2 (Short Sound of *i*)
Story: A Ring for Kim
Skills Practice: Review *-s* and *-'s*
Skills Practice: Adding *-s'*
Skills Practice: Ending Sounds -ng/g
Skills Practice: Ending Sounds -ng/n

45 **III. Writing**

Writing Lesson: Page 4
Homework: Page 5
Reading and Writing Evaluation

48 Lesson 2

48 **I. Conversation Skills**

Dialog (It's time for dinner.)
Vocabulary: Toys
Vocabulary: The Verbs *talk, whistle, sing*
Vocabulary: *house* and Names of Rooms
Vocabulary: Daily Activities (Verbs)
Structure Focus: *with* Phrases to Indicate Companion
Structure Focus: *with* Phrases to Indicate Instrument
Structure Focus: The Use of *for* to Indicate Purpose
Structure Focus: The Use of *or*
Vocabulary: The Verb *want*
Structure Focus: Information Questions with *Which*
Pronunciation: /i/ and /e/, /f/ and /v/
Oral Evaluation

59 **II. Reading**

Chart 2: Page 6 (Short Sound of *i*)
Story: The Hills' Dinner
Skills Practice: Adding and Subtracting *-ing*
Skills Practice: Beginning Sounds w/wh
Skills Practice: Beginning Consonant Blend *br-*

63 **III. Writing**

Checkup: Page 8
Writing Lesson: Page 9
Homework: Pages 10-11
Reading and Writing Evaluation

66 **Lesson 3**

66 **I. Conversation Skills**

Dialog (Kitty greets Jimmy)
Vocabulary: Buildings in a City
Vocabulary: Adjectives (*tall, short, low; big, little; young, new, old; pretty, handsome, ugly*)
Vocabulary and Structure Focus: Weather Expressions
Vocabulary: The Verb *need*
Vocabulary: Flowers
Vocabulary: Persons One Knows
Vocabulary: Chart and Story Words (Personal Titles and Names)
Structure Focus: Prepositional Phrases as Noun Modifiers
Structure Focus: *There is* and *There are*
Structure Focus: Questions with *Is there* and *Are there*
Structure Focus: Short Answers with *There* + *be*
Structure Focus: Past Tense of *be (was/were)*
Structure Focus: Past Tense Questions with *be (was/were)*
Structure Focus: Short Answers with *was* and *were*
Pronunciation: /ā/ and /a/, /w/ and /v/
Oral Evaluation

80 **II. Reading**

Chart 3: Page 12 (Vowel sound of *y*)
Story: In the City
Skills Practice: Subtracting *-ing*
Skills Practice: Words Ending in *-le*

82 **III. Writing**

Writing Lesson: Page 14
Skills Practice: Vowels and Consonants
Homework: Page 15
Reading and Writing Evaluation

84 **Lesson 4**

84 **I. Conversation Skills**

Dialog (Getting ready for dinner)
Vocabulary: Chart and Story Words
Vocabulary: The Kitchen
Vocabulary: The Use of *here* and *there*
Structure Focus: Making Requests with Imperatives
Structure Focus: Negative Requests
Vocabulary: Polite Replies to Requests
Structure Focus: Questions with *What* in Subject Position
Structure Focus: Short Answers to Questions with *What*
Vocabulary: The Verb *like*
Structure Focus: The Use of the Infinitive
Pronunciation: /o/ and /u/, /w/ and /g/
Oral Evaluation

94 **II. Reading**

Chart 4: Page 16 (Short Sound of *u*)
Story: Duck Hunting

96 **III. Writing**

Checkup: Page 18
Writing Lesson: Page 19
Skills Practice: Doubling the Final Consonant Before Adding *-ing*
Homework: Pages 20-21
Reading and Writing Evaluation

100 **Lesson 5**

100 **I. Conversation Skills**

Dialog (How do you come to school?)
Vocabulary: Verbs and Adjectives
Vocabulary: *get* + Adjectives
Vocabulary: Means of Transportation
Vocabulary: *get* with Means of Transportation
Vocabulary: The Story Word *brick*
Vocabulary and Structure Focus: The Verb *tell* + a Direct Quotation
Structure Focus: Past Tense of *have (had)*
Structure Focus: Past Tense Questions with *have,* and Short Answers
Structure Focus: Questions with *How* and Answers with *By*
Structure Focus: Using the Infinitive to Express Purpose
Structure Focus: The Use of *think* + a Clause
Pronunciation: /a/ and /o/, /p/ and /f/
Oral Evaluation

110 **II. Reading**

Chart 5: Page 22 (Short Sound of *u*)
Story: Uncle Bud's Truck Gets Stuck
Skills Practice: Beginning Consonant Blend *tr-*
Skills Practice: Beginning Consonant Blend *st-*

112 **III. Writing**

Writing Lesson: Page 24
Skills Practice: Dropping Final Silent *e* Before Adding *-ing*
Homework: Page 25
Reading and Writing Evaluation

115 **Lesson 6**

116 **I. Conversation Skills**

Dialog (Buying eggs)
Vocabulary: Food in Containers
Vocabulary: *fresh* and *stale*
Vocabulary: Simple Measurements
Vocabulary: The Chart Word *bell*
Vocabulary: Chart and Story Words *hens, nest*
Vocabulary: Adjectives (*sick, well, slow, fast*)
Vocabulary: *very* + Adjective
Vocabulary: The Verb *help*
Structure Focus: Past Tense of Regular Verbs
Structure Focus: Questions and Answers in the Past Tense
Structure Focus: *say* + a Direct Quotation
Structure Focus: *a lot of* with Count and Non-count Nouns
Structure Focus: *a lot of* and *many/much*
Structure Focus: *many, a few / much, a little*
Structure Focus: Questions with *How many* and *How much*
Structure Focus: The Future Tense with *will*
Structure Focus: Questions with *will*
Structure Focus: Negative Statements with *will not/won't*
Structure Focus: Short Answers with *will/won't*
Pronunciation: /ā/ and /e/
Pronunciation: Sounds of the Regular Past Tense Verb Endings
Oral Evaluation

133 **II. Reading**

Chart 6: Page 26 (Short Sound of *e*)
Story: Eggs to Sell
Skills Practice: Contrasting the Short Vowels *i* and *u*
Skills Practice: Contrasting the Short Vowels *e* and *u*
Skills Practice: Review of Words with *br-, pr-, tr-, st-, str-*

136 **III. Writing**

Checkup: Page 28
Writing Lesson: Page 29
Writing Lesson: Page 30
Homework: Pages 30-31
Reading and Writing Evaluation

138 Lesson 7

139 **I. Conversation Skills**

Dialog (Calling the doctor)
Vocabulary: Some Chart and Story Words
Vocabulary: *before* and *after, first* and *last*
Vocabulary: Aches and Pains
Vocabulary: *take* and *put* + Medicine
Vocabulary and Structure Focus: Adverbs
Structure Focus: Questions with *How* and Answers with Adverbs
Structure Focus: The Noun Substitutes *one* and *it*
Structure Focus: Negative Statements in the Past Tense
Structure Focus: *tell* + a Clause
Pronunciation: /s/ and /th/, /t/ and /th/ as in *thank*
Oral Evaluation

147 **II. Reading**

Chart 7: Page 32 (Short Sound of *e*)
Story: Mr. Hunt's Friends
Skills Practice: Beginning Consonant Blend *fr-*
Skills Practice: Contrasting the Short Vowels *e* and *i*

149 **III. Writing**

Writing Lesson: Page 34
Skills Practice: Adding *-s* to Verbs
Skills Practice: *man/men, woman/women*
Skills Practice: Addressing an Envelope
Homework: Page 35
Reading and Writing Evaluation

153 **Lesson 8**

154 **I. Conversation Skills**

Dialog (Emergency phone call)
Vocabulary: Some Chart and Story Words
Vocabulary: Containers for Carrying Things
Vocabulary: Chart and Story Words (*marry, happy*)
Vocabulary: Prepositions of Location
Vocabulary: Story Words (*standing with my back to ______*)
Structure Focus: The Definite and Indefinite Articles *the* and *a*
Vocabulary: The Modal *can*
Structure Focus: Statements and Questions with *can*
Structure Focus: Short Answers with *can/can't*
Structure Focus: Affirmative Past Tense Statements with Irregular Verbs (*went, did, drank, sat, gave, bought, taught*)
Structure Focus: Past Tense Questions with Irregular Verbs
Structure Focus: Adjective + *that* Clause
Vocabulary and Structure Focus: Making Introductions with Appositives
Pronunciation: /d/, voiced /th/, unvoiced /th/
Oral Evaluation

165 **II. Reading**

Chart 8-A: Page 36 (Short Sound of *a*)
Story: The Black Cat
Chart 8-B: Page 38 (Short Sound of *a*)
Story: Jack Will Marry Ann
Skills Practice: Beginning Consonant Blend *bl-*
Skills Practice: Contrasting *bl-* and *br-*
Skills Practice: Contrasting the Short Vowels *a* and *e*

168 **III. Writing**

Writing Lesson: Page 40
Skills Practice: Review Adding *-ing* to Verbs
Homework: Page 41
Reading and Writing Evaluation

170 **Lesson 9**

170 **I. Conversation Skills**

Dialog (Picnic in the park)
Vocabulary: Chart and Story Words (Factories)
Vocabulary: The Story Word *path*
Vocabulary: Seating
Vocabulary: The Simple Fractions *half* and *a quarter*
Structure Focus: *another one, the other one,* and *the others*
Structure Focus: *very, too,* and *enough*
Vocabulary: Future Time Expressions
Structure Focus: The Use of *be + going to* to Indicate Future Time
Structure Focus: Past Tense of Irregular Verbs (*rang, gave, drank, swam, sat, ran*)
Structure Focus: Negative Statements in the Past Tense
Pronunciation: /o/ and /uu/, /n/ and /ng/
Oral Evaluation

180 **II. Reading**

Chart 9: Page 42 (Short Sound of *a*)
Story: The Glass Factory
Skills Practice: Beginning Consonant Blend *gl-*
Skills Practice: Beginning Consonant Blend *gr-*
Skills Practice: Contrasting *gl-* and *gr-*
Skills Practice: Contrasting the Short Vowels *a* and *u*

183 **III. Writing**

Checkup: Page 44
Writing Lesson: Page 45
Skills Practice: Review Dropping Final Silent *e* Before Adding *-ing*
Homework: Pages 46-47
Reading and Writing Evaluation

185 Lesson 10

186 I. Conversation Skills

Dialog (Making an appointment with the doctor)
Vocabulary: Public Rooms
Vocabulary: Some Medical Terms
Vocabulary: The Verb *do*
Vocabulary: The Verbs *stop* and *drop*
Vocabulary: The Verb *fix*
Vocabulary: Ordinal Numbers
Vocabulary: Holidays in the United States
Structure Focus: Past Tense of Irregular Verbs (*got, ate, made, wore, tore, sold, told*)
Vocabulary: The Use of *ago*
Structure Focus: The Use of *and... too*
Structure Focus: The Use of *not...and...not either*
Structure Focus: The Use of *help* with Object + Verb
Pronunciation: /g/ and /ng/, Vowel + /r/
Oral Evaluation

198 II. Reading

Chart 10-A: Page 48 (Short Sound of *o*)
Story: At the Doctor's Office
Chart 10-B: Page 50 (Short Sound of *o*)
Story: Bob Oliver's Shop
Skills Practice: Beginning Consonant Blend *cl-*
Skills Practice: Beginning Consonant Blend *dr-*
Skills Practice: Beginning Consonant Blend *sp-*
Skills Practice: Contrasting the Short Vowels *a* and *o*
Skills Practice: Contrasting the Short Vowels *o* and *u*
Skills Practice: Review *MEN* and *WOMEN*

201 III. Writing

Writing Lesson: Page 52
Skills Practice: Review *-s* and *-ing* Verb Endings
Homework: Page 53
Homework: Singular and Plural Nouns
Reading and Writing Evaluation

203 **Lesson 11**

204 **I. Conversation Skills**

Dialog (Feeling better)
Vocabulary: Living Room Furniture
Vocabulary: The Word *person*
Vocabulary: *match, fire, burning*
Vocabulary: Injuries
Vocabulary: *first* and *then*
Vocabulary and Structure Focus: Regular Verbs, Present and Past Tenses
Vocabulary and Structure Focus: Irregular Verbs, Present and Past Tenses (*saw, said, heard, took, shook, put*)
Structure Focus: Past of *be* + Verb-*ing*
Structure Focus: Verb + Object + Infinitive
Structure Focus: Verb + Object + *not* + Infinitive
Structure Focus: Verb + Verb-*ing*
Structure Focus: Verb + Object + Verb-*ing*
Structure Focus: Prepositions + Verb-*ing*
Structure Focus: Passive Voice (*be* + Verb-*ed*)
Structure Focus: The *-er* Comparative Form of Adjectives
Structure Focus: Comparative Form of *good* and *bad*
Vocabulary and Structure Focus: *How do you feel?* and Replies
Pronunciation: /ō/ and /oi/, /ou and oi/
Oral Evaluation

220 **II. Reading**

Chart 11-A: Page 54 (Sound of *er, ir, ur*)
Story: Fern Gets Burned
Chart 11-B: Page 56 (Sound of *er, ir, ur*)
Story: Fern Gets Burned (Continuation on page 57)
Skills Practice: Review Words with /er/

225 **III. Writing**

Writing Lesson: Page 58
Skills Practice: Adding *-ed* to Verbs
Homework: Page 59 and Extra Worksheet
Reading and Writing Evaluation

229 **Lesson 12**

230 **I. Conversation Skills**

Dialog (Let's go to a movie.)
Vocabulary: Chart and Story Words
Vocabulary: Prepositions of Direction
Vocabulary: Verbal Phrases with *back*
Vocabulary: Driving a Car to Work
Vocabulary: Driving a Car Downtown
Vocabulary: Driving Home
Vocabulary: Car Trouble
Vocabulary: Adjectives with Opposite Meanings
(*far, near; large, small; expensive, cheap; dark, light; new, used)*
Structure Focus: *It's* + Distance *from...to....*
Structure Focus: Requests with *Let's*
Structure Focus: Negative Requests with *Let's*
Pronunciation: /ou/ and /ī/, /ou and /oi/
Oral Evaluation

239 **II. Reading**

Chart 12-A: Page 60 (Sound of *ar*)
Story: The Arthurs' Farm
Chart 12-B: Page 62 (Sound of *ar*)
Story: At the City Market
Skills Practice: Review Words with *ar*
Skills Practice: Agent Nouns with *-er*

243 **III. Writing**

Writing Lesson: Page 64
Homework: Page 65 and Extra Worksheet on Past Tense
Reading and Writing Evaluation

246 **Lesson 13**

247 **I. Conversation Skills**

Dialog (Getting to work)
Vocabulary: Recreation Places
Structure Focus: Questions with *What time*
Vocabulary: The Verb *find out*
Vocabulary: Frequency Adverbs
Structure Focus: Position of Frequency Adverbs
Structure Focus: The Use of *ever* and *never*
Vocabulary: *the same* and *different*
Structure Focus: Comparisons with *as...as*
Structure Focus: Verbs with No *-ing* Form in the Present Tense
Structure Focus: Short Answers to Yes/No Questions (Review)
Pronunciation: Intonation Drills
Oral Evaluation

262 **II. Reading**

Skills Practice: Review Short Vowels (Auditory Discrimination)
Skills Practice: Review Short Vowels (Minimal Pairs in Sentences)
Skills Practice: Review Words Ending with Consonant + *y*
Skills Practice: Review *wh* Contrasted with *w* and *h*
Skills Practice: Review *ng* Contrasted with *n* and *g*
Skills Practice: Review /er/ and /ar/

266 **III. Writing**

Writing Lesson: Pages 66-67
Skills Practice: Forming *What* Questions
Skills Practice: Forming the *-er* Comparative of Adjectives
Homework: Pages 68-69
Reading and Writing Evaluation

270 Introduction to *City Living*

271 Lesson 14 (*City Living*: Stories 1-2)

271 Story 1: Jack Black Comes to the City

272 I. Conversation Skills

Vocabulary: The Words *Mom* and *Dad*
Vocabulary: The Verb *get* (*receive*)
Vocabulary: Verbs That Show Affection
Vocabulary: The Verbs *smile at* and *laugh at*
Structure Focus: The Use of *up* in *coming up the street*
Structure Focus: The Use of *from* in *watching (someone) from (somewhere)*
Structure Focus: Indirect Object without *to*
Structure Focus: Verb + Object + Verb
Vocabulary and Structure Focus: The Use of the Verb *let*

280 II. Reading

General Instructions: Reading *City Living*
Story 1: Jack Black Comes to the City
Study Helps: Page 70, *Skill Book 2*

283 Story 2: In the Dress Shop

284 I. Conversation Skills

Vocabulary: Prices
Vocabulary: Fastening Clothing
Vocabulary: *without*
Vocabulary: *together* and *alone*
Vocabulary: Adjectives
Vocabulary: The Verb *fit*
Vocabulary: The Verb *match*
Vocabulary: The Verb *look* + Adjectives
Vocabulary: The Verbs *ask* and *answer*
Structure Focus: *ask* + Object + Infinitive
Structure Focus: The Use of *but*
Structure Focus: Passive Voice (Present Tense)

294 II. Reading

Story 2: In the Dress Shop
Study Helps: Page 70, *Skill Book 2*
Skills Practice: Adding *-es* to Verbs and Nouns
Checkup: Page 71

296 III. Writing

Writing Lesson: Page 72
Writing Lesson: Page 73
Homework: Page 74

297 Lesson 15 (*City Living*: Stories 3-5)

297 Story 3: Working in a Factory

297 **I. Conversation Skills**

Vocabulary: The Verb *lift*
Vocabulary: The Verb *fill* and the Adjectives *empty* and *full*
Vocabulary and Structure Focus: Expressions with *be* + *have-ing*
Structure Focus: Noun Clauses with *what, when,* and *where*
Structure Focus: Passive Voice (Present Tense)
Structure Focus: The Present Perfect Tense with *just*
Structure Focus: Full and Contracted Forms of the Present Perfect Tense

304 **II. Reading**

Story 3: Working in a Factory
Study Helps: Page 75, *Skill Book 2*

305 Story 4: City Traffic

305 **I. Conversation Skills**

Vocabulary: Giving Someone a Ride (a Lift)
Vocabulary: *traffic* (*heavy* and *light*)
Vocabulary: Asking for Directions
Vocabulary: Giving Directions
Structure Focus: *told* + Object + Information Words + Infinitive
Structure Focus: The Modal *must* in Affirmative Statements

310 **II. Reading**

Story 4: City Traffic
Study Helps: Page 75, *Skill Book 2*

311 Story 5: At the Market

311 **I. Conversation Skills**

Vocabulary: *ready* and *get ready*
Vocabulary: *person, animal, thing*
Vocabulary: *a list, a shopping list*
Vocabulary: *single, married, get married*
Vocabulary: The Verb *plan*
Vocabulary: The Verb *give...back*
Vocabulary: Other Ways of Expressing Time

317 **II. Reading**

Story 5: At the Market
Study Helps: Page 75, *Skill Book 2*
Checkup: Page 76

317 **III. Writing**

Writing Lesson: Page 77
Skills Practice: Adding *-es* to Nouns That End in Consonant + *y*
Homework: Page 78

319 Lesson 16 (*City Living*: Stories 6-7)

319 Story 6: The Puppy Got the Duck

319 **I. Conversation Skills**

Vocabulary: *in the park*
Vocabulary: *leave, left*
Structure Focus: Time Clauses with *when*
Structure Focus: The Use of *but* to Combine Parallel Sentences
Structure Focus: The Question *What happened?*

324 **II. Reading**

Story 6: The Puppy Got the Duck

325 Story 7: What Happened?

325 **I. Conversation Skills**

Vocabulary: The Noun *stitches* and the Verb *stitched up*
Vocabulary: *early, late, on time*
Vocabulary: *in a hurry*
Vocabulary: *Hurry up!*

328 **II. Reading**

Story 7: What Happened?

328 **III. Writing**

Writing Lesson
Skills Practice: Adding Endings to Verbs That End in Consonant + *y*

330 Oral Evaluation for Skill Book 2

340 Reading and Writing Evaluation for Skill Book 2

344 Conversation Skills Word List

350 Reading Word List

Acknowledgments

The authors wish to acknowledge with gratitude the help of the following persons:

– Volunteer tutors in the National Affiliation for Literacy Advance (NALA), a membership organization of Laubach Literacy International. Their pioneering efforts in ESOL-literacy tutoring led to the development of *The Laubach Way to English* and their experience has contributed to its content.

– Riorita Ceniza, an educational technologist, who provided a content analysis of the original manuscript and behavioral objectives for an *ESOL* program.

– Muriel Pierson, Jan Rose Sabey, tutors in California and Illinois, especially those at Lake View Presbyterian Church in Chicago, and countless students. Their encouragement and patient testing of ideas made this series of manuals possible.

– Daniel, Diana, and Peter Macero for their unfailing support and encouragement.

– The staff of New Readers Press and Laubach Literacy for their cooperation, especially Dr. Robert S. Laubach, Caroline Blakely, Priscilla Gipson, and the editor, Kay Koschnick, for her painstaking efforts, patience, and advice at every stage of the work.

Notes on typography and style:

- Slash marks around a letter or letters indicate the sound for which they stand. Thus, you say /g/ like the beginning consonant sound in *girl,* and /j/ like the beginning consonant sound in *jumping.*

  Letters in italics are read by their letter names, as: *a, b, c.*

- Although the authors recognize that there are teachers and students of both sexes, they have chosen, for the sake of clarity, to use the pronoun *she* to refer to the teacher and *he,* to the student.

  Conversation skills practices and their corresponding illustrations show both sexes in a variety of roles and activities.

About the Authors

Jeanette D. Macero

Jeanette D. Macero, associate professor of English at Syracuse University, has been involved with teaching ESOL at all levels for 20 years. She began her work at the English Language Institute at the University of Michigan, studying and working with Charles Fries and Robert Lado.

Mrs. Macero has organized and administered programs in ESOL, citizenship, and basic education for schools and community groups and has been consultant to several adult education departments in both universities and public school systems. She has trained ESOL teachers for the Peace Corps and has taught ESOL methodology to many native-speaking and non-native-speaking teachers. In addition, she was linguistic consultant and quiz writer for the easy English newspaper *News for You* at its inception.

In 1977, Mrs. Macero became president of the New York State ESOL-Bilingual Education Association. She is also the review editor for its publication *Idiom.* She is on the advisory panel of the National Affiliation for Literacy Advance (NALA) and is a member of Teachers of English to Speakers of Other Languages (TESOL), the National Association for Foreign Student Affairs (NAFSA), and the American Council on the Teaching of Foreign Languages (ACTFL).

Martha A. Lane

Martha A. Lane, as coordinator of Volunteer Reading Aides for Lutheran Church Women, helps communities to organize adult literacy and ESOL-literacy tutoring programs, in cooperation with other denominations and organizations, and conducts training workshops for tutors and tutor trainers.

Miss Lane has been tutoring students and training other tutors since 1968. She is certified as a Master Tutor Trainer by the National Affiliation for Literacy Advance. (NALA) and serves on that organization's ESOL committee.

She has a master's degree in magazine journalism from Northwestern University and was associate editor of *Together* magazine for six years. She is the author of *A Teacher's Guide to Teaching English as a Second Language with the New Streamlined English Series,* the predecessor to *The Laubach Way to English.*

Miss Lane is a member of Teachers of English to Speakers of Other Languages (TESOL), the National Association for Public Continuing and Adult Education (NAPCAE), the National School Volunteer Program, and the International Reading Association.

Introduction: What Is the 'Laubach Way to English'?

The Laubach Way to English is a series of manuals especially designed for teaching English to speakers of other languages (ESOL), particularly to functionally illiterate adults. These teacher's manuals provide a comprehensive beginning English program in listening, speaking, reading, and writing skills.

Each teacher's manual is correlated to a skill book in the Laubach Way to Reading series. The skill book is the student's text-workbook in reading and writing.

The Laubach Way to Reading series

The Laubach Way to Reading series is a systematic program of teaching carefully articulated, sequential reading and writing skills, beginning at the zero level of literacy. The learner progresses from the sounds and regular spellings of the basic consonants to those of the short vowels, the long vowels, and finally to irregular spellings and more difficult reading and writing skills.

The Laubach Way to Reading series

Skill Book 1: Sounds and Names of Letters
Skill Book 2: Short Vowel Sounds
Skill Book 3: Long Vowel Sounds
Skill Book 4: Other Vowel Sounds
Skill Book 5: Special Consonant Sounds

The "Laubach method"

The Laubach Way to Reading is a revision of the New Streamlined English series, which grew out of the work of the late Dr. Frank C. Laubach. Dr. Laubach spent more than 40 years of pioneering work in literacy education in 103 countries.

The "Laubach method" he developed starts with the known—the spoken word—and moves to the unknown—the written word—in easy steps that elicit the correct response from the student and reinforce it immediately. The emphasis is on learning by association rather than by rote memory. In the first five skill book lessons, sound-symbol relationships are taught with key words and pictures superimposed with letters. These pictorial memory association cues are phased out as the student attains independence in word attack skills. Lessons stress reading for meaning from the very beginning. Writing skills—beginning with the formation of letters—reinforce reading skills.

Meeting the needs of ESOL students

The skill books were originally written for adult native speakers of English with no reading skill. For many years, however, large numbers of volunteer tutors affiliated with Laubach Literacy International have been asked to teach ESOL students as well.

To improve its services to ESOL students, particularly the functionally illiterate, Laubach Literacy commissioned this series of manuals, the Laubach Way to English, to provide a comprehensive ESOL program.

Developing these manuals involved adapting the methods of teaching the reading and writing lessons to the easy wording a beginning ESOL student could understand. It also involved adding methods of teaching conversation skills.

Laubach Literacy selected as authors for the *ESOL Teacher's Manual for Skill Book 2* Martha A. Lane and Jeanette D. Macero. Together, they brought to the project both grass-roots experience with ESOL-literacy tutoring and expertise in teaching ESOL methodology.

The Laubach Way to English: A comprehensive ESOL program

The teacher's manual these authors developed provides comprehensive instructions for teaching listening, speaking, reading, and writing skills. Practice in the listening-and-speaking conversation skills includes dialogs, vocabulary, structures, pronunciation, and intonation. These skills are sequenced systematically so that the student has thorough aural-oral practice with vocabulary and structures before meeting them in the reading. Additional vocabulary and structures, not found in the reading, are provided for their usefulness in everyday life.

This manual accompanies the student workbook *Skill Book 2: Short Vowel Sounds* and the correlated reader *City Living.*

ESOL Illustrations for Skill Book 2, a teacher's picture book, must be used in conjunction with this manual. The pictures can be used to show the student the meaning of new vocabulary in the introductory units and in the conversation skills section of the lessons that follow.

In addition to conversation skills, the manual provides instructions for teaching the skill book lessons in reading and writing, as well as additional practice in word attack skills.

Throughout the lessons, the teacher's demonstrations and verbal instructions to the student are in a simple form for easy comprehension by the ESOL student.

Although designed specifically for teaching adults who are illiterate in their native language as well as in English, the Laubach Way to English can be used successfully with many other ESOL students. In particular, literate students whose native languages have writing systems other than the Roman alphabet should find the practice in basic reading and writing skills beneficial.

Each One Teach One, and classrooms too

Among other things, the "Laubach method" has traditionally meant "Each One Teach One," a volunteer tutor and a student, teaching and learning in an atmosphere of caring and compassion.

Accordingly, the methods described in the Laubach Way to English apply to a one-to-one teaching situation, but suggestions are offered for adapting the methods for classroom use, where necessary. Thus, the series is useful for ESOL-ABE classes in public schools as well as for tutoring programs.

For volunteer tutors and beginning teachers

The detailed step-by-step-instructions in the Laubach Way to English make it possible for both volunteer tutors and beginning ESOL teachers to use the manuals with ease and confidence.

General Procedures

This manual is meant to be used after the student has successfully completed the material in the *Skill Book 1* level of the Laubach Way to English series.

Placing the new student

A new student who seems to have some knowledge of English should not be placed directly in *Skill Book 2* without careful evaluation. Many times, a student has acquired some superficial fluency in carrying on simple conversations. This can be misleading, since often such a student does not have a mastery of the basic structural patterns of English.

It is best to administer both the Oral Evaluation (Parts I and II) and the Reading and Writing Evaluation for *Skill Book 1* to determine where in the series the student should begin. The teacher should evaluate the student's performance as directed.

Even if the student is ready to begin *Skill Book 2,* it would be wise to review any test items which caused him difficulty since each new lesson builds on all that has been taught in previous lessons.

Format of the lessons

The lessons in this manual are divided into three parts: Conversation Skills, Reading, and Writing.

The Conversation Skills section begins with a simple dialog, which the student will find useful in both the learning situation and his daily life. This is followed by the vocabulary items to be taught and the structural patterns in which the words are to be used. Next, there is a pronunciation practice to give the student some flexibility in making the sounds of English. This section ends wtih an oral evaluation, or review, of the new material.

In the Conversation Skills sections, the material in the left-hand column is for your own information. Do not read it to the student or explain it to him. The material in the right-hand column is what you are to say and do as you are teaching.

The Reading section begins with study of the skill book chart containing key words for the short vowel sound being studied. This is followed by the reading of the skill book story and oral questions to check the student's reading comprehension.

The Writing section tells how to use skill book exercises of various kinds: review of the story's content, study of word spellings, and writing words and sentences from dictation.

Both the Reading and Writing sections contain skills practices that augment the skill book with different kinds of reading and writing exercises.

Each lesson ends with a Reading and Writing evaluation.

The Reading and Writing sections have many different formats. Many times, however, the left-hand column, labeled "Do this," indicates what you are to point to as you say the script in the right-hand column, labeled "Say this."

Conducting the lessons

The instructions presented in this teacher's manual are very important. Even if you have had previous experience in teaching English as a second language, it is a good idea to review the steps for each lesson before you meet with your student. The material is arranged in increasing order of difficulty for your student—from imitation to practice to production without assistance. Therefore, do not skip any of the steps or rearrange them. Practice your part of the lesson so that you are familiar with your lines and cues. When you know exactly what to say and do, the lesson will move along at a lively pace and will not falter. Every minute will thus be used in a positive way.

The ideal situation is for you to speak less than a fourth of the time, thus giving your student ample time for imitation and practice. Although this may be difficult to do, it is a goal you should strive toward. Let the student do the work. Do not be too quick to supply the answer if the student hesitates. Give him the opportunity to think in English. If his response is less than perfect, you say it and have the student repeat after you. Always praise and encourage him, using words like *good, better,* and *fine* often.

In order to achieve a learning situation in which the student is doing most of the talking, you should become familiar with the gestures indicated throughout this manual; use them instead of words whenever possible. To keep the student's interest and attention, maintain eye contact with your student, smile, and be encouraging. Never scold or become impatient or show discouragement. Learning a language is a slow and steady process, not one in which dramatic leaps take place. You and your student will both feel a sense of achievement if the student can learn something new at each session.

You have undertaken a rewarding and challenging adventure. It is our hope that this manual aids you on your way.

Lesson 1

OBJECTIVES

When a student completes this unit, he should be able to:

1. Say and respond to a new dialog.
2. Identify some items of clothing and jewelry and use them with the verbs *wear, put on,* and *take off.*
3. Say the names of the basic colors *black, white, brown, yellow, green, red, blue* (review); and *silver, gold, gray, orange, purple* (new); and use *light* and *dark* with names of colors.
4. Use two modifiers before a noun, as: *big pet shop.*
5. Use the indirect object with verbs that take *to* (review) and the indirect object with verbs that take *for*, as: *get...for, buy...for.*
6. Make questions with *Who* in the subject position, such as *Who speaks English*?
7. Pronounce the vowel sounds /i/ and /ē/ as in *chip* and *cheap* and the consonant sounds /b/ and /v/ as in *berry* and *very*.
8. Read the following new words:
   Chart words: *Miss, sister, big, little, ring, finger*
   Story words: *it, gift, getting, giving*
   Instructions: *Study.*
9. Read a simple story, using the new chart and story words.
10. Use the noun endings *-s*, and *-'s*, and *-s'*.
11. Distinguish aurally between the ending sounds -ng/g and -ng/n and identify each sound with its symbol (letter or letters).
12. Write the new chart and story words.

VISUAL AIDS

1. Accompanying *ESOL Illustrations for Skill Book 2,* pp. 2-6.
2. A picture is only a good substitute for the object itself. If possible, have the following in the classroom:

a man's suit	a dress	a jacket	shoes	a silver watch
a sweater	a coat	a belt	3 rings	a gold watch

3. For the colors, use construction paper or the squares on p. 2 of *ESOL Illustrations 2.* Color them in ahead of time. You may want to paste gold and silver foil on the squares for gold and silver instead of coloring them in.
4. Color some of the items of clothing on pp. 4-6 of *ESOL Illustrations 2.* In the practice in various lessons that follow, we use: a light green coat, a red jacket, a blue sweater, a brown belt, gray pants, a yellow dress, a white blouse, and a purple skirt.

I. Conversation Skills

DIALOG

Clerk:	May I help you?
Liz:	Yes, I'd like to buy a gift for my mother. It's her birthday.
Clerk:	Here are some nice rings.
Liz:	This one is pretty. How much is it?
Clerk:	$12.95.
Liz:	I'll take it.

Instructions to the teacher

Note: The procedure for teaching the dialog is the same as in the *ESOL Manual for Skill Book 1.*

1. Teacher models the entire dialog—both the role of the clerk and the role of the customer (Liz)—two or three times while the student listens.

   Notice that you do not say the words *Clerk* and *Liz* while modeling the dialog.

   Indicate rings at the appropriate moment in the dialog.

   To indicate change of roles, shift your weight from one foot to the other and turn your body slightly.

2. Teacher models one line of the dialog and asks the student to repeat.

   Continue the same way with each speaker's part of the dialog.

   Class: In a class situation, first have the class repeat in unison. Then divide the class into groups and have each group repeat. With unison work of this kind, have the members of the class begin each line of the dialog exactly at the same moment, or there will be utter confusion.

Script for teaching

[Put up your hand in a Stop gesture to indicate that you want the student to listen, not repeat, at this time. Say: "Listen."]

May I help you?

Yes, I'd like to buy a gift for my mother.
It's her birthday.

Here are some nice rings.

This one is pretty.
How much is it?

$12.95. [Say: "Twelve ninety-five."]

I'll take it.

[Say: "Repeat," and use a Beckoning gesture to indicate that you want the student to say each line after you.]

Teacher: May I help you?
Student: May I help you?

Teacher: May I help you?
Student: May I help you?
Teacher: [Praise student. Say: "Good."]

Teacher: Yes, I'd like to buy a gift for my mother.
It's her birthday.
Student: Yes, I'd like to buy a gift for my mother.
It's her birthday.

[Indicating rings.]
Teacher: Here are some nice rings.
Student: Here are some nice rings.

Teacher: This one is pretty. How much is it?
Student: This one is pretty. How much is it?

Teacher: $12.95. [Say: "Twelve ninety-five."]
Student: $12.95.

One-to-one:

3. Teacher takes the role of clerk, and student takes the role of Liz in the dialog.

[Say the first line of the dialog. If the student begins to repeat after you, use the Stop gesture to indicate that you want him to listen. If the student cannot give you the second line of the dialog, prompt him. Gesture and say: "Listen," and then: "Repeat."]

4. Teacher and student reverse roles in the dialog.

Class:

3. In a class situation, have the members of the class say the dialog in unison, then in pairs.

   In a larger class, divide the class in half, with each half taking first one, then the other, role in the dialog.

   Then divide the class in quarters, ending with one-to-one practice.

   Keep the pace brisk. Remember to praise your student often.

VOCABULARY: Review of Chart and Story Words

This is Miss Jill Hill.
Jill is Kim's sister.
Jill is the big sister.
Kim is the little sister.

Jill gives a gift to Kim.
Jill gives a gift to her little sister.

1. Using the picture on p. 3 of *ESOL Illustrations 2,* the teacher models *This is Miss Jill Hill,* saying it several times.

[Say: "Listen," and use Stop gesture.]

2. Teacher models the sentence and asks the student to repeat.

Teacher: This is Miss Jill Hill.
Student: This is Miss Jill Hill.

Teacher: This is Miss Jill Hill.
Student: This is Miss Jill Hill.

[Beckon to the student to say the sentence again without your saying it. If he does, say: "Good!" If he cannot, continue having him imitate you.]

3. Teacher points to the picture of Miss Jill Hill and says, "Who is this?"

Teacher: Who is this?
Student: This is Miss Jill Hill.

[Continue in the same way with the next three items in the box. For the last two items, point to the gift and ask: "What's this?"]

Note: Use these three steps to teach the rest of the vocabulary.

Before introducing each new item, review the previous one by asking, "Who is this?"

Class: In a class situation, the teacher follows the procedure above, going from choral recitation to smaller groups to individual practice.

VOCABULARY: *wear, put on, take off*

I'm wearing a ring. I'm taking off my ring. I'm putting on my ring.

Teacher models the sentences several times, performing the action carefully to demonstrate the meaning. Have the student repeat after you.

[Say: "Listen to *wearing*." Indicating your ring, say: "I'm wearing a ring."]

[Do *taking off* and *putting on* in the same way, actually taking off the ring as you say the second sentence and putting it on for the third sentence.]

VOCABULARY: Articles of Clothing and Jewelry

This is a coat.	These are jeans.
This is a jacket.	These are pants.
This is a sweater.	These are glasses.
This is a belt.	These are shoes.
This is a ring.	
This is a watch.	These are clothes.

Using the pictures on pp. 4-5 of *ESOL Illustrations 2*, the teacher models the sentences. Do all of the singular sentences with *This* first, then all of the plural sentences with *These.*

Add as other new vocabulary only items of clothing that you or your student are wearing that are not listed here, as *a pants suit* or *a vest.*

[Indicating the picture of a coat, say: "Listen. This is a coat. Repeat. This is a coat."]

Teacher: This is a coat.
Student: This is a coat.

[Gesture for student to answer.]

Teacher: What's this?
Student: This is a coat.

[Continue in the same way with the remaining items, always reviewing items previously taught. Finally, indicating all the clothing, say: "These are clothes."]

The woman's wearing a dress.	The man's wearing a suit.
a blouse.	a shirt.
a skirt.	a tie.

Using the pictures on p. 6 of *ESOL Illustrations 2*, the teacher models first the sentences about the woman, then the sentences about the man. Have the student repeat.

[As you say the sentences, point to the articles of clothing being taught. Before you begin each new item, review items previously taught.]

DRILL: Substitution Drill with Visual Cues

1. Teacher asks questions, pointing to the various items of clothing on pp. 4-6 of *ESOL Illustrations 2*. Teacher gives the expected student response until the student can answer unassisted.

[Point to the picture of the dress.]

Teacher: What is the woman wearing?
She's wearing a dress.
Repeat. [Use Beckoning gesture.]
She's wearing a dress.
Student: She's wearing a dress.

Teacher: What is the man wearing?
Student: He's wearing a suit.

[Continue with the other clothing items. With some items, such as *coat*, practice with both *man* and *woman*.]

2. Continue the drill, using the question *What is the man taking off?*

[Point to the picture of the jacket.]

Teacher: What is the man taking off?
He's taking off his jacket. Repeat.
He's taking off his jacket.
Student: He's taking off his jacket.

Teacher: What is the woman taking off?
Student: She's taking off her ring.

[Continue with the rest of the clothing and jewelry items.]

3. Change the drill, using the same format and the question *What is the woman putting on?*

Note: If you feel the student needs more practice, ask: "What are you wearing?" eliciting a variety of answers. Use only items already taught.

You may also ask, "What are you putting on?" as you indicate you want the student to put on a sweater, ring, or watch. As the student puts on the item, have him say: "I'm putting on a ring."

VOCABULARY: Names of Colors with *light* and *dark*

This is gold. silver. gray. orange. purple.
This is light blue. dark blue.
These are colors.

1. Teacher reviews the colors taught in the *ESOL Manual for Skill Book 1: black, white, brown, yellow, red, green, blue.*

   Use construction paper or the squares on p. 2 of *ESOL Illustrations 2,* which you have colored in.

   Teacher: [Indicating color.]
   What color is this?
   Student: It's black.

2. Teacher models the sentences in the box several times, having the student repeat.

   Use construction paper or the squares on p. 2 of *ESOL Illustrations 2* to illustrate these new colors, also.

   [Say: "Listen to the colors."
   Point to the color as you say: "This is gold."]

   [Continue with the other colors in the box, ending with *light blue* and *dark blue.* Then, add: *light green, dark green; light gray, dark gray; light brown, dark brown.*]

   [Finally, point to all the colors and say: "These are colors."]

DRILL: Identification Drill

Using p. 2 of *ESOL Illustrations 2,* teacher asks questions which elicit the names of colors.

Ask for both new and review items.

Teacher	Student
[Indicating color.]	
What color is this? It's gray.	It's gray.
What color is this? It's dark blue.	It's dark blue.

[Continue as above. After the first two examples, do not prompt the student unless necessary.]

DRILL: Question and Answer Drill

Teacher asks questions that combine a review of the clothing taught and the colors. Use pp. 4-6 of *ESOL Illustrations 2,* which you have colored ahead of time. Do *not* point to the item you are asking about.

Teacher	Student
What color is the blouse?	It's white.
What color is the sweater?	It's blue.
What color are the pants?	They're gray.

[Continue with the remaining items.]

STRUCTURE FOCUS: Two Modifiers

This is a big pet shop.
This is a little gift shop.
This is a big dress shop.
This is a hot fish dinner.

Teacher models the sentences several times, having the student repeat.

Note: In English, nouns can be preceded by one, two, or more modifiers (adjectives or other nouns).

[Say: "Listen to *big pet shop*," then model the first sentence.]

[Continue in the same way with the remaining sentences.]

DRILL: Expansion Drill

Teacher models the key sentence, pauses, then gives the adjective to be added into the key sentence. Teacher repeats the entire (expanded) sentence and has the student repeat.

Continue in this way until the student can make the expanded sentences easily by himself.

Teacher	Student
This is a pet shop. big	
This is a big pet shop.	This is a big pet shop.
This is a pet shop. little	This is a little pet shop.
This is a gift shop. big	
This is a gift shop. little	
This is an English book. big	
This is a gold ring. little	
This is a Spanish book. little	
This is a cheese sandwich. big	
This is a fish dinner. hot	
This is a meat dinner. cold	

STRUCTURE FOCUS: Indirect Object with *to* (Review)

The woman	is giving	the book	to the boy.
The man	is selling	the book	to the girl.
The girl	is speaking	English	to the boy.
She	is showing	the books	to the students.

The teacher models the sentences several times, having the student repeat.

Note: Verbs like *give, sell, speak,* and *show* can take two objects: a direct object and an indirect object with *to*. Notice that the indirect object in the sentences being taught comes after the direct object.

[Before modeling the first sentence, say: "Listen to *to the boy*."]

[Continue to call attention to the indirect object in the same way before modeling each of the remaining sentences.]

DRILL: Expansion Drill

The teacher says the indirect object and the sentence. The student expands the sentence by adding the indirect object.

Teacher	Student
to the boy The woman's giving the book. The woman's giving the book to the boy. Please repeat. The woman's giving the book to the boy.	 The woman's giving the book to the boy.
to the boy. Jill's giving the book.	 Jill's giving the book to the boy.
to him Kim's speaking English.	 Kim's speaking English to him.
to them He's repeating the number.	
to the teacher The girl's showing the book.	
to the child The teacher's reading the book.	
to the boy The man's selling some apples.	

STRUCTURE FOCUS: Indirect Object with *for*

Kim	is getting	a gift	for her mother.
Jill	is buying	a ring	for her mother.
I	am opening	the door	for him.
She	is closing	the window	for the teacher.
They	are making	dinner	for their mother.
I	am signing	the paper	for you.

The teacher models the sentences, having the student repeat.

Signing is a new word here. Show the meaning by performing the action of signing your name on a piece of paper and giving it to the student.

Note: Verbs like *get, buy, open, close, make,* and *sign* often take two objects: a direct object and an indirect object with *for*. Notice that the indirect object in the sentences being taught comes after the direct object.

[Before modeling the first sentence, say: "Listen to *for her mother.*"]

[Continue to call attention to the indirect object in the same way before modeling each of the remaining sentences.]

DRILL: Expansion Drill

1. Teacher says the indirect object and the sentence. Student expands the sentence by adding the indirect object with *for*.

Teacher	Student
for the woman. We open the door. We open the door for the woman.	We open the door for the woman.
for the woman We close the door.	We close the door for the woman.
for Ann We're making lunch.	
for Mrs. Hill They're buying a ring.	
for the teacher I'm opening the window.	
for me Ann's getting the book.	
for mother They're making dinner.	
for us She's signing her name.	

2. This drill contains both verbs that take *to* and verbs that take *for*.

Teacher	Student
the boy Jill's giving the pen. Jill's giving the pen to the boy.	Jill's giving the pen to the boy.
the woman Bob's giving the pencil.	
her mother The girl's showing her dress.	
his girl friend The boy's buying a ring.	
Bob Jill's closing the door.	
the man The woman's repeating her telephone number.	

STRUCTURE FOCUS: Questions with *Who* in Subject Position

Jill	is the big sister.
Who	is the big sister?
Kim	is the little sister.
Who	is the little sister?
Ann and Glenn	are going home.
Who	is going home?

Teacher models the statement and the corresponding question several times, having the student repeat both.

[Say: "Listen to *Who.*"]

Note: In these questions, *Who* is a question word in the subject position. The answer to questions such as these will always be used in the subject position.

Notice that the verb is used in the third person singular in the question even when the answer to be given is plural.

The intonation of *Who* questions is the same as that of statements, that is, a falling intonation pattern (final).

DRILL: Transformation Drill

Student transforms a statement into a question with *Who* in the subject position.

Teacher	Student
Jill is the big sister.	
Who is the big sister?	
Please repeat.	
Who is the big sister?	Who is the big sister?
Kim is the little sister.	
Who is the little sister?	Who is the little sister?
Bob is wearing a ring.	
Ann is taking off her ring.	
Sue is putting on a light green coat.	
Glenn is buying a red jacket.	
Glenn and Will are wearing jeans.	
Ann and Bob are wearing old shoes.	
Ann and Glenn are going home.	

STRUCTURE FOCUS: Short Answers to *Who* Questions

Who speaks	English?	I do.
Who teaches	the class?	The teacher does.
Who wears	jeans?	Boys and girls do.
Who is	the little sister?	Kim is.
Who has	an English book?	I do.

Teacher models each question with its short answer several times, having the student repeat only the answer.

[Say: "Who speaks English?" Pause. "I do."
With a Beckoning gesture, indicate that you want the student to repeat "I do."]

DRILL: Short Answers (Free Reply)

Teacher asks questions which elicit short answers, such as *I do, Kim is,* and so on. Do not accept a one-word answer, such as *Kim*.

Teacher	Student
Who speaks English? I do.	I do.
Who studies English?	
Who wears jeans?	
Who has a watch?	
Who has a sister?	
Who repeats the words?	
Who is the big sister?	
Who is the little sister?	
Who is wearing a dress?	
Who is wearing jeans?	
Who is wearing a ring?	
Who is wearing a jacket?	

PRONUNCIATION: /ē/ and /i/

1. Teacher models first the vowel sound /ē/ as in *cheap,* then the vowel sound /i/ as in *chip*.

   Do not explain the meaning of the words. This is simple pronunciation practice.

   These vowel sounds are review, so drill them quickly.

[Say: "Listen to /ē/."
Repeat each word several times.]

eat	deep	heat
cheap	seat	team

[Have the student repeat the words above after you.]

[Say: "Listen to /i/."
Repeat each word several times.]

it	dip	hit
chip	sit	Tim

[Have the student repeat the words above after you.]

2. Teacher contrasts the two sounds, using minimal pairs, such as *cheap/chip*.

[Say: "Listen to *cheap, chip*."]

cheap	chip
deep	dip
seat	sit
leave	live
team	Tim

3. The student discriminates between the two sounds. Teacher tells the student that the vowel sound in *cheap* is "one," and the vowel sound in *chip* is "two."

   If the student makes a mistake, that is, if he says *cheap* is "two," the teacher repeats:
   "*Cheap* is one, *chip* is two."
   This will enable the student to hear the contrast again.

[Tell the student that *eat, cheap, deep, seat* are "one" (the first sound), and that *it, chip, dip, sit* are "two" (the second sound).]

[To help your student, write on the board the first two examples you use, with numerals.]

1	2
eat	it

Teacher		**Student**
eat	Say "one."	one
it	Say "two."	two
cheap	Say "one."	one
deep	Say "one."	one
chip	Say "two."	two

[Now have the student practice distinguishing the two sounds.]

Teacher	**Student**
cheap	one
dip	two
deep	one
eat	one
it	two
Tim	two

[Continue until the student can distinguish between the two sounds without confusion.]

4. Practice by saying one of the pair (*cheap*) and having the student say the other (*chip*).

[Pointing to yourself, say: "cheap." Indicating the student, say: "chip."]

Teacher	Student
cheap	chip
deep	dip
seat	sit
heat	hit
team	Tim

Teacher	Student
chip	cheap
dip	deep
sit	seat
hit	heat
Tim	team

Teacher	Student
cheap	chip
chip	cheap
sit	seat
team	Tim
dip	deep

5. Practice the sounds by using them in phrases and sentences. Do not explain vocabulary.

[Say: "Listen to *The ring is cheap.* Repeat. *The ring is cheap*."]

Teacher	Student
The gift is for Mrs. Hill.	The gift is for Mrs. Hill.

It's cheap.
Sit in this seat.
Eat some chips.
Tim is on the team.
It's a ship.
It's a sheep.

PRONUNCIATION: /b/ and /v/

Using steps 1-5 in the previous Pronunciation section, practice the sounds /b/ and /v/ as in *berry* and *very*.

Note: Both /b/ and /v/ are voiced sounds. The sound /b/ is made with the lips closed. The sound /v/ is made with the upper teeth on the lower lips. Direct your student to look at your lips and teeth to help him see as well as hear the difference.

/b/	/v/
bail	vale
berry	very
ban	van
Bic	Vic
dub	dove
curb	curve

Sentences

I'm from Indian Valley.
It's a brown berry.
That's very good.
It's a curve.
It's a curb.

ORAL EVALUATION

The teacher should have a notebook for recording the student's progress. Make notes about items that a student is having difficulty with.

1. Review items of clothing.

   If your student can identify 10 or more of these fairly quickly and with understandable pronunciation, then you can consider that he has learned them.

   [Asking the question *What is the woman (man) wearing?* point to the items of clothing on pp. 4-6 of *ESOL Illustrations 2.* Do not prompt your student until it is clear that he cannot name the item.]

2. Review the names of the colors.

   Student should be able to name all of them since they are mostly review items.

   [Using p. 2 of *ESOL Illustrations 2,* point to the various colors and ask: "What color is this?"]

3. Review the use of two modifiers before a noun.

   Student should be able to do this pattern with ease.

   [Do the Expansion Drill which follows Structure Focus: Two Modifiers.]

4. Review the indirect object with verbs that take *to* and with verbs that take *for.*

   Student should be able to do all this with some ease since it is mostly review.

   [Do part 2 in the Expansion Drill which follows Structure Focus: Indirect Object with *for.*]

5. Review questions and answers with *Who* in the subject position.

   This is an important structural pattern. Review it at your next class session if your student has difficulty.

   [Do the Transformation Drill that follows Structure Focus: Questions with *Who* in Subject Position. Have the student answer the questions as well.]

II. Reading

If you have not already done so, go over the results of the Reading and Writing Evaluation for *Skill Book 1* with your student. Be sure that he understands anything he did incorrectly.

CHART 1: Page 2

All the charts in *Skill Book 2* are taught in the same way. Have the student read everything on the page, including headings and page numbers. Always go from the *known* (review of the key word at the top of the page—such as *in*) to the *unknown* (the new words). Let your student sound out each new word for himself as much as possible. Point out any differences between how the words are spelled and how they are pronounced. Be sure that the student sounds out each word correctly, according to the sounds of the letters that he learned in *Skill Book 1.*

The pictures in the charts from now on are just hints of what the new words mean. Do *not* tell or ask your student anything about the pictures. Instead, go directly to the first column of words.

Your instructions to the student for the three columns of words in each chart are:

Column 1: Please read.

Column 2 (in red): [Point to the letter or letters for each sound.]
What is the sound?

[Point to the vowel being studied.]
What is the vowel sound?

Column 3: Please read.

The instructions below tell how to teach the entire chart page for Lesson 1.

Do this:	**Say this:**
	Teacher: Please open your book to page 2.
Point to *Lesson 1*.	Teacher: Please read. Student: Lesson 1.
Point to key word *in*.	Teacher: Read. Student: In.
Point to *i* under *in*.	Teacher: What's the sound of this letter? Student: /i/. Teacher: What's the name of this letter? Student: *i*.
Point to *i* at top right of page.	Teacher: *I* is a vowel. Please repeat. *I* is a vowel. Student: *I* is a vowel.

Line 1

Point to *Miss* in the first column of words.	Teacher: Please read. Student: Miss. [If the student cannot read the new word, do not tell him. Instead, go right on to the next column. He should be able to sound out the word for himself in the next column.]
Point to *Miss* in red column. Point to the sounds of the word one at a time, exactly as the word is divided: *M...i...ss*. Be sure your student says each sound correctly.	Teacher: What is the sound? Student: /m/. Teacher: What is the sound? Student: /i/. Teacher: What is the sound? Student: /s/.
Point back to *i* in red column.	Teacher: What is the vowel sound? /i/. What is the vowel sound? [Gesture to student to answer.] Student: /i/. [Since this is the first time you are asking this question, give the answer to help the student understand. After this, do not give the answer.]
Point to *Miss* in last column.	Teacher: Read. Student: Miss. Teacher: Good! [Correct the student's pronunciation here, if he needs help with it.]

Do this:	Say this:

Line 2

Point to *sister* in the first column of words.	Teacher: Please read. Student: Sister.
Point to the sounds of the word in the next (red) column one at a time, exactly as the word is divided: *s...i...s...t...er.*	Teacher: What is the sound? Student: /s/. Teacher: What is the sound? Student: /i/. Teacher: What is the sound? Student: /s/. Teacher: What is the sound? Student: /t/. Teacher: This sound is /er/. What is the sound? Student: /er/.
Point back to *i* in red column.	Teacher: What is this vowel sound? Student: /i/. Teacher: Good!
Point to *sister* in the last column.	Teacher: Read. Student: Sister.

Line 3

Point to *big* in the first column.	Teacher: Please read. Student: Big.
Point to the sounds in the next column, one at a time: *b...i...g*.	Teacher: What is the sound? Student: /b/. Teacher: What is the sound? Student: /i/. Teacher: What is the sound? Student: /g/.
Point back to *i* in red column.	Teacher: What is the vowel sound? Student: /i/. Teacher: Good!
Point to *big* in the last column.	Teacher: Read. Student: Big.

Line 4

Point to *little* in the first column.	Teacher: Please read. Student: Little.
Point to the sounds in the next column, one at a time: *l...i...tt...u...l.*	Teacher: What is the sound? Student: /l/.../i/.../t/.../u/.../l/.
Point back to *i* in red column.	Teacher: What is this vowel sound? Student: /i/. Teacher: Good!
Point to *little* in the last column.	Teacher: Read. Student: Little.

Line 5

Point to *ring* in the first column of words.

Teacher: Please read.
Student: Ring.

Point to the sounds in the next column, one at a time: *r...i...ng*.

Teacher: What is the sound?
Student: /r/.

Teacher: What is the sound?
Student: /i/.

Teacher: The sound for *ng* is /ng/. What is the sound?
Student: /ng/.

Point back to *i* in red column.

Teacher: What is the vowel sound?
Student: /i/.

Point to *ring* in the last column.

Teacher: Read.
Student: Ring.

Line 6

Point to *finger* in the first column of words.

Teacher: Please read.
Student: Finger.

Point to the sounds in the next column, one at a time: *f...i...ng...g...er*.

Teacher: What is the sound?
Student: /f/.

Teacher: What is the sound?
Student: /i/.

Teacher: What is the sound?
Student: /ng/.

Teacher: What is the sound?
Student: /g/.

Teacher: What is the sound?
Student: /er/.

Teacher: Good!

Point back to *i* in red column.

Teacher: What is this vowel sound?
Student: /i/.

Point to *finger* in the last column.

Teacher: Read.
Student: Finger.

Review

Point to each word on the chart, one at a time, going down the last column.

Teacher: Read.
Student: Miss...sister...big...little...ring...finger.

Teacher: Very good!

STORY: A Ring for Kim

Note: To aid the student's comprehension, before you begin to teach the story, write the names of the two girls on the story illustration. Label the taller girl Jill. Label the shorter girl Kim.

Teach every story in *Skill Book 2* exactly as you have taught each story since Lesson 6 of *Skill Book 1.*

1. Help the student sound out new words that appear in the story, but not in the chart. The new story words here are *it, gift, getting, giving.*
2. Ask the student to read the first paragraph silently.
3. Ask questions to check the student's comprehension of the paragraph. Be sure to use only question forms that he has previously practiced. Allow him to give short answers when appropriate.
4. Ask the student to read the first paragraph aloud. If he cannot read it fairly smoothly or if he makes major pronunciation errors, you read it and have him imitate you, one line at a time. Then have the student read the paragraph aloud again.
5. Do the rest of the story as you did the first paragraph, one or two paragraphs at a time.
6. Read the story to your student, sentence by sentence. Speak at a normal rate and with natural intonation. Slowing down would cause unnatural stress on some words. Have the student repeat each sentence after you. Have him say it, not read it. Have him say each sentence several times, until he is imitating your intonation as well as your pronunciation.
7. Now have the student read the entire story—including the title—aloud.

Comprehension questions that you may use for the Lesson 1 story are given below.

	Teacher	**Student**
Paragraph 1	[Point to the tall girl in the story illustration.] Who is this?	(Miss) Jill Hill.
	[Point to the short girl in the story illustration.] Who is this?	(Miss) Kim Hill.
Paragraph 2	Who is the big sister?	Jill is.
	Who is the little sister?	Kim is.
Paragraph 3	Where are the sisters?	They're in a gift shop.
	Is it a little gift shop?	No, it isn't. (It's a big gift shop.)
	Whose gift shop is it?	Miss Oliver's.
Paragraph 4	What is Kim doing?	She's getting a gift for Mrs. Hill.
	What is Jill doing?	She's getting a gift for Kim.
Paragraph 5	Who is giving the gift to Kim?	Jill is.
	What is the gift?	A ring.
	Is the ring big?	No, it's little.
Paragraph 6	Where does Kim put the ring?	On her little finger.
Paragraph 7	Who thanks Jill?	Kim does.
	What does Kim thank Jill for?	The ring.

SKILLS PRACTICE: Review *-s* and *-'s*

Write the following words in a column on the blackboard:

girl
sister
ring
Kim
gift
Hill

Have your student read the words.

Now, write *s* and *'s* on separate index cards. Make the letters the same size as the letters on the board. Place the letter on the left edge of the card.

1. Point to *girl* in the column.

   Say: The girls are Americans.
   The girls are Americans.

   Place the *s* card after *girl* to form *girls* and repeat the sentence.

2. Point to *girl* in the column again.

   Say: The girl's ring is gold.
   The girl's ring is gold.

   Place the *'s* card after *girl* to form *girl's* and repeat the sentence.

3. Now give the two cards to your student. First, point to the word. Then read the sentence for that word. Beckon to the student to place the correct card after the word. Repeat the sentence if necessary.

sister	This is his sister's book.
sister	Ed has two sisters.
ring	The rings are on the table.
Kim	Kim's dish is little.
gift	Mrs. Hill gets five gifts.
Hill	Mr. Hill's coat is big.
Hill	The Hills live on this street.

   If the student forms the correct word, say "Good!"

   If the student hesitates very long or makes a mistake, repeat the sentence and point to the correct card. Let him place the card after the word. Then repeat the sentence again.

SKILLS PRACTICE: Adding *-s'*

Write the sentences in the box on a piece of paper for your student. Group the sentences as shown. (If you have a class, make ditto copies and also write the sentences on the blackboard.) Do this beforehand.

A.	The girl has a ring. The girl's ring is little.	Ann has a ring. Kim has a ring. Jill has a ring. The girls' rings are little.
B.	The bird has two eggs. Bob picks up the eggs. Bob has the bird's eggs.	The birds have two eggs. Bob picks up the eggs. Bob has the ________ eggs.
C.	Kim has a ring. Ed picks up the ring. Ed has his sister's ring.	Kim has a ring. Her sister has a ring. Ed picks up the rings. Ed has his ________ rings.
D.	Mr. Oliver is in his tent. Mr. Oliver's tent is little.	The Hills are in the tent. The ________ tent is big.

Do this:	**Say this:**
Set A	
Point to the first group of sentences, at left.	Teacher: Please read. Student: [Reads first two sentences.]
Point to *ring* in *The girl's ring is little.*	Teacher: Whose ring is this? Student: The girl's.
Underline the *'s* in *girl's*.	Teacher: This means *one girl* has a ring.
Point to the second group of sentences, at right.	Teacher: Please read. Student: [Reads the next four sentences.]
Point to *rings* in *The girls' rings are little.*	Teacher: Whose rings are these? Student: The girls'.
Underline the *s'* in *girls'*.	Teacher: This means some *girls* have rings.

Set B

Point to the first group of sentences.

Teacher: Please read.
Student: [Reads first three sentences.]

Point to the second group of sentences.

[Help the student read the first sentence, as *have* is a new reading word for him.]

Teacher: The birds have two eggs.
Please read.
Student: [Reads.]

[When the student comes to the blank, beckon to him to say the missing word, *birds'*. Prompt him only if necessary.]

Point to *eggs* in last sentence.

Teacher: Whose eggs are these?
Student: The birds'.

Point to the blank.

Teacher: Write *birds'*.
Student: [Writes *birds'* in the blank.]

Point to *bird's* in first group.

Teacher: Is this one bird?
Student: Yes.

Point to *birds'* in second group (the word the student has written).

Teacher: Is this one bird?
Student: No.

Set C

Do Set C in a similar way.

Set D

Point to the first group of sentences.

Teacher: Please read.
Student: [Reads first two sentences.]

Point to *The Hills* in second group.

Teacher: *The Hills* means the Hill family.
Mr. Hill, Mrs. Hill, and their children are the Hills.

Point to second group of sentences.

Teacher: Please read.

[Beckon to student to say the missing word, *Hills'*, when he comes to it. Then have him write it in the blank.]

Note: This exercise will help prepare the student to read and understand sentences with *the Hills* and *the Hills' dinner* in the story in Lesson 2.

SKILLS PRACTICE: Ending Sounds -ng/g

Step 1: Write the following endings and words on the blackboard or on paper. Line up the words with the endings exactly as shown.

-ng	-g
wing	wig

Step 2: Pronounce each word several times, having the student repeat after you. Point to the word as you pronounce it.

Step 3: Cover up all but the *ng* in *wing*.

Say: "*Wing* ends with the sound /ng/. *Wing*. *Wing* ends with the letters *ng*."

Step 4: Cover up all but the *g* in *wig*.

Say: "*Wig* ends with the sound /g/. *Wig*. *Wig* ends with the letter *g*."

Step 5: Point to *wing*, then *wig*, pronouncing each. Have the student repeat each word.

Step 6: Point to *wing*, then *wig*. Say: "Please read."

Step 7: Pronounce the words in random order. Have the student point to the word you are saying.

Step 8: Point to the words in random order. Say: "Please read."

Step 9: Erase *wing* and *wig*, and write the next pair (*ring* and *rig*) under the correct headings. Be sure to line up the words under the headings.

Repeat the eight steps above with each of the following minimal pairs. Be sure to have only one minimal pair showing at a time.

-ng	-g	-ng	-g
ring	rig	sang	sag
ping	pig	lung	lug
bang	bag	hung	hug
hang	hag	rung	rug

Step 10: Erase the last minimal pair, but leave the endings *-ng* and *-g* on the board.

Review by reading words in random order and asking the student to point to the ending sound of the word. (If you read *sang,* for example, the student should point to *-ng*.)

SKILLS PRACTICE: Ending Sounds -ng/n

Following the same 10 steps, contrast the ending sounds /ng/ and /n/, using the minimal pairs and headings shown here. Work with only one pair at a time.

-ng	-n	-ng	-n
wing	win	sung	sun
sing	sin	bang	ban
king	kin	fang	fan
thing	thin	rang	ran
		tang	tan

III. Writing

WRITING LESSON: Page 4

Do this:	Say this:
Point to heading.	Teacher: Writing Lesson. Please read. Student: Writing Lesson.

Study

Point to *study* at top right of page.	Teacher: This word is *study*. Read: *study*. Student: Study.
Point to *Study* under *Writing Lesson.*	Teacher: Read. Student: Study. Teacher: Good!

1. Miss

Ask student to turn back to Chart 1 on page 2. Then point to *Miss* in last column.	Teacher: Please turn to page 2. Read this word. Student: Miss. Teacher: What is the beginning sound? Student: /m/. Teacher: What is the name of the letter? Student: *Capital M.* Teacher: What is the vowel sound? Student: /i/. Teacher: What is the ending sound? Student: /s/. Teacher: What letters make the sound /s/? Student: *s...s.*
Ask student to turn to page 4. Then point to number 1 under *Study.*	Teacher: Please turn to page 4. Write *Miss.* Student: [Writes *Miss* after number 1.]

2. sister

Point to *sister* in last column of the chart on page 2.	Teacher: Please read this word. Student: Sister. Teacher: What is the ending sound? Student: /er/. Teacher: What letters make the sound /er/? Student: *e...r.*
Point to number 2 under *Study.*	Teacher: Please turn to page 4. Write *sister.*

3. big

Point to *big* in last column of the chart on page 2.	Teacher: Please read. Student: Big.
Point to number 3 under *Study.*	Teacher: Please turn to page 4. Write *big.*

4. little

Point to *little* in last column of the chart on page 2.

Teacher: Please read.
Student: Little.

Teacher: What's the beginning sound?
Student: /l/.

Point to *i* in *little*.

Teacher: What's this vowel sound?
Student: /i/.

Point to the two *t*'s.

Teacher: You write two *t*'s,
but they have one sound.
What is the sound?
Student: /t/.

Point to *ul* in red column.
Point to *le* in last column.

Teacher: *Little* ends with the sound /ul/.
Write that sound like this: *l...e.*

Point to number 4 under *Study.*

Teacher: Please turn to page 4.
Write *little.*

5. ring

Point to *ring* in last column of the chart on page 2.

Teacher: Please read.
Student: Ring.

Teacher: What's the beginning sound?
Student: /r/.

Teacher: What's the vowel sound?
Student: /i/.

Teacher: What's the ending sound?
Student: /ng/.

Teacher: What letters make the sound /ng/?
Student: *n...g.*

Point to number 5 under *Study.*

Teacher: Please turn to page 4.
Write *ring.*

6. finger

Point to *finger* in last column of the chart on page 2.

Teacher: Please read.
Student: Finger.

Teacher: What's the beginning sound?
Student: /f/.

Teacher: What's the vowel sound?
Student: /i/.

Point to *fing g er* in red column.
Point to *finger* in last column.

Teacher: *Finger* sounds like this.
But write only one *g*.

Teacher: What's the ending sound?
Student: /er/.

Teacher: What letters make the sound /er/?
Student: *e...r.*

Point to number 6 under *Study*.

Teacher: Please turn to page 4.
Write *finger.*

Listen and write

Do this:	**Say this:**
Point to the heading *Listen and write.*	Teacher: Please read. Student: Listen and write.

Have your student cover the words he has just written in the Study section. Then dictate the same words in this order:

1. big	4. sister
2. Miss	5. little
3. ring	6. finger

Have your student check his work against the chart on page 2 or the Study section. Have him correct any mistakes.

Write

Have your student read aloud the next heading, *Write*, and the three names. Then have him write the names indicated. Be sure that he writes capital letters and periods where needed.

HOMEWORK: Page 5

Have your student read aloud everything on the page. Ask him to write the words two times and the sentences one time, at home.

READING AND WRITING EVALUATION

1. Write the sentences below on the board, spacing the words as shown here. (Do not write the letters at the beginning of the sentences; they are just here to indicate the order to you.)

   Have your student circle the correct word and read the complete sentence. Use the first sentence to demonstrate what you want the student to do. Then let him do the other three by himself. The student should be able to complete all of the last three sentences correctly.

   a. The girl is / has a pan.

   b. The ring is finger. / little.

   c. Jill gives the gift to / it Kim.

   d. This is Miss Olivers / Oliver's gift shop.

2. Dictate the following words for your student to write: *it, getting, giving, little, finger.*

   The student should be able to write at least three out of five correctly.

MORE READING

You may want to use the supplementary reader *More Stories 2* with your student. It contains three stories correlated to each lesson of *Skill Book 2.* The stories reinforce the new words in each lesson. Vocabulary and grammatical structures are controlled.

If your student needs extra reading practice, you may help him read some of these stories in class. If he is able to read independently, he may enjoy and benefit from reading the stories at home.

Lesson 2

OBJECTIVES

When a student completes this unit, he should be able to:

1. Say and respond to a new dialog.
2. Say the chart words plus vocabulary concerning toys, the home, and daily activities.
3. Use *with* phrases to indicate companion (*with Jill*) and instrument (*with a spoon*).
4. Use *for* to indicate purpose.
5. Use *or*, as in: "Is this a blouse *or* a shirt?"
6. Use the word *want*.
7. Use *which* in information questions.
8. Pronounce the vowel sounds /i/ and /e/ as in *bid* and *bed* and the consonant sounds /f/ and /v/ as in *fan* and *van*.
9. Read and write the numbers 10-100 by tens.
10. Read the following new words:
    Chart words: *kitchen, whistle, sitting, singing, bringing, dinner*
    Story words: *with, Hills'*
    Instructions: *Fill in the letters. Fill in the words.*
11. Read a simple story, using the new chart and story words.
12. Read some variants of known verbs formed by dropping or adding *-ing*.
13. Distinguish aurally between the beginning sounds w/wh and identify each sound with its symbol.
14. Read some words beginning with the consonant blend *br-*.
15. Write the new chart and story words.

VISUAL AIDS

1. *ESOL Illustrations 2*, pp. 7-11.
2. If readily available, bring in a whistle, a bat and ball, a top, a doll.
3. Bring two knives, two forks, and two spoons.
4. Have a book of matches for the Skills Practice on the sounds w/wh.

REVIEW

Review any items your student had difficulty with when doing the Oral Evaluation in Lesson 1.

I. Conversation Skills

DIALOG

Mrs. Hill:	It's time for dinner.
Mr. Hill:	Good. I'm hungry. What are we having?
Mrs. Hill:	We're having a fish dinner tonight.
Mr. Hill:	Good. I like fish.

Teacher models the dialog, using the procedure outlined in Lesson 1, and having the student repeat.

VOCABULARY: Toys

These are toys.
Ed has a whistle. Jill has a bat and a ball. Kim has a top. Kim has a doll.

Teacher models these sentences several times, using p. 7 of *ESOL Illustrations 2*. Have the student repeat.

[As you point to p. 7 of *ESOL Illustrations 2*, indicate the bat and ball, top, whistle, and doll, and say: "These are toys." Then pointing to each one individually, say: "Will has a whistle," and so on.]

DRILL: Identification Drill

Pointing to p. 7 of *ESOL Illustrations 2*, teacher asks questions which elicit the names of the toys.

Teacher	Student
What are these?	These are toys.
What does Ed have?	He has a whistle.
What does Kim have?	
What does Jill have?	
What does the girl have?	
What are these?	

VOCABULARY: The Verbs *talk, whistle, sing*

Kim and Jill are talking. I'm whistling. I'm singing.

Teacher models the sentences several times, having the student repeat. Demonstrate the meaning of the words by talking, whistling, and singing. These verbs are necessary for the story.

[Demonstrate the meaning of the verbs. As you model each sentence, say: "Listen to *talking*," and so on.]

[Continue with the remaining items.]

DRILL: Identification Drill

Teacher performs the action and asks the student to identify it.

Teacher	Student
[Whistle.]	
You're whistling.	You're whistling.
[Sing.]	You're singing.
[Talk.]	You're talking.

[If the student does not know how to respond, ask: "What am I doing?"]

VOCABULARY: *house* and Names of Rooms

This is a	house.
This is the	kitchen.
	dining room.
	bathroom.
	living room.
	bedroom.
	closet.

Using pp. 8-11 of *ESOL Illustrations 2*, teacher models the sentences several times, having the student repeat.

[Point to the appropriate picture as you say: "This is a house," and so on.]

DRILL: Identification Drill

[Pointing to pp. 8-11 of *ESOL Illustrations 2*, ask: "What is this? This is a house. Please repeat. This is a house."]

[Continue asking about the remaining vocabulary, prompting only if necessary.]

VOCABULARY: Daily Activities (Verbs)

The Hills	live	in this house.
Mrs. Hill	cooks	in the kitchen.
The Hills	eat and drink	in the dining room.
Jill	washes her hands	in the bathroom.
Kim	brushes her teeth	in the bathroom.
They	sit and talk	in the living room.
They	watch television	in the living room.
They	sleep	in the bedroom.
Ed	puts his clothes	in the closet.

Teacher models the sentences several times, having the student repeat. Use pp. 8-11 of *ESOL Illustrations 2.*

DRILL: Question and Answer Drill with Visual Cues

1. Teacher asks questions eliciting the names of the rooms.

[Pointing to the appropriate pictures in *ESOL Illustrations 2*, pp. 9-11, ask the following questions.]

Teacher	Student
Where do the Hills live?	They live in this house.
Where does Mrs. Hill cook?	
Where do the Hills eat?	
Where does Kim brush her teeth?	
Where do they watch television?	
Where do they sleep?	
Where does Ed put his clothes?	

2. Teacher asks questions eliciting appropriate answers concerning the daily activities being taught. If the student cannot answer, point to the appropriate picture on pp. 9-11 of *ESOL Illustrations 2.*

Teacher	Student
What does Mrs. Hill do in the kitchen?	She cooks.
What do the Hills do in the dining room?	
What do the Hills do in the bathroom?	
What do the Hills do in the living room?	
What do the Hills do in the bedroom?	

DRILL: Free Reply

Teacher asks questions eliciting answers about the student's daily activities. The replies will be varied.

Teacher	Student
When do you cook?	I cook (in the morning and at night).
When do you eat lunch?	
When do you wash your hands?	
When do you watch television?	
When do you sit and talk in the living room?	
When do you brush your teeth?	
When do you sleep?	
When do you eat breakfast?	

STRUCTURE FOCUS: *with* Phrases to Indicate Companion

Jill is in the kitchen	with	Mrs. Hill	now.
Kim is sitting	with	Ed	now.
Mr. Hill is eating dinner	with	his wife and children	now.
Mrs. Hill is watching television	with	Mr. Hill	now.

Teacher models the sentences several times, having the student repeat. Use pp. 9-10 of *ESOL Illustrations 2* if needed.

[Say: "Listen to *with*."]

Note: *With* is followed by a noun or object pronoun. The *with* phrase comes after the object or the place expression. The word order of *with* phrases causes the student difficulty.

DRILL: Expansion Drill

Have the student put the *with* phrase into the sentence in the correct word order.

[Say: "with Mrs. Hill." Pause.
"Jill is in the kitchen." Pause.
"Jill is in the kitchen now." Pause.
"Jill is in the kitchen with Mrs. Hill now." Please repeat.
"Jill is in the kitchen with Mrs. Hill now."

Teacher	Student
with Kim Jill is in the kitchen.	Jill is in the kitchen with Kim.
with Kim Jill is watching television now.	
with Glenn Liz is going downtown now.	
with Jill Mrs. Hill is eating lunch.	
with Ed Kim is going to church.	
with her Jill is going shopping now.	
with us He's going downtown.	
with him Jill is playing ball now.	

STRUCTURE FOCUS: *with* Phrases to Indicate Instrument

I eat potatoes	with a fork.
I eat soup	with a spoon.
I cut meat	with a knife.
I eat olives	with my fingers.

Teacher models the sentence several times, having the student repeat. Use the fork, spoon, and knife you have brought with you to illustrate the vocabulary.

The verb *cut* is a new word here, too.

[Say: "Listen to *with a fork*."
Show the fork as you say the sentence.]

[Continue in the same way with the rest of the items.]

DRILL: Expansion Drill

Teacher has the student put the *with* phrase into the sentence in the correct word order. Hold up the item to help the student learn the vocabulary.

Teacher	Student
with a fork I eat meat. I eat meat with a fork.	I eat meat with a fork.
with a fork I eat potatoes.	I eat potatoes with a fork.
with a spoon I eat soup.	
with a spoon I put sugar in my coffee.	
with a knife I cut meat.	
with a knife I cut bread.	
with my fingers I eat olives.	

Cultural note:

If it seems appropriate, especially for those students who use eating utensils other than knives, forks, and spoons, show the student how most people in the United States hold knives, forks, and spoons. Demonstrate how we cut meat by shifting the fork from our left hand while cutting to the right hand while eating. Have the student try it himself.

Do *not* insist that the student use the utensils your way. Simply demonstrate. Avoid making any value judgments.

STRUCTURE FOCUS: The Use of *for* to Indicate Purpose

He's	going shopping	<u>for</u> a ring.
He's	bringing a dish	<u>for</u> the fish.
I'm	going downtown	<u>for</u> a gift.

Teacher models the sentences several times, having the student repeat.

[Say: "Listen to *for*."]

Note: The word *for*, as it is used here, indicates purpose. It follows the object or place expression in a sentence.

The word *bringing* is new here.

DRILL: Expansion Drill

Teacher has the student put the *for* phrase into the sentence in the correct word order.

Teacher	Student
a gift He's going downtown.	He's going downtown for a gift.
a fish He's going downtown.	
a dog He's going to the pet shop.	
a ring He's going to the gift shop.	
an apple He's going to the kitchen.	
a glass of water Kim's going to the kitchen.	
a dress Jill's going to the dress shop.	
a book Ed's going to the teacher.	
lunch He's going home.	

STRUCTURE FOCUS: The Use of *or*

Is this	a ring	or a watch?	It's a ring.
Is the gift shop	big	or little?	It's big.
Are we going	home	or downtown?	Home.

Teacher models the questions and answers several times, having the student repeat both.

[Say: "Listen to *or*."]

Do not overemphasize *or*, which is usually pronounced as if it were part of the preceding word.

Note: The word *or* joins words which are grammatically alike: nouns *(ring or watch)*, adjectives *(big or little)*, and so on.

DRILL: Question and Answer Drill

1. Teacher asks questions containing *or* to elicit a choice from the student.

[Using the objects themselves or ***ESOL Illustrations 2***, pp. 4-5 and p. 2, ask: "Is this a ring or watch? It's a ring. Repeat. It's a ring."]

Teacher	**Student**
Is this a watch or a ring?	It's a watch.
Is this a sweater or a jacket?	It's a sweater.
Are these pants or jeans?	They're pants.
Is this a knife or a fork?	
Is this yellow or orange?	
Is this light blue or dark blue?	
Are you going home or downtown?	
Are you going home or shopping?	

2. Student asks questions containing *or* which the teacher or another student answers.

   For further practice, if needed, use vocabulary about money. Supply some nickels, dimes, quarters, and so on.

[Pointing to two pictures or objects, indicate by using a Beckoning gesture that you want the student to ask the questions. Prompt him at first by saying, "Is this . . . ," encouraging him to complete the question.]

Teacher	**Student**
[Hold up or indicate the objects.]	
a blouse or a shirt	Is this a blouse or a shirt?
It's a shirt.	
a suit or a jacket	
red or orange	
purple or blue	
white or gray	
light brown or dark brown	
a fork or a spoon	
a spoon or a knife	

VOCABULARY: The Verb *want*

I	want	a piece of paper.
I	want	my book.
The teacher	wants	her pencil.
The teacher	wants	her sweater.

Teacher models sentences several times, having the student repeat.

[Say: "Listen to *want*."]

Place the items in different parts of the room so they are not readily available. Get the item and hold it, demonstrating that you "want" it. Don't have all the items set out before you; for example, look for your pencil in your purse or pocket.

DRILL: Multi-Slot Substitution Drill with Vocal Cues

Teacher	Student
I want a piece of paper.	I want a piece of paper.
a book	I want a book.
She	She wants a book.
The teacher	The teacher wants a book.
a pencil	The teacher wants a pencil.
her sweater	The teacher wants her sweater.
a pen	The teacher wants a pen.
I	I want a pen.
a glass of water	I want a glass of water.
a cup of coffee	I want a cup of coffee.

STRUCTURE FOCUS: Information Questions with *Which*

I have a red pen and a black pen. Which pen do you want?	The red pen.
I have an English book and a Spanish book. Which book do you want?	The English book.

Teacher models each statement, question, and answer several times, having the student repeat all three.

[Say: "Listen to *Which*."]

Note: In information questions, *Which*—plus an optional noun—is followed by the question word order: *Which (pen) do you want?*

Questions beginning with *Which* ask about one of a group. *Which* is more specific than *What*. Both speaker and listener share an understanding of what the choices are when *Which* is used.

Information questions beginning with *Which* use a falling intonation pattern (final) similar to that used for statements.

DRILL: Transformation Drill

Student is asked to transform a statement into an information question with *Which*. After giving two examples, simply give the statement. Prompt the student only if necessary.

[Say: "Mary is reading the English book. Which book is Mary reading?" Using a Beckoning gesture, say: "Please repeat. Which book is Mary reading?"]

Teacher	Student
Ann is reading the Spanish book.	Which book is Ann reading?
Glenn is buying the English book.	Which book is Glenn buying?
He is in the gift shop.	Which shop is he in?
Ann is in the pet shop.	Which shop is Ann in?
Kim is wearing her gold ring.	Which ring is Kim wearing?
Mary lives in the little white house.	Which house does Mary live in?
The girls play with the big dog.	Which dog do the girls play with?
Will plays with the brown ball.	Which ball does Will play with?
Glenn and Liz live in the big gray house.	Which house do Glenn and Liz live in?
Ann looks at the yellow dress.	Which dress does Ann look at?

DRILL: Question and Answer Drill

Teacher elicits questions using *Which* plus *or*.

Student makes the question, and the teacher or another student responds.

If the student knows this vocabulary, you may not need to use illustrations.

[Pointing to the picture of the jacket and sweater, say: "the jacket/the sweater." Pause. "Which do you want, the jacket or the sweater?" Beckon for the student to repeat, and say: "Which do you want, the jacket or the sweater?"]

[After the student repeats the question, *you* answer the question (or have another student do so).]

Teacher	Student
the jacket/the sweater	Which do you want, the jacket or the sweater?
The sweater.	
the coat/the jacket the blouse/the shirt the tie/the belt	
the gold watch/the silver watch	
the green olives/the black olives	
the orange/the apple coffee/milk water/milk	

PRONUNCIATION: /i/ and /e/, /f/ and /v/

1. See the Pronunciation section in Lesson 1 for the steps to follow in teaching the vowel sounds /i/ and /e/ as in ***bid*** and ***bed***.

   These vowel sounds are review, so drill them quickly.

[Say: "Listen to /i/ and /e/."]

/i/	/e/	Sentences
bid	bed	Bill, give me the bell.
till	tell	It's a red pin.
hid	head	Give me the check.
chick	check	Tell Jill to go to bed.
bitter	better	She hid her head.
bill	bell	

2. Following the same procedure, teach the consonant sounds /f/ and /v/.

   The sounds /f/ and /v/ are both made with the upper teeth on the lower lip. The sound /f/ is unvoiced, whereas the sound /v/ is voiced.

[Say: "Listen to /f/ and /v/."]

/f/	/v/	Sentences
fan	van	He failed.
fail	vale	He has a lot of friends.
few	view	This veal is good.
safer	saver	I feel fine.
leaf	leave	This fan is safer.
feel	veal	This is a fine view.

READING AND WRITING

Teacher models the counting of the numbers 10-100 by tens, having the student repeat. This is review.

[Say: "Please repeat."]

Teacher: 10, 20, 30, 40, 50, 60, 70, 80, 90, 100
Student: 10, 20, 30, 40, 50, 60, 70, 80, 90, 100

[After the student can say the numbers understandably, write each number, 10-100, on paper or on the board as you and he say it. Write the numbers exactly as taught on p. 66 of *Skill Book 1*.]

Teacher: This is 10. What's this?
Student: It's 10.
Teacher: Good. Please write 10.

[Continue with 20-100.]

[When the student has written all the numbers, have him read 10-100 again.]

ORAL EVALUATION

1. Review the vocabulary on toys. Student should be able to identify all of these fairly quickly.

   [Using p. 7 of *ESOL Illustrations 2,* have your student identify the toys.]

2. Review the words *talk, whistle,* and *sing,* all of which are necessary for the story.

   [Do the Identification Drill following Vocabulary: The Verbs *talk, whistle, sing.*]

3. Review the rooms of a house and the daily activities taught. Student should be able to identify five of the rooms and seven of the daily activities.

   [Do the Question and Answer Drill with Visual Cues following Vocabulary: Daily Activities.]

4. Review *with* (companion) and *with* (instrument). Be sure the student can use these *with* phrases in the correct order in the sentence.

   [Do the Expansion Drills following the two Structure Focus sections dealing with *with* phrases.]

5. Review the use of *for* to indicate purpose. Be sure the student can use the *for* phrases in the correct order in the sentence.

   [Do the Expansion Drill following Structure Focus: The Use of *for* to Indicate Purpose.]

6. Review questions with *which* plus *or*.

   [Have the student do the Question and Answer Drill following Structure Focus: Information Questions with *Which*. Have the student answer the questions this time.]

II. Reading

Before you begin the chart, check and correct the student's homework from Lesson 1. If it is not completed, have him complete it now.

CHART 2: Page 6

Remember that *Skill Book 2* charts are taught differently from *Skill Book 1* charts. The pictures are just visual clues. The student always tries to sound out new words for himself. Point out any differences between how words sound and how they are spelled.

Do this:	**Say this:**
	Teacher: Please open your book to page 6.
Point to *Lesson 2.*	Teacher: Please read. Student: Lesson 2.
Point to key word *in.*	Teacher: Read. Student: In.
Point to *i* under *in.*	Teacher: What's the sound of this letter? Student: /i/.
	Teacher: What's the name of this letter? Student: *i.*
Point to *i* at top right of page.	Teacher: *I* is a vowel. Please repeat. *I* is a vowel. Student: *I* is a vowel.

Line 1

Do this:	Say this:
Point to *kitchen* in the first column of words.	Teacher: Please read. Student: Kitchen.
In the red column, point to the sounds of the word, one at a time, exactly as the word is divided: *k...i...ch...e...n.*	Teacher: What is the sound? Student: /k/. Teacher: What is the sound? Student: /i/. Teacher: What is the sound? Student: /ch/. Teacher: What is the sound? Student: /e/. Teacher: What is the sound? Student: /n/.
Point back to *i* in red column.	Teacher: What is this vowel sound? Student: /i/. Teacher: Good!
Point to *kitchen* in last column.	Teacher: Please read. Student: Kitchen.

Line 2

Note: Although many native speakers of English distinguish between the sounds /w/ and /wh/, many others do not. That is, they tend to say *wistle* instead of *whistle*. Please, for the student's sake, always make as much distinction between the two sounds as possible, even if this is not part of your normal speech. This will help the student learn the spelling differences.

The sound /wh/ is unvoiced. To say it correctly, say it with a puff of air—just as if you were blowing out a candle.

There is more work on the sounds /w/ and /wh/ in the Skills Practice in this lesson.

Do this:	Say this:
Point to *whistle* in the first column of words.	Teacher: Please read. Student: Whistle.
In the red column, point to the sounds of the words, one at a time, exactly as the word is divided: *wh...i...s...u...l.*	Teacher: This sound is /wh/. What is the sound? Student: /wh/. Teacher: What is this sound? Student: /i/. Teacher: What is this sound? Student: /s/. Teacher: What is this sound? Student: /u/. Teacher: What is this sound? Student: /l/. Teacher: Good!
Point back to *i* in red column.	Teacher: What is this vowel sound? Student: /i/.
Point to *whistle* in last column.	Teacher: Please read. Student: Whistle.

Lines 3-6

Teach the rest of the chart in exactly the same way. Then review by asking the student to read each word from the last column once more. Finally, have him read the page number.

(The sound /wh/ is the only new sound or spelling in this chart.)

STORY: The Hills' Dinner

To teach the story, follow steps 1-7 in the Story section of Lesson 1.
Help the student sound out the new story words: *with, Hills'.*
Use the questions below to check the student's comprehension.

	Teacher	Student
Paragraph 1	Where is Mrs. Hill? Who is with her? Is the kitchen big?	She's in the kitchen. Jill is. Yes, it is.
Paragraph 2	What's Ed doing? Where is Kim?	He's sitting in the kitchen. She's in the kitchen (with Ed).
Paragraph 3	What does Ed have? What is Ed doing? Whose whistle is it?	He has a whistle. He whistles. *or* He's whistling. It's Ed's.
Paragraph 4	What is Mrs. Hill doing? Who is singing with her?	She's singing. Kim and Jill are.
Paragraph 5	What is Mr. Hill bringing for dinner? Is the fish big or little?	He's bringing a fish. It's big.
Paragraph 6	Who is bringing a dish? Who is bringing a pan?	Ed is. Jill is.
Paragraph 7	What are the Hills having for dinner?	They're having fish.

SKILLS PRACTICE: Adding and Subtracting *-ing*

Write the following words and have the student read each pair (without and with the *-ing* ending).
Write one form *under* the other so that what is added or subtracted is visually clear.
Write the words in the order shown. Do *not* explain at this time how to add or drop any ending.

look looking	fish fishing	jump jumping	kick kicking	study studying	listen listening
singing sing	bringing bring	sitting sit	getting get	giving give	

SKILLS PRACTICE: Beginning Sounds w/wh

Note: The letters *wh* form a consonant digraph. A consonant digraph is a combination of two consonants producing a single sound. In *Skill Book 1,* the student learned the consonant digraphs *sh, ch, th.*

The following exercise will help the student hear and pronounce the difference between /w/ and /wh/ and identify each sound with its symbol.

To help your student pronounce /wh/ correctly, light a match and hold it directly in front of his mouth as he repeats after you a /wh/ word like *which.* He will be pronouncing the /wh/ sound correctly when he blows out the match as he says the word.

Step 1: Write *w* and *wh.* Space them apart.

Step 2: Model a minimal pair: *witch* and *which.* Pronounce each word several times, pointing to *w* or *wh.* The student listens.

(Do *not* write the words for the student in this exercise.)

Step 3: Pronounce the two words again. Have the student repeat each word after you and point to *w* or *wh.*

Step 4: Say the words in random order. Have the student point to the correct symbol (*w* or *wh*) for the word you are saying.

Step 5: Point to the symbols *w* and *wh* in random order. Have the student say the word.

Continue in the same way with the following minimal pairs. Do *not* write the words for your student nor explain what they mean.

/w/	/wh/	/w/	/wh/	/w/	/wh/
we	whee	we'll	wheel	wet	whet
wear	where	wig	whig	wale	whale
wit	whit	wine	whine	weather	whether

SKILLS PRACTICE: Beginning Consonant Blend *br-*

Note: The letters *br* form a consonant blend. In a consonant blend, two or three consonants are sounded together, but each of these sounds is still heard distinctly. In this way, a blend is different from a digraph, which has just one sound.

This manual includes exercises on many different consonant blends, taught in the way described below.

Step 1: Write *ring* and *bring* as shown below. Be careful to line up the words and to underline the *r* and *br* exactly as shown.

ring
bring

Step 2: Point to and pronounce each word, first *ring,* then *bring.* Repeat a few times. The student listens.

Step 3: Point to and pronounce each word, having the student repeat. Do *ring,* then *bring.* Repeat a few times.

Step 4: Point to each word, beckoning for the student to say it. Do *ring,* then *bring.* Repeat a few times.

Repeat these four steps with the following pairs, one pair at a time.
(You may, however, leave all the pairs showing on the blackboard or paper. It is not necessary to erase each time you start a new pair.) Be sure to line up the words and underline the letters as shown.

rag	rim	rat	ran
brag	brim	brat	bran

III. Writing

CHECKUP: Page 8

Do this:	Say this:
Point to *Checkup*.	Teacher: Please read. Student: Checkup.
Point to the new words in red at the top of the page.	Teacher: Read. Student: Fill...letters...words. [If the student cannot read the words, help him sound them out. When the sound is different from the spelling, sound the word out according to the respelling in parentheses.]

Fill in the letters

Now point to the first set of instructions in black.	Teacher: Read. Student: Fill in the letters. Teacher: Good! Please fill in the letters.

When the student has finished the top half of the page, check his work. Ask him to read each word, then give the name and sound of the letters he wrote.

Fill in the words

Point to the second set of instructions in black.	Teacher: Read. Student: Fill in the words. Teacher: Good! Please fill in the words.

When your student has finished this section, ask him to read each sentence aloud. Check his spelling carefully. Then ask him to read the page number aloud.

WRITING LESSON: Page 9

Note: In *Skill Book 2,* the Writing Lesson consists of three parts. In the Study section, the student analyzes the spelling of the chart words from that lesson and writes them. In Listen and Write, the student writes words and sentences from dictation. In the section called Write, the student copies words, phrases, and sentences.

Do this:	Say this:
Point to heading.	Teacher: Please read. Student: Writing Lesson.

Study

Point to *Study*.	Teacher: Read. Student: Study.
	Teacher: Please turn to page 6. Look at the word *kitchen.* What is the first sound? Student: /k/.
	Teacher: What is the name of the letter? Student: *k*.
Pantomime the meaning of *silent* by putting your finger to your lips.	Teacher: One letter is silent. It doesn't have a sound. What letter is silent? Student: *t*.
	Teacher: Good! Turn to page 9. Write *kitchen* by number 1.

Help your student study and write each chart word the same way. Be sure to point out all silent letters, double consonants, and anything else that will help him remember the spelling of a word.

Listen and write

Before beginning this section, have the student cover up the words he has just written in the Study section. Then dictate the words in this order:

1. dinner
2. whistle
3. kitchen
4. sitting
5. bringing
6. with

Write

Ask your student to read aloud the heading *Write.* Then have him read aloud the name *Ed Hill* and the two sentences before he copies them. Check his work carefully to be sure that he has used capital letters correctly and has put a period at the end of each sentence.

HOMEWORK: Pages 10-11

Ask your student to read aloud everything on page 10. Have him read the instructions on page 11. Ask him to do pages 10 and 11 at home and to read the chart and story in this lesson again at home.

READING AND WRITING EVALUATION

1. Write the following letters on the board and ask the student to give the sound of each: *ch, wh, tt, ng, nn, er.*

   The student should be able to give at least four correct sounds.

2. Write the following words and ask your student to read them: *with, bring, whistle, singing, whistles.*

   The student should be able to read at least three words correctly.

3. Dictate these words: *sitting, dinner, sing, kitchen, singing, with.*
   The student should be able to write at least four words correctly.

4. Write the following exercise—with the instructions and the words to be completed—as shown.

   Fill in the letters.

   M__ ss
   s__ ster
   w__ th

   The student should be able to read and follow the instructions, and complete all three words correctly.

MORE READING

In the supplementary reader *More Stories 2,* the stories for Lesson 2 may be read in class or suggested for reading at home.

Lesson 3

OBJECTIVES

When a student completes this lesson, he should be able to:

1. Say and respond to a new dialog.
2. Identify the names of some kinds of buildings, such as *library* and *hospital*; some adjectives, such as *old* and *new; flowers;* and persons one knows, such as *neighbor* and *boss.*
3. Use expressions like *It's windy* to describe the weather.
4. Use the verb *need.*
5. Use prepositional phrases as noun modifiers.
6. Use the patterns *There is...* and *There are... ."*
7. Use the past tense of the verb *be* (*was, were*) in statements, questions, and short answers.
8. Pronounce the vowel sounds /ā/ and /a/ as in *pain* and *pan* and the consonant sounds /w/ and /v/ as in *wet* and *vet.*
9. Read the following new words:
   Chart words: *lily, city, windy, Kitty, Jimmy, building, picture*
   Story words: *Ms., King, Fisher, pretty.*
10. Read a simple story, using the new chart and story words.
11. Read more variants of known verbs formed by adding or dropping *-ing.*
12. Read known words ending with *-le* (*uncle, little, whistle*).
13. Distinguish between vowels and consonants.
14. Write the new chart and story words.

VISUAL AIDS

1. Some current U.S. postage stamps and some letters in stamped, addressed envelopes.
2. Some snapshots of your family members and friends. If possible, include a picture of a baby.
3. A little book, a cup, and a glass.
4. A calendar for the current month.
5. *ESOL Illustrations 2*, pp. 12-20.
6. Before class, make the Vowel-Consonant Chart as directed in the Skills Practice in *III. Writing.*

REVIEW

Review any items your student had difficulty with during the Oral Evaluation in Lesson 2.

I. Conversation Skills

DIALOG

Kitty:	Hi, Jimmy. Come on in.
Jimmy:	Hi, Kitty. It's windy out.
Kitty:	Yes, and I think it's going to rain too.
Jimmy:	I hope not. I have to go to the post office. Would you like to come with me?
Kitty:	Yes, thanks. I'd like to.

Teacher models the dialog, using the procedure outlined in Lesson 1. Use p. 20 of *ESOL Illustrations 2* to explain *windy* and *rainy* and p. 16 for *post office.*

VOCABULARY: Buildings in a City

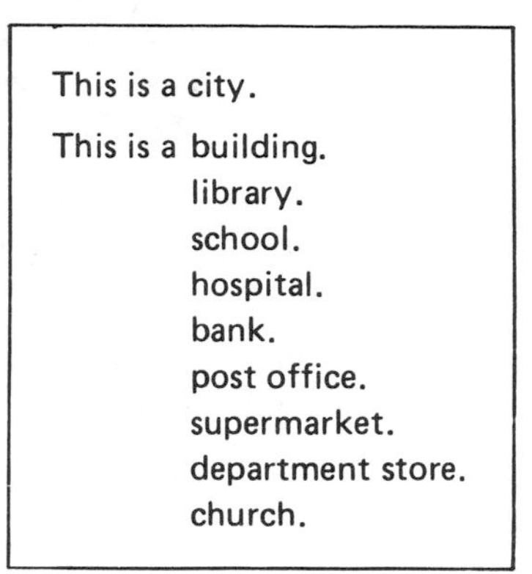

This is a city.

This is a building.
library.
school.
hospital.
bank.
post office.
supermarket.
department store.
church.

1. Teacher models the sentences several times, having the student repeat. Use pp. 14-17 of *ESOL Illustrations 2.*

[Indicating the pictures, say the sentences one by one.]

This is a city.
Kitty lives in a big building in the city.
Kitty goes to the library for books.

Kitty goes to the English classes at the school.
Kitty goes to the hospital in the afternoon. She's a nurse.

Kitty and Jimmy put money in the bank.
They send letters and buy stamps at the post office.
They buy milk and bread at the supermarket.

They buy clothes at the department store.
They go to church on Sunday.

2. Teacher models the sentences several times, having the student repeat. Use pp. 14-17 of *ESOL Illustrations 2* and the postage stamps and letters to explain the vocabulary items.

[Indicating the pictures, say the sentences one by one.]

DRILL: Identification Drill

Use pp. 14-17 of *ESOL Illustrations 2.*

[Pointing to the pictures, ask: "What's this? This is a city. Please repeat. This is a city."]

DRILL: Question and Answer Drill

1. Teacher asks questions with *Where* which will elicit the vocabulary being taught.

[Say: "Where does Kitty live? She lives in a big building. Please repeat. She lives in a big building."
Point to the appropriate picture]

Teacher	Student
Where does Kitty go for books?	She goes to the library.
Where does Kitty go for English classes?	
Kitty is a nurse. Where does she work?	
Where do Kitty and Jimmy put their money?	
Where do they buy bread?	
Where do they send letters and buy stamps?	
Where do they go on Sunday?	
Where do they buy clothes?	

2. Teacher asks the student about where he buys clothes, stamps, and so on.

Teacher	Student
Where do you buy stamps?	I buy them at the post office.
Where do you buy bread?	
Where do you go for books?	
Where do you buy milk?	
Where do you go for English classes?	
Where do you go on Sunday?	

VOCABULARY: Adjectives

The man is tall.	The child is short.
The building is tall.	The building is low.
The man is big.	The child is little.
The building is big.	The building is little.
The woman is young.	The man is old.
The building is new.	The building is old.
The woman is pretty.	The building is ugly.
The man is handsome.	The building is ugly.

Teacher models the sentence in the pairs given, as: *tall* and *short.* Using pp. 18-19 of *ESOL Illustrations 2,* have the student repeat after you.

[Say: "Listen to *tall* and *short*," and model the sentence. Have the student repeat.]

[Say: "Listen to *tall* and *low*," and model the sentence. Have the student repeat.]

[Continue in the same way with the remaining vocabulary items.]

DRILL: Reply and Rejoinder Drill

Teacher asks questions containing one adjective *(tall)* which will elicit a negative short answer. Then have the student give the correct information in a sentence which contains an opposite adjective (*short*). Use objects and pp. 18-19 of *ESOL Illustrations 2*.

[Holding up a little book, ask:
"Is this a big book? No, it isn't. It's little.
Please repeat. No, it isn't. It's little."]

Teacher	Student
[Hold up an old pencil.]	
Is this a new pencil?	No, it isn't. It's old.
Is this a little window?	
Is this a low building?	
Is she an old woman?	
Is he a young man?	
Is the woman ugly?	
Is the man ugly?	
Is this an old chair?	
Is this a big ring?	
Is this a new penny?	
Is he a short boy?	
Is she a tall girl?	

VOCABULARY and STRUCTURE FOCUS: Weather Expressions

It's windy.
It's sunny.
It's rainy.
It's snowy.
It's hot.
It's cold.

Teacher models sentences several times, having the student repeat. Use p. 20 of *ESOL Illustrations 2.*

Note: The construction with *It* plus *be* is used to express weather conditions. This same construction has already been introduced with time expressions.

You may add one other adjective that describes the weather on the day you are teaching this lesson, such as *cloudy, hazy,* or *foggy.*

[Point to the appropriate picture on p. 20 of *ESOL Illustrations 2* as you say: "It's windy. It's sunny," and so on.]

DRILL: Substitution Drill with Visual Cues

Pointing to a picture on p. 20 of *ESOL Illustrations 2,* ask about the weather.

[Point to the appropriate picture on p. 20 of *ESOL Illustrations 2* as you ask:
"How is the weather today? It's windy. Repeat. It's windy."]

[Continue with the remaining items.]

VOCABULARY: The Verb *need*

It's cold.	I need a coat.
It's rainy.	I need an umbrella.
It's snowy.	I need boots.
It's sunny.	I need a hat.

Teacher models the pairs of sentences several times, having the student repeat. Use p. 20 of *ESOL Illustrations 2* to explain the new vocabulary items.

[Say: "Listen to *need*."]

DRILL: Making Sentences

Teacher gives student a sentence about the weather plus a cue as to what a person needs during such weather, for example: "It's rainy," and the cue "umbrella." Student forms the sentence "I need an umbrella."

Teacher		Student
It's rainy.	umbrella	
I need an umbrella.		I need an umbrella.
It's warm.	coat	
I don't need a coat.		I don't need a coat.
It's rainy.	umbrella	I need an umbrella.
It's snowy.	boots	
It's sunny.	umbrella	
It's cold.	coat	
It's windy.	jacket	
It's snowy.	hat	

VOCABULARY: Flowers

This is a lily.

These are roses.
These are flowers.

Teacher models the sentences, having the student repeat. Use pp. 12-13 of *ESOL Illustrations 2.*

[Say: "Listen to *lily*," as you point to the picture. Beckon to the student to repeat. Continue in the same way with *roses* and *flowers*.]

VOCABULARY: Persons One Knows

My sister	has a picture of her baby.
My friend	has a lily on the table.
My girl friend	is pretty.
My boy friend	is handsome.
My neighbor	has roses.
My boss	has flowers on his desk.

Teacher models the sentences, having the student repeat. Use pp. 12-13 of *ESOL Illustrations 2.*

The word *picture* is also new here; it can be explained easily with the illustration on p. 12.

[Say: "Listen to *baby*."
Model the sentences and beckon for the student to repeat.]

[Continue in the same way with the remaining items.]

DRILL: Identification Drill with Visual Cues

Teacher indicates the various illustrations of persons one knows to elicit the names.

[Pointing to the picture of *friend*, say:
"Who's this? This is a friend. Please repeat. This is a friend."]

[Continue in the same way with all the items.]

DRILL: Substitution Drill with Vocal Cues

1. Teacher takes out pictures (snapshots) of relatives, friends, a baby, and shows them to the student. Change the drill to fit the pictures you have on hand.

[Showing whatever pictures you have with you, identify them, using the pattern, "This is a picture of my ________." Have the student repeat after you.]

[Showing the pictures again, ask: "What is this?" Have the student answer by saying, "This is a picture of your ________." Be sure he uses the correct pronoun.]

2. Teacher may continue the drill by asking the student to show some of his own pictures. Use the question and answer patterns shown here.

Teacher: Do you have a picture of your ________?
Student: [Showing picture.]
This is a picture of my ________.

VOCABULARY: Chart and Story Words (Personal Titles and Names)

This is Kitty King.
<u>Ms</u>. King is a nurse.

This is Jimmy Fisher.
<u>Mr</u>. Fisher is a factory worker.

Teacher models each pair of sentences, having the student repeat. Use p. 16 of *ESOL Illustrations 2*.

The names *Ms. Kitty King* and *Mr. Jimmy Fisher* are used in the Lesson 3 story.

[Say: "Listen to *Ms.*," and say the first pair of sentences. Continue in the same way with *Mr.* and the second pair of sentences.]

STRUCTURE FOCUS: Prepositional Phrases as Noun Modifiers

This is a picture <u>of</u> <u>Kitty</u> <u>King</u>.
This is a building <u>on</u> <u>Main</u> <u>Street</u>.
This is a man <u>with</u> <u>his</u> <u>son</u>.

Teacher models the sentences several times, having the student repeat.

Note: Prepositional phrases *(of Kitty King)* follow the nouns they modify.

[Say: "Listen to *of Kitty King,*" and say the sentence. Continue in the same way with the phrases underlined above.]

DRILL: Combining Sentences

The teacher gives two statements which the student combines into one, using a prepositional phrase to modify the noun.

[Say: "This is a picture. This is Kitty King." Pause. "This is a picture of Kitty King. Please repeat. This is a picture of Kitty King."]

Teacher	Student
This is a picture. This is my sister's baby.	This is a picture of my sister's baby.
This is a picture. This is Kitty King.	This is a picture of Kitty King.
This is a picture. This is my boy friend.	This is a picture of my boy friend.
This is a building. The building is on Main Street.	This is a building on Main Street.
This is a bank. The bank is on Beacon Street.	This is a bank on Beacon Street.
This is a clock. The clock is on the wall.	This is a clock on the wall.
This is a woman. The woman is with her baby.	This is a woman with her baby.
This is a man. The man is with his son.	This is a man with his son.
This is a lily. The lily is on the table.	This is a lily on the table.

STRUCTURE FOCUS: *There is* and *There are*

There is	a	picture	on the table.
There is	some	coffee	in the cup.
There are	some	chairs	in the room.
There are	ten	students	in the class.

Teacher models the sentences several times, having the student repeat. Place one of the pictures you have brought with you on the table.

[Say: "Listen to *There is,*" and model the sentences.]

[Then say: "Listen to *There are.*"]

Note: In this pattern, the word *there* is in the subject position. The word has no meaning in itself.

The word *some* may be used with *There is* and a non-count noun or with *There are* and a plural count noun.

DRILL: Substitution Drill with Vocal Cues

1. Drill with *There is.*

Teacher	Student
There is a pen on the table.	There is a pen on the table.
book	There is a book on the table.
pencil	
picture	
orange	
some water	

2. Drill with *There are.*

Teacher	Student
There are pens on the table.	There are pens on the table.
some cups	
dishes	
pans	
two apples	
some books	

3. Drill with both *There is* and *There are.*

Teacher	Student
There is a cup on the table.	There is a cup on the table.
some cups	
some paper	
some cheese	
some spoons	
some forks	
some bread	

DRILL: Making Statements

Teacher begins the drill by giving a word which identifies something in the room (known vocabulary).

The student must use the word in a sentence beginning with *There is* or *There are.*

After the student has done a few sentences in this way, encourage him to make up his own sentences, using this pattern.

You may begin modeling the contracted form *There's* in this drill.

Teacher	Student
a book	
There's a book on the table.	There's a book on the table.
two windows	There are two windows in the room.
a door	
a blackboard	
some pencils	

STRUCTURE FOCUS: Questions with *Is there* and *Are There*

	There	is	a	bank	on Main Street.
Is	there		a	bank	on Main Street?
	There	is	some	sugar	in the coffee.
Is	there		any	sugar	in the coffee?
	There	are	some	pet shops	downtown.
Are	there		any	pet shops	downtown?

Teacher models the statement and the corresponding question several times, having the student repeat.

Note: In the question form, *any* is used with a non-count noun or with a plural count noun.

[Say: "Listen to *Is there*," before modeling the first two statements and questions.]

[Say: "Listen to *Are there*," before modeling the last statement and question.]

DRILL: Transformation Drill

The student transforms a statement into a question. The student must also change *some* or a number in the statement to *any* in the question.

You may use the contracted form *There's* in this drill.

Teacher	Student
There's a bank on Main Street.	Is there a bank on Main Street?
There's an orange on the table.	Is there an orange on the table?
There are some cups on the table.	Are there any cups on the table?
There are three hospitals in this city.	Are there any hospitals in this city?
There's some bread on the table.	Is there any bread on the table?
There's a post office on Main Street.	
There's a library downtown.	
There are some apples in the kitchen.	
There's some soup in that dish.	
There are two windows in the bedroom.	

STRUCTURE FOCUS: Short Answers with *There + be*

Is there	a	table	in the room?	Yes,	there is.
Are there	any	pens	on the table?	No,	there aren't.

Teacher models each question and its answer several times, having the student repeat both.

[First say: "Listen to *Yes, there is.*"
Then say: "Listen to *No, there isn't.*"]

DRILL: Short Answer Drill

Teacher asks the student questions to which he can give short affirmative and negative answers.

The student should answer according to what he sees in the room in which you have class. Use the cup and the glass (both empty) to elicit negative answers.

Listen carefully to be sure that your student says *there* instead of *they*, a common error.

[Say: "Is there a chair in this room? Yes, there is. Please repeat. Yes, there is."]

Teacher	Student
Is there a table in the room?	Yes, there is.
Is there a window in the room?	
Are there two doors in the room?	
Are there any dogs in the room?	
Is there any coffee in the cup?	
Are there any children in the room?	
Is there any water in the glass?	
Are there any books on the table?	
Is there any milk in the glass?	

STRUCTURE FOCUS: Past Tense of *be* (*was/were*)

I am cold today.	I was cold yesterday.
It is hot today.	It was hot yesterday.
She is at home today.	She was at home yesterday.
You are at school today.	You were at school yesterday.
We are at school today.	We were at school yesterday.
We are in class today.	They were in class yesterday.

Teacher models the present tense form (which the student already knows) and its corresponding past tense form (a new item).

Indicate by using a calendar the meaning of *today* and *yesterday.*

[Say: "Listen to *was,*" and model the sentences with *was.*]

[Say: "Listen to *were,*" and model the sentences with *were.*]

DRILL: Multi-Slot Substitution Drill with Vocal Cues

Teacher	Student
I was in class yesterday.	I was in class yesterday.
at home	
I was at home yesterday.	I was at home yesterday.
She	
at the bank	
They	
He	
You	
It is cold today.	It is cold today.
yesterday	
It was cold yesterday.	It was cold yesterday.
She	
at home	
today	
at the bank	

DRILL: Transformation Drill

Student changes a present tense statement into a past tense statement.

Teacher	Student
It is cold.	It was cold.
She is tall.	
The buildings are new.	
The building is ugly.	
You are in class today.	
They are going downtown today.	
I am in class today.	
Bob is handsome.	
It is windy today.	

STRUCTURE FOCUS: Past Tense Questions with *be* (*was/were*)

	You were	in class yesterday.
Were	you	in class yesterday?
	He was	at the bank yesterday.
Was	he	at the bank yesterday?

Teacher models the statement and question, having the student repeat the question.

Note: When making questions with *was* and *were*, use question word order: *was* or *were* comes before the subject word.

Use a rising intonation when making questions with *was* and *were*.

[Say: "Listen to *Were*."
Say both the statement and the question, beckoning the student to repeat: "Were you in class yesterday?"]

DRILL: Transformation Drill

Teacher gives the statement and has the student transform (change) the statement into a question.

Teacher	Student
You were in class yesterday.	Were you in class yesterday?
They were in class yesterday.	
We were at the post office yesterday.	
They were at the bank yesterday.	
I was cold.	
It was sunny.	
She was pretty.	
There was a picture on the desk.	
There are some pencils on the desk.	

STRUCTURE FOCUS: Short Answers with *was* and *were*

Was Ann at the bank?	Yes, she was.
Were you in class yesterday?	No, I wasn't.
Were they at work yesterday?	No, they weren't.

Teacher models the question and short answer, having the student repeat only the answer.

[Say first: "Listen to *Yes, she was.*"
Then say: "Listen to *No, I wasn't.*"]

DRILL: Short Answers (Free Reply)

1. Student gives a short answer to questions with *was* and *were*.

Teacher	Student
Were you in class yesterday?	(Yes, I was.)
Was the student in class?	(No, he wasn't.)
Was Kitty at the supermarket yesterday?	
Were Kitty and Jimmy at the bank?	
Were you at the post office yesterday?	
Was your boss at work?	
Were we at the library yesterday?	
Was Glenn in church on Sunday?	
Was it hot yesterday?	

2. Student gives a short answer to questions with *is/are, was/were,* and *do/does.*

   This is a review exercise since questions with *is/are* and *do/does* were practiced in *ESOL Manual 1.*

Teacher	Student
Do you have a pen?	(Yes, I do.)
Does the boy live in that building?	(No, he doesn't.)
Are you tall?	(No, I'm not.)
Was that a sweet orange?	
Do you drink coffee?	
Is the coffee hot?	
Was the water cold?	
Do you have a sister?	
Does the girl go downtown every day?	
Were you at home yesterday?	
Is this your book?	
Was Ann downtown yesterday?	
Were we in school on Sunday?	
Are you reading?	
Do you need a piece of paper?	

PRONUNCIATION: /ā/ and /a/, /w/ and /v/

1. See the Pronunciation section in Lesson 1 for the steps to follow in teaching the vowel sounds /ā/ and /a/ as in *pain* and *pan*.

   These vowel sounds are review, so drill them quickly.

[Say: "Listen to /ā/ and /a/."]

/ā/	/a/	Sentences
pain	pan	It's a big plane.
cape	cap	I'd like a snack.
aid	add	Take this home.
pace	pass	It's a black cat.
Kate	cat	I ate the cake.

2. Following the same procedure, teach the consonant sounds /w/ and /v/ as in *wet* and *vet*.

   Note: The sounds /w/ and /v/ are voiced sounds. In making /w/, the lips are round, whereas in making /v/, the upper teeth are on the lower lip.

[Say: "Listen to /w/ and /v/."]

/w/	/v/	Sentences
wet	vet	Go west.
wine	vine	They went wild.
west	vest	His vest is wet.
rowing	roving	The wine is good.
wane	vane	Van will do it.
		He visited the Warings.

ORAL EVALUATION

1. Review the vocabulary on buildings in a city and the corresponding activities. Student should be able to identify eight of the buildings and all the activities fairly quickly.

   [Using pp. 14-17 of *ESOL Illustrations 2*, do the Question and Answer Drill which follows Vocabulary: Buildings in a City.]

2. Review the adjectives introduced. Student should be able to use eight of these fairly quickly.

   [Do the Reply and Rejoinder Drill which follows Vocabulary: Adjectives.]

3. Review expressions to describe the weather. Student should be able to describe all of these fairly quickly.

   [Using p. 20 of *ESOL Illustrations 2*, ask: "How is the weather today?"]

4. Review the verb *need*. This is an essential vocabulary item.

   [Using p. 20 of *ESOL Illustrations 2,* do the Making Sentences Drill following Vocabulary: The Verb *need*.]

5. Review the vocabulary on flowers and on naming persons one knows. Student should be able to identify *lily* and *girl friend* for the story, and at least three other items.

   [Do the Identification Drill with Visual Cues which follows Vocabulary: Persons One Knows.]

   [Then, point to the flowers and ask: "What is this?" and "What are these?"]

6. Review the use of prepositional phrases as noun modifiers. Student should be able to do these fairly quickly.

   [Do the Combining Sentences Drill following Structure Focus: Prepositional Phrases as Noun Modifiers.]

7. Review the use of *there is* and *there are* in questions and short answers.

   [Do the Transformation Drill following Structure Focus: Questions with *Is there* and *Are there*. Have the student answer each question.]

8. Review the use of *was* and *were* in statements and questions. This is a vital pattern for the student to know.

   [Do the Transformation Drills after Structure Focus: Past Tense of *be* and Past Tense Questions with *be*.]

9. Review making short answers with *am, is, are, was, were, do,* and *does.* It is extremely important that your student be able to answer the questions, giving the correct short answer without much hesitation. This drill will practice material he has learned in the past as well as new material and is basic to future lessons.

   [Do part 2 in the Short Answers (Free Reply) Drill which follows Structure Focus: Short Answers with *was* and *were*.]

II. Reading

Check your student's homework from Lesson 2. Have him quickly read everything on both pages to you.

CHART 3: Page 12

Note: The vowel sound for *y* in an unstressed syllable at the end of a word is somewhere between the short *i* sound and the long *e* sound. Pronounce words ending in *y* as you would naturally say them, and use the same pronunciation when you say the vowel sound /y/ by itself. But refer to the sound as the vowel sound for *y,* not the short *i* sound or the long *e* sound.

At this time, do *not* mention that *y* may sometimes have another vowel sound, as in *cry.* For your own information, *y* has this long *i* sound when it comes at the end of a stressed syllable.

Teach this chart exactly as you did the previous ones, except introduce the key word like this.

Do this:	Say this:
Point to the picture of the lily.	Teacher: This is a lily. What is this? Student: This is a lily.
Point to the key word *lily.*	Teacher: This word is lily. Read: *lily.* Student: Lily.
Cover all but the final *y* in *lily.*	Teacher: *Lily* ends with the sound /y/. What sound does *lily* end with? Student: /y/.
Point to the red *y* under *lily.*	Teacher: *Lily* ends with the letter *y.* What letter does *lily* end with? Student: *y.*
Again, cover all but the final *y* in *lily.*	Teacher: *Lily* ends with the vowel sound /y/. *Lily* ends with the letter *y.* In *lily, y* is a vowel.
Point to *y* at top right of page.	Teacher: What is the name of this letter? Student: *y.*
	Teacher: The vowel sound of *y* is /y/. What is the vowel sound of *y?* Student: /y/.
Point to the final *y* in *lily.*	Teacher: What is this vowel sound? Student: /y/.
	Teacher: Good!

Do the rest of the chart as you did the previous charts in this book. Your instructions to the student for the three columns of words are:

Column 1:	Please read.
Column 2 (in red):	[Point to the letter or letters for each sound.] What is the sound? [Point to the vowel sound being studied.] What is the vowel sound?
Column 3:	Please read.

You will want to point out these things to your student about the new chart words.

city:	In *city, c* has the sound /s/. In *city, y* has the vowel sound /y/.
windy:	In *windy, y* has the vowel sound /y/.
Kitty:	*Kitty* has two *t*'s, but they have one sound: /t/. In *Kitty, y* has the vowel sound /y/.
Jimmy:	*Jimmy* has two *m*'s, but they have one sound: /m/. In *Jimmy, y* has the vowel sound /y/.
building:	In *building*, the *u* is silent [finger over lips]. The letters *ng* make the sound /ng/.
picture:	In *picture*, you say /k/-/ch/, but you write *c, t.* In *picture*, you say /er/, but you write *u, r, e.* The letters *ure* make the sound /er/.

Note: Whenever you teach a new name—as a chart word or a story word—tell whether it is a man's name, a woman's name, or a family name. Also, point out that the name begins with a capital letter.

STORY: In the City

Teach the story the same way as the previous ones in this book. The new story words are: *Ms., King, Fisher, pretty.*

Use the questions below to check the student's comprehension. Many short answers are shown here, but the student may also answer with full sentences. Either way is all right.

	Teacher	Student
Paragraph 1	Is the city big or little?	It's big.
	Is the city windy?	Yes, it is.
Paragraph 2	Where does Kitty King live?	She lives in the windy city.
	Where does Jimmy Fisher live?	He lives in the windy city.
Paragraph 3	Where does Kitty live?	She lives in this big building.
	Where does Jimmy live?	He lives in a big building.
	Does Jimmy live in Kitty's building?	No, he doesn't.
	Does a city have big buildings?	Yes, it does.
Paragraph 4	Who is visiting Kitty?	Jimmy Fisher is.
	What is Jimmy giving to Kitty?	A lily.
Paragraph 5	Is the lily pretty?	Yes, it is.
	Does Kitty thank Jimmy for the lily?	Yes, she does.
Paragraph 6	What is Kitty giving to Jimmy?	Her picture.
	Is it a picture of Kitty?	Yes, it is.
	Does Jimmy thank Kitty for the picture?	Yes, he does.

SKILLS PRACTICE: Subtracting *-ing*

Write the following words, lined up as shown. Ask your student to read first the *-ing* form, then the root, as: *visiting, visit.*

visiting	bringing	singing	getting	giving	living	whistling
visit	bring	sing	get	give	live	whistle

Do *not* explain anything about adding or subtracting the ending at this point.

SKILLS PRACTICE: Words Ending in *-le*

Step 1: Write the following words on the board.
Line up and underline all the final *-le*'s as shown.

little
uncle   ul
whistle

Step 2: Ask the student to read each word.

Step 3: Pointing to the *le* in the three words, say: "At the end of a word, *le* has the sound /ul/."

Write *ul* to the right of the three words.

Pointing to the *le* in each word, say: "*Little, uncle, whistle.*"

III. Writing

WRITING LESSON: Page 14

Study

First, read the headings. Then, help your student study each chart word. Point out all the differences between how the words are said and how they are written. Study also the new story word *pretty*.

Have the student write the following words in the Study section:

1. city
2. Kitty
3. Jimmy
4. building
5. picture
6. pretty

Listen and write

Have your student cover the words he has written in the Study section. Then dictate the following words for him to write:

1. lily
2. windy
3. pretty
4. city
5. building
6. picture

Write

Have your student copy the names and the phrase at the bottom of the page. Be sure he uses capital letters correctly and understands why they are necessary in each case. Finally, have him read the page number.

SKILLS PRACTICE: Vowels and Consonants

In this exercise, you will review the meaning of *vowel* and teach the meaning of *consonant*. Then, you will teach the student to use the symbols *V* and *C* to stand for *vowel* and *consonant.* This is preparation for exercises in the next lessons on adding *-ing* to verbs.

Before class, write the Vowel-Consonant Chart shown here on paper (on large chart paper for a class). Make the chart as neat as you can. Line up the letters exactly as shown here. Save this chart for use in the next lessons; the student will need to refer to it.

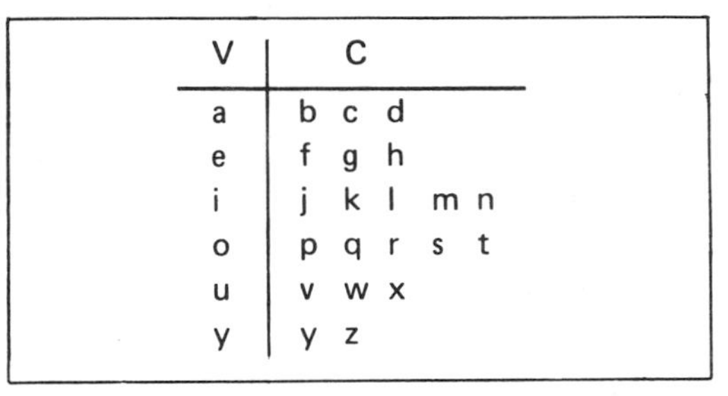

Step 1: Pointing to the column of vowels, say:
"These are vowels. *A* is a vowel, *E* is a vowel," and so on, through "*Y* is a vowel."

Step 2: Point to the letters to the right of the vertical line, and say: "These are consonants.
B is a consonant. *C* is a consonant. *H* is a consonant. *T* is a consonant.
Y is a consonant or a vowel." (Point to both *y*'s.)

Step 3: Point to all the vowels, and ask: "What are these?"
When student answers, "Vowels," point to the heading *V*. Say: "Good! Vowels."

Step 4: Point to all the consonants and ask: "What are these?"
When student answers, "Consonants," point to the heading *C*. Say: "Good! Consonants."

HOMEWORK: Page 15

Ask the student to read everything on this page to you. Ask him to write the homework at home and to read the first three charts and stories at home.

READING AND WRITING EVALUATION

1. Write these words: *city, windy, Kitty, Jimmy.* Have the student read each word. Then, point to the *y* in each word, and ask: What is the vowel sound of *y*?

   The student should be able to read all four words correctly and to give /i/ as the vowel sound of *y*.

2. Write the following sentences on the board, spacing the words as shown. Have the student circle the correct word and read the sentence.

   The lily is pretty. / windy.

   The buildings in a city / river are big.

   Kitty lives in / on a big building.

   The student should be able to complete at least two sentences correctly.

3. Dictate the following words for the student to write: *city, Jimmy, windy, building, lily, pretty, picture.*
   The student should be able to spell five correctly.

MORE READING

In *More Stories 2,* the stories for Lesson 3 may be read in class or suggested for reading at home.

Lesson 4

OBJECTIVES

When a student completes this lesson, he should be able to:

1. Say and respond to a new dialog.
2. Identify chart and story words.
3. Identify objects in a kitchen.
4. Use *here* and *there*.
5. Use the imperative form of the verb.
6. Give polite responses to requests.
7. Use *What* as the subject in questions, such as "What is in the kitchen?" and give short answers.
8. Use the verb *like.*
9. Use the infinitive after the verbs *want, need,* and *like.*
10. Pronounce the vowel sounds /o/ and /u/ as in *dock* and *duck* and the consonant sounds /w/ and /g/ as in *wet* and *get*.
11. Read the following new words:
    Chart words: *gun, duck, hunting, sun, son, cut, cutting*
    Story words: *hit, mud, bring.*
12. Read a simple story, using the new chart and story words.
13. Double the final consonant before adding *-ing* to a verb, when appropriate.
14. Write the new chart and story words.

VISUAL AIDS

1. *ESOL Illustrations 2*, pp. 21-22.
2. Bring sufficient pieces of candy to class to help demonstrate vocabulary.
3. Before class, make the two charts as directed in the Skills Practice in *III. Writing.*

REVIEW

Review any items your student had difficulty with during the Oral Evaluation in Lesson 3.

I. Conversation Skills

DIALOG

Mother:	Jill, please help me make dinner. Please cut the bread with this knife.
Jill:	Sure, Mom.
Mother:	Thank you. Put the bread on the table, and call everyone to dinner.
Jill:	Ed, Kim, Dad! It's time for dinner.
Mother:	Wash your hands, Ed. Hurry. We're ready for dinner.

Teacher models the dialog, using the procedure outlined in Lesson 1.

VOCABULARY: Chart and Story Words

The sun is up.
Glenn Hill is hunting with his son.
They are hunting ducks with guns.

Ed hits a duck.
The duck is in the mud.

Ed picks up the duck.
He brings the duck to the tent.
Ed cuts up the duck.

Teacher models the sentences several times, having the student repeat. Use p. 21 of *ESOL Illustrations 2*. These words are necessary for the story.

DRILL: Question and Answer Drill

Teacher asks questions which elicit answers using the vocabulary being taught. Use p. 21 of *ESOL Illustrations 2* to prompt the student.

[Say: "Where is the sun? The sun is up. Repeat. The sun is up."]

Teacher	Student
Where is the sun?	The sun is up.
What is Glenn Hill doing?	
Who is Glenn hunting with?	
What are Glenn and his son hunting?	
What are they hunting with?	
What does Ed hit?	
Where is the duck?	
Where does Ed bring the duck?	
What does Ed do to the duck?	

VOCABULARY: The Kitchen

This is a kitchen.

There is a pan on the stove.
There are cups in the sink.
There is a rug on the floor.
There is a light on the ceiling.
There is a telephone on the wall.

There are dishes in the cabinet.
There is bread on the counter.
There is milk in the refrigerator.

Using p. 22 of *ESOL Illustrations 2*, teacher models the sentences several times, having the student repeat.

[As you say the vocabulary items, point to the appropriate part of the picture.]

DRILL: Identification Drill

Teacher has the student identify the kitchen items on p. 22 of *ESOL Illustrations 2.*

[Varying the order of presentation and pointing to the item, ask: "What's this?" Prompt your student only when necessary.]

DRILL: Question and Answer Drill

[Ask: "Where are the cups? The cups are in the sink. Please repeat. The cups are in the sink."]

Teacher	Student
Where are the dishes?	The dishes are in the cabinet.
Where is the pan?	
Where is the light?	
Where is the milk?	
Where are the cups?	
Where is the bread?	
Where is the telephone?	
Where is the rug?	
What is this? [Indicate the entire kitchen.]	

VOCABULARY: The Use of *here* and *there*

This is my watch.	It is here.
That is my watch.	It is there.

Teacher models the sentences several times, having the student repeat.

Note: *Here* is used to designate at or in *this* place whereas *there* is at or in *that* place.

[Say: "Listen to *here.*" Indicating your watch near you, say the first sentence above.]

[Then place your watch at some distance from yourself. Say: "Listen to *there*." Indicating your watch, say the second sentence.]

DRILL: Question and Answer Drill

Set some objects near the student, and others at a distance. Ask questions which will elicit answers containing *here* or *there*, as appropriate.

Teacher	Student
[Indicating the object.]	
Where is your book?	It's here.
Where is the door?	It's there.
Where is the window?	
Where is the blackboard?	
Where is your pen?	
Where is your pencil?	

STRUCTURE FOCUS: Making Requests with Imperatives

Please open	the window.
Please close	your book.
Bring	the book to me.
Have	a piece of candy.
Come	here.

Teacher models the sentences several times, having the student repeat. Perform the action as you say the sentences.

[Say: "Listen to ***Please open the window***," indicating by opening the window and beckoning, that you want the student to do so.]

[Follow the same procedure with the remaining items.]

Candy, a new word here, will be easy to demonstrate by giving the student a piece of candy as you say the sentence.

Note: Requests (with *please*), commands, and directions are formed by using the basic form of the verb.

Do not teach alternate polite forms, such as "Would you please ...," at this time.

The verb *come* is new here.

DRILL: Making Requests

Teacher gives a noun and has the student use it to make a request.

If the student cannot do so, prompt him.

[Say: "The door." Pause. "Please open the door. Repeat. Please open the door."]

Teacher	**Student** (Possible requests)
the book	(Please close the book.)
the window	(Please close the window.)
a piece of candy	(Have a piece of candy.)
a glass of water	(Drink a glass of water.)
the chair	(Please sit in the chair.)
your sandwich	(Eat your sandwich.)
English	(Please speak English.)
your coat	(Please take off your coat.)

DRILL: Acting on a Request

Teacher makes a polite request and indicates that the student is to do what has been requested. Ask him to explain what he is doing. If the student does not understand, show him what to do by doing it yourself and answering the question. Help him only as long as—or if—it is necessary.

[After making sure the student's book is closed, say: "Please open your book." Indicate with a motion of your hand that you want the student to open his book. As he performs the action, ask: "What are you doing?" expecting the student to answer, "I'm opening my book."]

[Repeat this for each of the requests.]

Teacher	**Student**
Please close your book. What are you doing?	[Performs action.] I'm closing my book.
Please close the door. What are you doing?	[Performs action.] I'm closing the door.
Please open the window. What are you doing?	
Please throw away that paper. What are you doing?	
Please pick up your pencil. What are you doing?	
Please look at the clock (your watch). What are you doing?	
Please sign your name. What are you doing?	
Please say "Hello." What are you saying?	
Please take off your watch (ring). What are you doing?	
Please put on your watch (ring). What are you doing?	

STRUCTURE FOCUS: Negative Requests

Please don't speak Spanish now.
Please don't look at your book.
Please don't go home now.
Please don't go there.

Teacher models the sentences several times, having the student repeat.

[Say: "Listen to *Please don't*."]

Note: Negative requests, directions, and commands are formed by using *don't* with the imperative form of the verb.

DRILL: Transformation Drill

Student transforms an affirmative request into a negative one.

[Say: "Please open your book. Please don't open your book. Repeat. Please don't open your book."]

Teacher	Student
Please speak Chinese.	Please don't speak Chinese.
Please give her the money.	
Please sign your name.	
Please open the window.	
Please look at your book.	
Please cut up the duck.	
Please bring the duck to the tent.	
Please thank me.	
Please put the glass on the table.	

VOCABULARY: Polite Replies to Requests

Request	Polite Reply
Please open the door for me.	All right.
Please close the window.	OK.
Have a cup of coffee.	Yes, thanks.
Have a piece of candy.	No, thank you.
Please don't speak Spanish in class.	I'm sorry.
Please don't look at your book.	OK, I won't.

Teacher models the request and its corresponding polite reply several times, having the student repeat both.

[Say: "Listen to *All right*," then repeat the request and reply.]

DRILL: Polite Replies

Teacher makes request and elicits polite affirmative and negative replies.

Accept any answer that is appropriate.

Teacher	Student
Please close the window.	OK. *or* All right.
Please open your book.	
Have a cup of coffee.	
Please don't speak Spanish in class.	
Please put the glass on the table.	
Please don't go home now.	
Please don't look at my book.	
Have a piece of candy.	

STRUCTURE FOCUS: Questions with *What* in Subject Position

A pan	is	on	the stove.
What	is	on	the stove?
The milk	is	in	the refrigerator.
What	is	in	the refrigerator?
The cups	are	in	the sink.
What	is	in	the sink?

Teacher models the statement and the corresponding question several times, having the student repeat both.

[Say: "Listen to *What*."]

Note: In these questions, *What* is a question word in the subject position. The verb in the question is in the third person singular even when the answer to be given is plural.

The intonation of *What* questions is the same as that of statements, that is, a falling intonation pattern (final).

DRILL: Transformation Drill

Student transforms a statement into a question using *What* in the subject position.

All of the questions should be in the third person singular (*What is*).

Teacher	Student
The milk is in the refrigerator.	What is in the refrigerator?
The meat is in the refrigerator.	What is in the refrigerator?
A pen is on the table.	
A clock is on the wall.	
A table and chairs are in the room.	
A rug is on the floor.	
A pencil is on the table.	
My pen and pencil are on the table.	
My coat is on the chair.	
His shoes are on the floor.	

STRUCTURE FOCUS: Short Answers to Questions with *What*

What is on the stove?	A pan.
What is on the floor?	A rug.
What is in the cabinet?	The dishes.

Teacher models the question and its short answer, having the student repeat only the answer.

[Say: "What is on the stove? A pan. Please repeat. A pan."]

DRILL: Short Answers

Teacher asks questions with *What* in subject position which elicit a short answer from the student.

[Using p. 22 of *ESOL Illustrations 2*, ask the following questions. Some require a plural answer.]

Teacher	Student
What is in the refrigerator?	Milk.
What is on the stove?	A pan.
What is in the sink?	Cups.
What is on the wall?	
What is on the ceiling?	
What is on the floor?	
What is in the cabinet?	
What is on the counter?	

VOCABULARY: The Verb *like*

I like apples.	I don't like oranges.
I like meat.	I don't like fish.
I like dogs.	I don't like cats.
I like my boss.	I don't like his wife.

Teacher models each contrasting pair of sentences—affirmative and negative—several times, having the student repeat both.

[Say: "Listen to *like* and *don't like*."]

Demonstrate the meaning of *like* by smiling broadly and *don't like* by frowning, wrinkling your nose, and shaking your head.

DRILL: Question and Answer Drill

Teacher asks a question with *like*, giving two choices.

Student answers by telling which of the two he likes. He then gives a negative statement as well.

Teacher	Student
Do you like cats or dogs?	(I like cats.) (I don't like dogs.)
Do you like apples or oranges?	
Do you like meat or fish?	
Do you like roses or lilies?	
Do you like bananas or oranges?	
Do you like skirts or jeans?	
Do you like Bob or Jim?	
Do you like Jill or Kim?	

STRUCTURE FOCUS: The Use of the Infinitive

I want to buy a jacket.
I need to buy some bread.
I like to go shopping.

Teacher models the sentences several times, having the student repeat.

[Say: "Listen to *to buy*."]

Be sure that the student hears and pronounces *to*, but do not stress the word as you say it.

Note: Verbs like *want, need,* and *like* can be followed either by a noun (*I want a pen*) or by an infinitive (*I want to buy a pen*).

The infinitive is *to* plus the simple form of the verb.

Not all verbs can be followed by an infinitive. For example, consider *I enjoy singing.*

DRILL: Completing Sentences

Teacher gives the student a verb phrase, such as *buy a jacket*, and the beginning of the sentence, such as *I want*.

Student puts these together in a sentence with an infinitive, such as *I want to buy a jacket.*

Teacher	Student
buy a jacket I want	
I want to buy a jacket.	I want to buy a jacket.
buy a coat She wants	
go fishing I like	
buy some new shoes He needs	
wear jeans I like	
go hunting Glenn likes	
study English I need	
walk home I want	
watch television We want	
go to the bathroom The child needs	
wash her hands She needs	

DRILL: Transformation Drill

Teacher gives an affirmative statement with *want, need,* or *like* plus an infinitive.

Student transforms it into a negative statement.

Teacher	Student
I like to cook.	
I don't like to cook.	I don't like to cook.
I like to wash dishes.	I don't like to wash dishes.
We want to go home now.	
You need to wear a coat today.	
I need to go to the supermarket today.	
Kitty wants to have lunch now.	
He wants to throw away his old jacket.	
We like to watch television.	
They need to buy a new stove.	

PRONUNCIATION: /o/ and /u/, /w/ and /g/

1. See the Pronunciation section in Lesson 1 for the steps to follow in teaching the vowel sounds /o/ and /u/ as in *dock* and *duck.*

[Say: "Listen to /o/ and /u/."]

/o/	/u/	Sentences
dock	duck	The coffee is hot.
cot	cut	The bus is late.
not	nut	The baby sucks his thumb.
cop	cup	The sun is hot.
stock	stuck	It's a mud hut.
		Cut up the duck.

2. Following the same procedure, teach the consonant sounds /w/ and /g/ as in *wet* and *get.*

[Say: "Listen to /w/ and /g/."]

/w/	/g/	Sentences
wet	get	She's a good woman.
wait	gate	Would you wait?
will	gill	Will you get me the gun?
we're	gear	Go west.
west	guest	Will's in the garden.
		We're guests.

ORAL EVALUATION

1. Review the chart and story words. Student should be able to say all of these fairly quickly since these words are necessary for the story.

   [Do the Question and Answer Drill following Vocabulary: Chart and Story Words.]

2. Review the vocabulary concerning the kitchen. Student should be able to identify eight of these fairly quickly.

   [Using p. 22 of *ESOL Illustrations 2,* have the student identify the items.]

3. Review the use of *here* and *there*.

   [Do the Question and Answer Drill following Vocabulary: The Use of *here* and *there*.]

4. Review making and politely answering requests. Have the student make a polite request, which you carry out; then switch roles. Make some of the requests negative.

   Review this pattern at the next class session if the student hesitates and cannot either make the request or respond to it.

   [Follow this procedure.]

   Student: Please open your book.
   Teacher: OK. [Performing action.]

   [Reverse roles.]

   Teacher: Please don't open the window.
   Student: All right. [*Not* performing action.]

5. Review questions with *What* in subject position and the corresponding short answers. In a class situation, have one student make the question and another give the answer.

   [Use p. 22 of *ESOL Illustrations 2* if necessary.]

   Teacher: A pan is on the stove.
   Student: What is on the stove? A pan.

6. Review the infinitive. This is an introduction to the infinitive and should be drilled at the next class session if the student has difficulty remembering to use *to* plus the simple form of the verb.

   [Do the Completing Sentences Drill following Structure Focus: The Use of the Infinitive.]

II. Reading

Check your student's homework from Lesson 3 before beginning the chart.

CHART 4: Page 16

Teach this chart in the same way you taught the previous charts. ("Read. What is the sound? What is the vowel sound? Read.") Be sure to have the student read everything on the page, from the heading and key word to the page number.

Point out these things about the spelling of the chart words:

sun/son: After doing the lines for *sun* and *son* on the chart, point to the word *sun* next to the picture
Say: "*Sun* with a *u* means this sun." Point to the picture.

Point to the word *son* next to the picture.
Say: "*Son* with an *o* means this son." Point to the picture.

duck: In *duck,* the letters *ck* make one sound: /k/.

hunting: The letters *ng* make the sound /ng/.

Cover the *-ing,* and say: "I hunt every day."
Uncover the *-ing,* and say: "I'm hunting now."

cut, cutting: Point to the word *cut* next to the picture.
Say: "Cut the paper."

Point to the word *cutting* next to the picture.
Say: "I am cutting the paper."

Pointing to *cut*, say: "*Cut* has one *t*."
Pointing to *cutting*, say: "*Cutting* has two *t*'s.

STORY: Duck Hunting

Teach the story in the usual way, following the steps described in Lesson 1. The new story words are: *hit, mud, bring.*

Use the following comprehension questions. Either short or long answers are acceptable.

	Teacher	Student
Paragraph 1	Who has a gun?	Mr. Hill does.
	Is the gun big or little?	It's big.
Paragraph 2	What is Mr. Hill doing?	He's hunting.
	Who is with Mr. Hill?	Ed is.
	Who is Ed?	Ed is Mr. Hill's son.
	What is Ed doing?	He's hunting ducks.
	Do Mr. Hill and Ed have guns?	Yes, they do.
Paragraph 3	What is Mr. Hill looking at?	The sun.
	What is Ed looking at?	The sun.
Paragraph 4	What does Ed do?	He hits a duck.
	What does Ed yell?	"I hit a duck!"
Paragraph 5	Where is the duck?	It's in the mud.
	Who picks up the duck?	Ed does.
Paragraph 6	Who brings the duck to the tent?	Ed does.
	Who cuts up the duck?	Ed does.
Paragraph 7	Who thanks Ed for cutting up the duck?	Mr. Hill does.

After reading the story, have a conversation with your student about hunting. Use as many of the suggested questions below as apply, depending on the answers the student gives.

Teacher	Student
Do you go hunting?	[Gives free replies.]
What do you hunt?	
Where do you hunt?	
Who goes hunting with you?	
Do you have a gun?	
Is it big or little?	
Do you hunt with your gun?	

If your student does not hunt, substitute similar questions about *fishing, sailing, swimming, camping,* or *hiking*. All of these were taught as vocabulary in *ESOL Manual 1.*

III. Writing

CHECKUP: Page 18

Ask your student to read this page silently and to write the answers. When he has finished the page, ask him to read aloud everything on the page (headings, instructions, his answers, the page number). Check his work carefully. Be sure he uses capital letters only where they are needed.

WRITING LESSON: Page 19

Study

Help your student study and write the chart and story words shown below. Point out every difference between the spelling of the word and how it is said.

1. duck
2. pick
3. cutting
4. son

Listen and write

Dictate the following words for the student to write:

1. gun
2. mud
3. cut
4. up
5. hunting
6. sun [Give a sentence as a cue: *The sun is up*.]

Check the student's work carefully. Then, cover the top two-thirds of the page and dictate this second group of words for the student to write at the bottom of the page. Check the student's spelling carefully. Correct any mistakes in a positive way.

1. cut
2. cutting
3. pick
4. picking
5. duck
6. son [Give a sentence: *Ed is Mr. Hill's son.*]

SKILLS PRACTICE: Doubling the Final Consonant Before Adding *-ing*

Before class, prepare the two charts shown in boxes in this Skills Practice. Write them fairly large on a sheet of paper, lining up the headings and words exactly as shown. (If you have a class, make a large wall chart and individual copies for each student.) Do not write in the word shown in handwriting at right.

Have the Vowel-Consonant Chart that you wrote in Lesson 3 available for the student to look at, if he wishes, as you do this exercise.

	C V C	+ C	i n g	
get	g e t	t	i n g	getting
cut	c u t	t	i n g	
put	p u t	t	i n g	
run	r u n	n	i n g	
hit	h i t			
sit	s i t			

Do this:	Say this:
1. Point to *get* at left.	Teacher: Please read. Student: Get.
Point to *g* in *get* under *CVC*.	Teacher: Is this a vowel or a consonant? Student: A consonant. Teacher: [Pointing to *C* over the *g*.] Good! A consonant.
Point to *e* in *get* under *CVC*.	Teacher: Is this a vowel or a consonant? Student: A vowel. Teacher: [Pointing to *V* over the *e*.] Good! A vowel.
Point to *t* in *get* under *CVC*.	Teacher: Is this a vowel or a consonant? Student: A consonant. Teacher: [Pointing to *C* over the *t*.] Good! A consonant.
Point, one at a time, to the letters *g, e, t* under *CVC*.	Teacher: Consonant, vowel, consonant.
2. Point to *cut* at left.	Teacher: Please read. Student: Cut.
Point to the letters *c, u, t* under *CVC*, one at a time.	Teacher: Consonant, vowel, consonant. [Beckon for student to say this with you.]
3. Do the rest of the words—*put, run, hit, sit*—as you did *cut* in step 2.	
4. Point to *get* under *CVC*, then run your finger under *getting* under the headings.	Teacher: Get. Getting.
Point to *g, e, t*. Point to the second *t*. Point to *i, n, g*.	Teacher: Consonant, vowel, consonant; [pause] consonant; [pause] *i, n, g*.
Run your finger under *getting*.	Teacher: Getting.
Point to the blank at right.	Teacher: Please write *getting*. Student: [Writes *getting* in the blank.]
5. Do *cutting, putting,* and *running* the same way as in step 4.	
6. With *hit* and *sit*, have the student first complete the words on the chart, and then write them again in the blanks at the right.	

Note: The formula used here, *CVC + C + ing*, applies only to one-syllable words.

Words ending in *x* are an exception to this rule. In such words, the final consonant is not doubled. Compare *get, getting* with *fix, fixing*, for example.

The student has not yet learned to read any verbs ending in *x*, so this exception will not be a problem for him.

Do not try to explain any of this to the student, since he does not have the vocabulary to understand your explanation. Let him learn from the pattern shown in the chart.

With this second chart, you will contrast for the student verbs that do *not* require doubling of the final consonant because they already end with two consonants. You will teach this chart in the same way you taught the previous one.

	C V C C	+ i n g	
hunt	h u n t	i n g	hunting
fish	f i s h	i n g	
sing	s i n g	i n g	
bring	b r i n g	i n g	
jump	j u m p		
kick	k i c k		

Do this:	**Say this:**
1. Point to *hunt* at left.	Teacher: Please read. Student: Hunt.
Point to *h* in *hunt* under *CVCC*.	Teacher: Is this a vowel or a consonant? Student: A consonant. Teacher: [Pointing to *C* over the *h*.] Good! A consonant.
Point to *u* in *hunt* under *CVCC*.	Teacher: Is this a vowel or a consonant? Student: A vowel. Teacher: [Pointing to *V* over the *u*.] Good! A vowel.
Point to *n* in *hunt* under *CVCC*.	Teacher: Is this a vowel or a consonant? Student: A consonant. Teacher: [Pointing to *C* over the *n*.] Good! A consonant.
Point to *t* in *hunt* under *CVCC*.	Teacher: Is this a vowel or a consonant? Student: A consonant. Teacher: [Point to *C* over the *t*.] Good! A consonant.
Point, one at a time, to the letters *h, u, n, t* under *CVCC*.	Teacher: Consonant, vowel, consonant, consonant.
2. Point to *fish* at left.	Teacher: Please read. Student: Fish.
Point to the letters *f, i, s, h* under *CVCC*, one at a time.	Teacher: Consonant, vowel, consonant, consonant. [Beckon for student to say this with you.]
3. Do the rest of the words—*sing, bring, jump, kick*—as you did *fish* in step 2.	
4. Point to *hunt* under *CVCC*, then run your finger under *hunting* under the same heading.	Teacher: Hunt. Hunting.
Point to *h, u, n, t*. Point to *i, n, g*.	Teacher: Consonant, vowel, consonant, consonant; [pause] *i, n, g*.
Run your finger under *hunting*.	Teacher: Hunting.
Point to the blank at right.	Teacher: Please write *hunting*. Student: [Writes *hunting* in the blank.]

5. Do *singing* and *bringing* the same way as in step 4.

   With *bringing,* cover the *b* and point to *r, i, n, g*
   as you say, "Consonant, vowel, consonant, consonant."

6. With *jump* and *kick,* have the student first complete
   the words on the chart, and then write them again
   in the blanks at the right.

HOMEWORK: **Pages 20-21**

Ask your student to read everything on page 20 to you. Ask him to write both pages at home. In addition, ask him to write a sentence about guns or hunting.

READING AND WRITING EVALUATION

1. Write the following sentences, as shown. Ask your student to circle the right word and read the sentence. The student should be able to answer both correctly.

A duck is a bird. / fish.	Mr. Hill has a son. / sun.

2. Write these consonant combinations: *ck, ng, tt.* Ask your student to say the sound of each. The student should be able to say at least two with little or no hesitation.

3. Ask your student to write these words:

hunting	bringing	hit	cut	mud
hunt	bring	hitting	cutting	son [Give a sentence.]

   The student should be able to write at least seven words correctly.

MORE READING

In the supplementary reader *More Stories 2,* the stories for Lesson 4 may be read in class or suggested for reading at home.

Lesson 5

OBJECTIVES

When a student completes this unit, he should be able to:

1. Say and respond to a new dialog.
2. Say some new verbs and related adjectives.
3. Say some expressions using *get* plus adjectives, such as *getting hungry*.
4. Identify methods of transportation and use them with *get in, get out of, get on,* and *get off.*
5. Use the story word *brick*.
6. Use the verb *tell* with a direct quotation.
7. Make statements and questions with the past tense of *have.*
8. Answer questions with *How,* using *by* in the answers.
9. Use the infinitive to express purpose.
10. Use the structures, "I think it's funny," and "I don't think it's funny."
11. Pronounce the vowel sounds /a/ and /o/ as in *lack* and *lock* (review) and the consonant sounds /p/ and /f/ as in *pig* and *fig.*
12. Read the following new words:
    Chart words: *truck, stuck, funny, comes, mother, brother*
    Story words: *Bud, Buck, from, some, does, think, bricks.*
13. Read a simple story, using the new chart and story words.
14. Drop the final silent *e* before adding *-ing* to verbs.
15. Read some words beginning with the consonant blend *tr-*.
16. Write the new chart and story words.

VISUAL AIDS

ESOL Illustrations 2, p. 8 and pp. 23-27.

REVIEW

Review any items your student had difficulty with when doing the Oral Evaluation in Lesson 4.

I. Conversation Skills

DIALOG

Teacher:	How do you come to school?
Student:	I come by bus.
Teacher:	How much does it cost?
Student:	50¢.
Teacher:	Do you have a car?
Student:	No, I don't. I always take the bus.

Teacher models the dialog, using the procedure outlined in Lesson 1.

Use the picture of a bus on p. 26 of *ESOL Illustrations 2,* if necessary.

VOCABULARY: Verbs and Adjectives

The girl laughs.	It's funny.
The girl cries.	It's sad.
Ann eats the apple.	It's good.
Ann throws away the egg.	It's bad.

Teacher models the pairs of sentences several times, having the student repeat. Demonstrate the actions to get the meanings across.

[Say: "Listen to *laugh* and *funny*." Say the sentences and beckon for your student to repeat.]

[Continue in the same way with the remaining vocabulary items.]

DRILL: Question and Answer Drill

Performing the action, the teacher asks questions which elicit the verbs and adjectives.

[As you laugh, ask: "What am I doing?" Pause. "You're laughing." Pause. "Why?" Pause. "It's funny."]

[Continue by performing the actions (*cry, eat, throw something away*), having your student give the answers.]

Teacher	**Student**
What am I doing?	You're crying.
Why?	It's sad.

VOCABULARY: *get* + Adjectives

The man is getting thin.	He doesn't like to eat.
The woman is getting fat.	She likes to eat.
The man is getting old.	He's seventy.
The taxi is getting stuck in the mud.	It doesn't go.
The boy is getting tired.	He wants to sleep.
The girl is getting thirsty.	She wants to drink a glass of water.
The girl is getting hungry.	She wants to eat lunch.

Teacher models the pairs of sentences several times, having the student repeat. Dramatize to illustrate the meaning of the words, and use p. 23 of *ESOL Illustrations 2*.

Note: *Get*, as it is used here, means *become.*

[Say: "Listen to *getting*." Pause. "The girl is getting hungry. She wants to eat lunch."]

[Continue giving the sets of examples.]

DRILL: Rejoinders

Teacher gives a statement and an adjective that elicit from the student a statement with *getting* plus the adjective.

Teacher	Student
The girl wants to eat lunch. hungry She's getting hungry.	She's getting hungry.
The girl wants to drink a glass of water. thirsty	She's getting thirsty.
The boy wants to sleep. tired	
The man is seventy. old	
The woman likes to eat. fat	
The man doesn't like to eat. thin	
The truck doesn't go. stuck	
The girl wants to eat dinner. hungry	
The man wants to drink a cup of coffee. thirsty	

VOCABULARY: Means of Transportation

This is a car.
taxi.
boat.
truck.

This is a bus.
an airplane.
a train.
a bicycle.

Using pp. 24-27 of *ESOL Illustrations 2*, the teacher models the sentences several times, having the student repeat.

DRILL: Identification Drill

[Pointing to the illustrations on pp. 24-27 of *ESOL Illustrations 2*, say: "What's this? It's a car." Student repeats: "It's a car."]

VOCABULARY: *get* with Means of Transportation

The man is getting in	the car.
	the taxi.
	the truck.
	the boat.
The man is getting out of	the taxi.
	the car.
	the truck.
	the boat.
The man is getting on	the bus.
	the train.
	the airplane.
	the bicycle.
The man is getting off	the airplane.
	the train.
	the bus.
	the bicycle.

Teacher models the sentences several times, having the student repeat. Use pp. 24-27 of *ESOL Illustrations 2.*

Note: We use *get in* (enter) and *get out of* (leave) with vehicles that can hold only a few passengers.

We use *get on* (enter) and *get off* (leave) with vehicles that can hold either many passengers or just a single passenger (bicycle, horse, and so on).

[Say: "Listen to *getting in*. The man is getting in the car. The man is getting in the taxi."]

[Continue with *truck* and *boat*.]

[Do the rest of the items the same way.]

DRILL: Substitution Drill with Vocal Cues

Teacher	Student
John's getting on the bus.	John's getting on the bus.
train	John's getting on the train.
car	John's getting in the car.
bicycle	
airplane	
taxi	
truck	
boat	
John's getting out of the taxi.	John's getting out of the taxi.
car	John's getting out of the car.
bus	John's getting off the bus.
train	
truck	
bicycle	
airplane	
boat	

VOCABULARY: The Story Word *brick*

These are bricks.
This is a brick house.
This is a brick wall.
He is making a brick wall.

Teacher models the sentences several times, having the student repeat. Use p. 8 of *ESOL Illustrations 2* to help the student understand the words *brick* and *wall*.

[Say: "Listen to *bricks, brick*."]

[Ask: "What are these?" and "What is this?"]

Note: The word *brick* is taught here as a noun (*These are bricks*) and as a modifier (*This is a brick wall*).

VOCABULARY and STRUCTURE FOCUS: The Verb *tell* + a Direct Quotation

Mrs. Hill tells Ed,	"Brush your teeth."
Mrs. Hill tells Ed,	"Put your clothes in the closet."
Ann tells Bob,	"Put the milk in the refrigerator."

Teacher models the sentences several times, having the student repeat.

[Say: "Listen to *tells*."]

DRILL: Substitution Drill with Vocal Cues

Student substitutes the quotation in the key sentence.

Teacher	Student
Mrs. Hill tells Ed, [pause] "Brush your teeth,"	Mrs. Hill tells Ed, "Brush your teeth."
"Wash your hands."	Mrs. Hill tells Ed, "Wash your hands."
"Put your clothes in the closet."	
"Put the milk in the refrigerator."	
"Put the cups in the sink."	
Kitty tells Jimmy, [pause] "Sit down."	Kitty tells Jimmy, "Sit down."
"Come in."	
"Please open the window for me."	
"Have a cup of coffee."	

STRUCTURE FOCUS: Past Tense of *have (had)*

I	had breakfast	at 7 o'clock.
You	had lunch	at noon yesterday.
He	had dinner	at 6 o'clock last night.
We	had class	yesterday morning.
You	had class	yesterday afternoon.
They	had class	last night.

Teacher models the sentences several times, having the student repeat.

[Before you begin to model the sentences with *had*, say: "I have breakfast every day." Pause. Then say: "Listen to *had*."]

DRILL: Multi-Slot Substitution Drill

Teacher	Student
We had lunch yesterday.	We had lunch yesterday.
You	You had lunch yesterday.
dinner	You had dinner yesterday.
I	I had dinner yesterday.
They	They had dinner yesterday.
breakfast	They had breakfast yesterday.
She	She had breakfast yesterday.
He	He had breakfast yesterday.
lunch	He had lunch yesterday.
We	We had lunch yesterday.

STRUCTURE FOCUS: Past Tense Questions with *have*, and Short Answers

I	had breakfast at 7 o'clock.	
Did I	have breakfast at 7 o'clock?	Yes, you did.
He	had class yesterday afternoon.	
Did he	have class yesterday afternoon?	Yes, he did.
They	had a Spanish class last night.	
Did they	have a Spanish class last night?	No, they didn't.

Teacher models statement, question, and short answer several times, having the student repeat all three.

[Say: "Listen to *Did*."]

Note: Use *did* to make questions in the past tense. Students may have difficulty remembering to use *have* (not *had*) in the question form. We use a rising intonation pattern with this type of question.

DRILL: Transformation Drill

Student transforms a statement in the past tense into a question in the past tense.

Teacher	Student
He had an apple.	Did he have an apple?
I had a cup of coffee.	
They had a class.	
She had two children.	
We had a dog.	
Jill had Ann's book.	
You had Bob's pen.	
Ann had lunch with Bob.	
Ann and I had dinner.	

DRILL: Short Answers (Free Reply)

1. Student answers questions using *Yes, I did* or *No, I didn't.* In a class session, use your students' names.

Teacher	Student
Did you have dinner last night?	(Yes, I did.)
Did you have Ann's jacket?	(No, I didn't.)
Did we have class last night?	
Did the teacher have class yesterday morning?	
Did you have Bob's pen?	
Did Ann have your sweater?	
Did Bob have your book?	
Did you have class yesterday afternoon?	

2. Student answers questions using *did/didn't, was/wasn't, were/weren't.*

Teacher	Student
Did you have coffee this morning?	(Yes, I did.)
Were you in class yesterday?	(No, I wasn't.)
Was Bob here yesterday?	
Did Ann have your pen?	
Were you at home last night?	
Did you have breakfast this morning?	
Did you have lunch with Ann yesterday?	
Was Bob at home yesterday?	
Did Ann and Bob have a class?	
Were you with Bob?	

STRUCTURE FOCUS: Questions with *How* and Answers with *By*

How do you go to work?	By bus.
How do you go downtown?	By car.
How do you go to Puerto Rico?	By plane.
How does Glenn go to Indian Valley?	By train.
How does Uncle Bud come here?	By truck.

Teacher models the sentences several times, giving the question and the answer. Have the student repeat both after you.

[Say: "Listen to *How* and *By*."]

Note: If the student wants to indicate *by walking*, teach him to say *I walk*. Advanced students could be taught *on foot.*

DRILL: Transformation Drill

The student transforms a statement into a question with *How.*

Teacher	**Student**
She goes to work by bus.	How does she go to work?
Ann goes downtown by taxi.	How does Ann go downtown?
Glenn goes home by train.	
The women go to Puerto Rico by plane.	
Uncle Bud comes here by truck.	
The girls go to school by bus.	
They go shopping by car.	

DRILL: Short Answer Drill

Teacher asks questions with *How* which elicit answers with *By*.

Teacher	**Student**
How does Ann go to the library?	By bus.
How does Glenn go home?	By train.
How does Uncle Bud come here?	
How do the girls go to school?	
How do you come to school?	
How do the men go to Italy?	
How do they go shopping?	
How does Ann go to the bank?	
How does Jimmy go to the post office?	

STRUCTURE FOCUS: Using the Infinitive to Express Purpose

I'm going to class	to learn	English.
I'm going downtown	to buy	a coat.
Jimmy is going home	to visit	his mother.
We come to school	to learn	English.
Uncle Bud comes to the city	to visit	the Hills.

Teacher models the sentences several times, having the student repeat.

[Say: "Listen to *to learn.*"]

Note: In these sentences, *to* (*in order to*) is used to express purpose. It answers the question *Why*.

DRILL: Question and Answer Drill

Teacher asks questions with *Why* to elicit answers with *to.*

Teacher	Student
Why does Uncle Bud come to the city?	He comes to visit the Hills.
Why do we come to school?	
Why is Jimmy going home?	
Why are you going downtown?	
Why does Jimmy go to the bank?	
Why does Kitty go to the supermarket?	

STRUCTURE FOCUS: The Use of *think* + a Clause

I think	it's sad.
She thinks	it's funny.
I think	the apple is good.
She thinks	the orange is sour.

Teacher models the sentences several times, having the student repeat.

[Say: "Listen to *think*."]

DRILL: Question and Answer Drill

1. Teacher asks a question which elicits an affirmative answer.

Teacher	Student
What does she think? [Pause.] funny	She thinks it's funny.
What do you think? sad	I think it's sad.
What do we think? old	We think it's old.
What do they think? new	
What does Jimmy think? funny	
What does Kitty think? good	

2. Teacher asks a question which elicits a negative form of the verb *think*, as: *I don't think*.

Teacher	Student
What do you think? [Pause.] funny I don't think it's funny.	I don't think it's funny.
What do you think? sad	I don't think it's sad.
What does Kitty think? The apple is sweet.	Kitty doesn't think the apple is sweet.
What does Jimmy think? The orange is sour.	
What do you think? The meat is good.	
What do Ann and Bob think? The coffee is hot.	

PRONUNCIATION: /a/ and /o/, /p/ and /f/

1. See the Pronunciation section in Lesson 1 for the steps to follow in teaching the vowel sounds /a/ and /o/ as in *black* and *block*.

   This is review, so it should be drilled quickly.

[Say: "Listen to /a/ and /o/."]

/a/	/o/	Sentences
cad	cod	My socks are black.
lack	lock	It's a dock.
cap	cop	He has a black hat.
band	bond	It's in Ann's pocket.
hat	hot	It's a map.
		It's a mop.

2. Following the same procedure, teach the consonant sounds /p/ and /f/ as in *pat* and *fat*.

   Note: Both /p/ and /f/ are unvoiced, but /p/ is made with both lips, whereas /f/ is made with the upper teeth on the lower lip.

[Say: "Listen to /p/ and /f/."]

/p/	/f/	Sentences
pad	fad	It doesn't fit.
pig	fig	Peter is funny.
pony	phony	He painted the picture.
pup	puff	I'd like a cup of coffee.
wipe	wife	It's a ship.
		The pail is full.

ORAL EVALUATION

1. Review verbs and adjectives introduced. Student should be able to understand and use all of them.

   [Do the Question and Answer Drill following Vocabulary: Verbs and Adjectives.]

2. Review *get* plus adjectives. Student should be able to identify *get stuck* (for the story) and five others.

   [Do the Rejoinder Drill following Vocabulary: *get* + Adjectives.]

3. Review means of transportation and *get in, get out of, get on,* and *get off.* Student should be able to identify six means of transportation with the correct form of *get.*

   [Using pp. 24-27 of *ESOL Illustrations 2,* teacher asks: "What is the man doing?" Student responds: "The man is getting in (or out of) the car."]

4. Review past tense statements and questions with *have.* This basic pattern will be studied with other verbs in later lessons.

   [Do the Transformation Drill and the Short Answers (Free Reply) Drill following Structure Focus: Past Tense Questions with *have,* and Short Answers.

5. Review making questions with *How* and giving short answers with *By.* This is a review, so the student should be able to answer quickly.

   Teacher: She goes to work by bus.
   Student: How does she go to work? By bus.

   [Continue in the same way, using the Transformation Drill following Structure Focus: Questions with *How* and Answers with *By.* Have the student answer the questions, too, this time.]

6. Review the use of the infinitive (as, *to learn*) to express purpose.

   [Do the Question and Answer Drill following Structure Focus: Using the Infinitive to Express Purpose.]

7. Review the use of *think* plus a clause. This pattern is necessary for the story.

   [Do both parts of the Question and Answer Drill following Structure Focus: The Use of *think* + a Clause.]

II. Reading

Check your student's homework for Lesson 4. If he has not finished, have him do so now, before you begin the reading for Lesson 5.

CHART 5: Page 22

Teach this chart in the same way you taught the chart for Lesson 1.
("Read. What is the sound? What is the vowel? Read.")

Point out these things about the new chart words.

truck: [Point to *tr.*] Say these two sounds together very quickly: *truck.*
The letters *ck* make one sound: /k/.

stuck: [Point to *st.*] Say these two sounds together very quickly: *stuck.*
The letters *ck* make one sound: /k/.

funny: The letters *nn* make one sound: /n/. You write two *n*'s.
Funny ends with *y.* The vowel sound of *y* is /y/.

comes: The vowel sound is /u/, but you write *o.*
Comes ends with the sound /z/, but you write *s.*
The *e* is silent [finger over lips].

mother: This vowel sound [point] is /u/, but you write *o.*
The letters *th* make one sound: /t̲h̲/. [Say the voiced sound.]
The letters *er* make the sound /er/.

brother: [Point to *br.*] Say these two sounds together very quickly: *brother.*
This vowel sound [point] is /u/, but you write *o.*
The letters *th* make one sound: /t̲h̲/. [Say the voiced sound.]
The letters *er* make the sound /er/.

STORY: Uncle Bud's Truck Gets Stuck

First, help the student sound out the new story words: *Bud, Buck, from, some, does, think, bricks.*

The first paragraph of the story may be very hard for an ESOL student to understand, even though he has been using the words for family relationships orally for a long time now. To help him understand, *before* you begin the story, write the following paragraph and ask your student to read it aloud. You may also wish to draw and label stick figures for the characters, as shown.

Mrs. Hill has a brother.
Her brother is Bud Buck.
Mrs. Hill has a son.
Her son is Ed.
Bud Buck is Ed's uncle.

Now, continue teaching the story according to the seven steps outlined in Lesson 1. Use the questions below to check the student's comprehension.

	Teacher	Student
Paragraph 1	Who is Ed's mother?	Mrs. Hill is.
	Who is Mrs. Hill's brother?	Bud Buck is.
	Who is Ed's uncle?	Bud Buck is. (Mr. Buck is.)
Paragraph 2	Where does Bud Buck live?	He lives in the city.
	How does Bud come from the city?	He comes from the city in his truck. [If the student answers, "By truck," accept that answer.]
	Why does Bud come from the city?	He comes to visit the Hills.
	Is Bud's truck big or little?	It's big.
Paragraph 3	What is in Uncle Bud's truck?	Some bricks.
	Who are the bricks for?	They're for Mr. and Mrs. Hill.
	Who brings the bricks from the city?	Uncle Bud does. (Bud Buck does.)
Paragraph 4	Whose truck gets stuck?	Mr. Buck's. (Bud's, Uncle Bud's.)
	Where does the truck get stuck?	It gets stuck in the mud.
	Who thinks it is funny?	Ed does.
	Does Ed's mother think it is funny?	No, she doesn't.
Paragraph 5	Who tells Ed, "Put some bricks in the mud"?	Ed's mother does. (His mother, Mrs. Hill.)
Paragraph 6	Who puts some bricks in the mud?	Ed and his mother.
	What does Uncle Bud do?	He brings the truck to the building.
	Does Mrs. Hill thank her brother?	Yes, she does.

SKILLS PRACTICE: Beginning Consonant Blend *tr-*

Step 1: Write *ruck* and *truck* as shown below. Be careful to line up the words and to underline the *r* and *tr* as shown.

ruck

truck

Step 2: Point to and pronounce each word, first *ruck*, then *truck*. Repeat a few times. The student listens.

Step 3: Point to and pronounce each word, having the student repeat. Do *ruck*, then *truck*. Repeat a few times.

Step 4: Point to each word, beckoning for the student to say it. Do *ruck*, then *truck*.

Repeat these four steps with the following pairs, one pair at a time. (You may leave all the pairs showing on the blackboard.) Be sure to line up the words and underline the letters as shown.

rap	rot	ram	rip
trap	trot	tram	trip

SKILLS PRACTICE: Beginning Consonant Blend *st-*

Note: Spanish-speaking students may add a vowel sound before the *st*, pronouncing *stuck* as *es-tuck*. Other students may put a vowel between the *s* and *t*, saying something like *suh-tuck.*

To correct both problems, have the student prolong the /s/ sound: *sssstuck*. (This technique will also help with other *s* blends, like *sn-, sm-,* and *sp-*.)

Following the four steps in the previous Skills Practice, work with these pairs of words, one pair at a time.

tuck	top	tab	tub	till
stuck	stop	stab	stub	still

III. Writing

WRITING LESSON: Page 24

Study

Help your student study the spelling of the following words before writing them. Point out that in each word *o* has the vowel sound /u/.

1. mother
2. brother
3. comes
4. does
5. some
6. from

Listen and write

Dictate the following words, and then the two sentences, for the student to write. Check his work carefully for capital letters, the *-'s* ending, and the periods.

1. truck
2. stuck
3. Mr. Buck
4. brick
5. think
6. funny

1. The truck is in the mud.
2. Bud is Mrs. Hill's brother.

SKILLS PRACTICE: Dropping Final Silent *e* Before Adding *-ing*

Do this:	Say this:
Write the word *come*.	
Point to *come.*	Teacher: Please read. Student: Come. Teacher: One letter is silent. What is it? Student: *e*.

Draw a line through the *e*, like this: *come̸*.

Now, write the following minichart. Line up the words exactly as shown. Draw a blank to the right of *coming.*

c o m e
c o m e̸
c o m ing ___coming___

Do this:	Say this:
Point to *come*.	Teacher: Please read. Student: Come.
Point to *come̸*.	Teacher: What letter is silent? Student: *e.*
Point to *coming*.	Teacher: Please read. Student: Coming.
Point to blank.	Teacher: Please write *coming.* Student: [Writes *coming* in the blank.]

Write *give.* Using the same steps, demonstrate how to write *giving.* Then do the same with *live* and *living.*

HOMEWORK: Page 25

Ask your student to read everything on the page, then to write it at home.

If you think that your student could and should be doing more homework, write out five simple questions about this lesson's story and ask him to write the answers at home. Be sure to read through the questions with him first. Suggested questions are given below. For practice, the student should write full sentences rather than short answers.

1. Who has a truck?
2. What is in the truck?
3. Where does the truck get stuck?
4. Who thinks it is funny?
5. Where does Ed put the bricks?

READING AND WRITING EVALUATION

1. Write the following sentences, as shown. Ask your student to circle the right word and then read the sentence. He should answer two correctly.

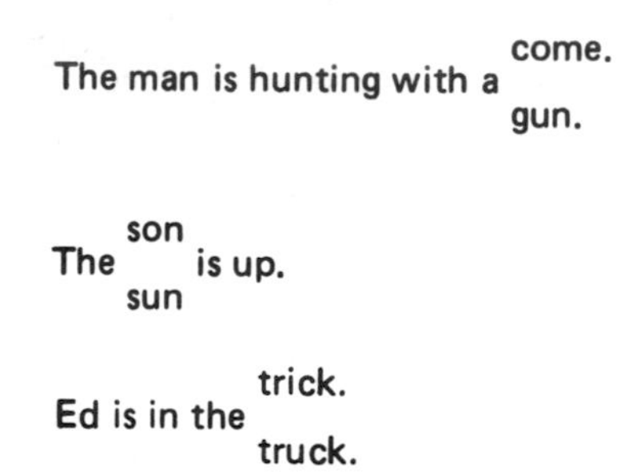

come.
The man is hunting with a
gun.
son
The is up.
sun
trick.
Ed is in the
truck.

2. Write the following words and ask your student to read them. He should be able to read four correctly.

son	stuck	bricks
truck	bringing	building

3. Dictate the following sentences for the student to write. He should not make more than three errors.

Uncle Bud's truck is stuck.
It is stuck in the mud.

MORE READING

In the supplementary reader *More Stories 2,* the stories for Lesson 5 may be read in class or suggested for reading at home.

Lesson 6

OBJECTIVES

When a student completes this unit, he should be able to:

1. Say and respond to a new dialog.
2. Say some new vocabulary: chart and story words, food in containers, some simple measurements, and some adjectives.
3. Use *very* as an intensifier with an adjective.
4. Use the verb *help*.
5. Use some regular verbs in the past tense in affirmative statements, questions, and answers.
6. Use *say* plus a direct quotation.
7. Use *a lot of* with plural count nouns and with non-count nouns.
8. Use *many, much, a little,* and *a few* with count and non-count nouns.
9. Make questions using *How much* and *How many.*
10. Make statements and questions with *will.*
11. Use *will* and *won't* in short answers.
12. Pronounce the vowel sounds /ā/ and /e/ as in *gate* and *get*, and pronounce the /t/, /d/, and /ud/ forms of the past tense ending.
13. Read the following new words:
    Chart words: *bell, hens, cents, help, twelve, seventy*
    Story words: *Fred, fresh, Ellen, will, very, many.*
14. Read a simple story, using the new chart and story words.
15. Read some words contrasting the short vowels *i* and *u*, *e* and *u*.
16. Read some words beginning with the consonant blends *br-, pr-, tr-, st-, str-.*
17. Write the new chart and story words.
18. Write questions, using the question mark.

VISUAL AIDS

1. *ESOL Illustrations 2,* pp. 28-37.
2. Food containers: egg carton, one-pound coffee can, cereal box.
3. Measuring containers: a one-cup measuring cup, a quart container, and a half-gallon container. (Empty milk cartons would be suitable for the quart and half-gallon containers.)
4. Something new and something old, such as coins.
5. In the picture of the hens and eggs in *ESOL Illustrations 2,* p. 33, color some of the big eggs and some of the little eggs brown.
6. To increase your own knowledge of the metric system, which many of your students already know, ask your local extension office for free informative materials on the metric system.
7. A calendar.

REVIEW

Review any items your student had difficulty with when doing the Oral Evaluation in Lesson 5.

I. Conversation Skills

DIALOG

Salesclerk:	May I help you?
Fred:	Yes, I'd like some fresh eggs.
Salesclerk:	How many would you like?
Fred:	I'll take two dozen.
Salesclerk:	Here they are. . .two cartons.
Fred:	How much are they?
Salesclerk:	$2.25, please.
Fred:	Thank you.

Teacher models the dialog, using the procedure outlined in Lesson 1.

VOCABULARY: Food in Containers

This is a carton of eggs.
can of coffee.
box of cereal.
bottle of soda.
six-pack of beer.
carton of ice cream.
package of cookies.
pack of cigarettes.
carton of cigarettes.
jar of jelly.

Teacher models the sentences several times, having the student repeat. Use *ESOL Illustrations 2*, pp. 28-29.

Note: If, in your part of the country, *soda* is called *pop* (or something else), teach the commonly used term.

DRILL: Identification Drill

Use *ESOL Illustrations 2*, pp. 28-29.

[Pointing to the illustrations one by one, ask: "What's this?"]

DRILL: Question and Answer Drill with Silent Cues

Using *ESOL Illustrations 2*, pp. 28-29, teacher asks the student, "What do you want to buy?"

Do not accept the name of the food alone as the answer; insist on "a carton of eggs," not just "eggs."

Teacher	Student
What do you want to buy?	I want to buy a carton of eggs.
What do you want to buy?	I want to buy a six-pack of beer.

[Continue with the rest of the vocabulary items.]

VOCABULARY: *fresh* and *stale*

This is a new package of cookies.	The cookies are fresh.
This is an old package of cookies.	The cookies are stale.
This is a new loaf of bread.	The bread is fresh.
This is an old loaf of bread.	The bread is stale.

Teacher models sentences several times, having the student repeat only the sentences containing the words *fresh* and *stale*. If the student has difficulty with *new* and *old*, show him something new (such as a new penny) and something old (an old penny).

[Say: "Listen to *fresh*. This is a new package of cookies. The cookies are fresh. Please repeat. The cookies are fresh."]

[Introduce *stale* in the same way.]

DRILL: Statement and Rejoinder Drill

Teacher makes a statement containing *new* or *old*, and student replies with a statement containing *fresh* or *stale*.

Teacher	Student
This is new meat.	The meat is fresh.
These are new eggs.	The eggs are fresh.
This is old bread.	The bread is stale.
This is old beer.	The beer is stale.
This is a new sandwich.	
This is new cereal.	
This is an old sandwich.	
This is a new loaf of bread.	
This is a new cup of coffee.	
These are old cookies.	

VOCABULARY: Simple Measurements

This	is	a cup.
One pint	is	two cups.
One quart	is	four cups.
One half-gallon	is	two quarts.
One gallon	is	four quarts.
This meat weighs		four pounds.
Jill weighs		100 pounds.

Teacher models sentences several times, having the student repeat. Use pp. 30-31 of *ESOL Illustrations 2* and the containers you have brought with you.

[Say: "Listen to *pint*," as you point to a pint.]

[Continue with the remaining items.]

Note: If your student seems confused, you may tell him that:

1 pint = .47 liters
1 quart = .95 liters
1 pound = .454 kilograms

DRILL: Identification Drill

Using p. 30-31 of *ESOL Illustrations 2* and the containers you have brought with you, have the student identify the measurement.

Note: These measurements will be drilled again in a later section of this lesson.

[Pointing to the appropriate illustration or item, say: "What's this? It's a pint."]

[Continue with the remaining items.]

DRILL: Substitution Drill with Vocal Cues

Teacher models the key sentence, then says only the cue.

Teacher	Student
I'm buying a quart of milk.	I'm buying a quart of milk.
a pint of ice cream	I'm buying a pint of ice cream.
10 pounds of potatoes	
a half-gallon of milk	
a pound of coffee	
seven pounds of meat	
a half-gallon of ice cream	
five pounds of sugar	
a pound of butter	

VOCABULARY: The Chart Word *bell*

The church bell	is ringing.	It's time for church.
The dinner bell	is ringing.	It's time for dinner.
The doorbell	is ringing.	Please go to the door.
The telephone	is ringing.	Please answer the phone.

Teacher models the two sentences, having the student repeat both. Use p. 32 of *ESOL Illustrations 2.*

Note: The student will learn from this exercise that we use the verb *ring* with *telephone* but not the noun *bell*. That is, we do not say **telephone bell.*

[Pointing to the illustration, say: "Listen to *bell, ringing*." Pause. "The church bell is ringing. It's time for church. Please repeat."]

[Continue with the remaining items in the same way.]

DRILL: Statement and Rejoinder Drill

Teacher makes a statement. Student agrees, making another statement with the verb *ring.*

Teacher	**Student**
It's time for church.	Yes, the church bell is ringing.
It's time for dinner.	
Please answer the doorbell.	
Please answer the telephone.	

[Repeat the drill.]

VOCABULARY: Chart and Story Words *hens, nest*

These are hens.
The hens are sitting on their nests.
We get eggs from hens.

Teacher models the sentences several times, having the student repeat. Use *ESOL Illustrations 2,* p. 33.

[Say: "Listen to *hens, nests.*"]

DRILL: Expansion Drill

Student adds adjectives to the sentences given.

Model the first answer in each group, "The hens. . ." and "We get eggs. . .," so the student will know which noun to modify with the adjectives.

Teacher	Student
The hens are sitting on their nests.	
Big, white	
The big white hens are sitting on their nests.	The big white hens are sitting on their nests.
The hens are sitting on their nests.	
Small, white	The small white hens are sitting on their nests.
The hens are sitting on their nests.	
Small, black	
We get eggs from hens.	
Big, white	
We get big white eggs from hens.	We get big white eggs from hens.
We get eggs from hens.	
Small, white	
We get eggs from hens.	
Big, brown	
We get eggs from hens.	
Small, brown	

VOCABULARY: Adjectives

The girl is in bed.	She's <u>sick</u>.
The girl is getting up.	She's <u>well</u>.
The boy walks to the store.	He's <u>slow</u>.
The boy runs to the store.	He's <u>fast</u>.

Teacher models the sentences several times, using *ESOL Illustrations 2*, pp. 34-35, and demonstrating the meaning of *fast* and *slow*. Have the student repeat the sentences with the adjectives.

[Say: "Listen to *sick*. The girl is in bed. She's sick. Please repeat. She's sick."]

[Continue in the same way with the remaining adjectives.]

DRILL: Question and Answer Drill

Indicating the pictures on pp. 34-35 of *ESOL Illustrations 2*, the teacher asks questions which elicit the adjectives being taught.

Teacher	Student
Is the girl sick or well?	She's sick.
Is the boy fast or slow?	
Is the girl sick or well?	
Is the boy fast or slow?	

VOCABULARY: *very* + Adjective

He's <u>very</u> sick.
He's <u>very</u> well.
He's <u>very</u> slow.
He's <u>very</u> fast.

Teacher models the sentences several times, having the student repeat.

[Say: "Listen to *very*."]

Demonstrate the difference between *slow* and *very slow* *fast* and *very fast.*

Note: The word *very* is an intensifier.

DRILL: Expansion Drill

Student adds the word *very* before the adjective in the sentence.

Teacher	**Student**
He's sick.	He's very sick.
He's slow.	He's very slow.
The house is big.	
The kitchen is little.	
The boy is fast.	
The girl is sick.	
The woman is sad.	
The bread is fresh.	
The beer is stale.	
The meat is fresh.	
The cookies are stale.	

VOCABULARY: The Verb *help*

The little girl	wants to put on her coat.	Please <u>help</u> her.
The children	want to take off their boots.	Please <u>help</u> them.
The old woman	wants to get on the bus.	Please <u>help</u> her.

Teacher models the sentences, having the student repeat only the sentences with *help*.

[Say: "Listen to *help*. The little girl wants to put on her coat. Please help her. Repeat. Please help her."]

DRILL: Statement and Rejoinder

Teacher says a sentence, and student makes a sentence using *help*.

Teacher	Student
The little girl wants to put on her coat.	Please help her.
The little girl wants to put on her sweater.	
The children want to put on their boots.	
The old man wants to get off the bus.	
The old woman wants to get on the bus.	
The little boy wants to put on his shoes.	
The little girl wants to take off her coat.	

STRUCTURE FOCUS: Past Tense of Regular Verbs

I	<u>opened</u>	this door yesterday.
You	<u>studied</u>	English last night.
We	<u>looked at</u>	the English book.
We	<u>helped</u>	him with his English.
Ellen	<u>walked</u>	home yesterday.
You	<u>repeated</u>	the words.
They	<u>needed</u>	some new clothes last month.

Teacher models the sentences several times, having the student repeat. Listen for the correct pronunciation of the verb ending.

Note: The past tense of regular verbs is usually formed by adding a *-d* or *-ed* to the base form of the verb. The ending is pronounced /t/, /d/, or /ud/. For details, see the Pronunciation section of this lesson.

[Before you begin modeling the sentences say: "I open this door every day." Pause. Say: "Listen to *opened.* I opened this door yesterday." Then continue with the rest of the sentences.]

DRILL: Substitution Drill with Vocal Cues

This drill may be omitted for more advanced students.

Teacher	Student
He opened the book yesterday.	He opened the book yesterday.
closed	
looked at	
picked up	
liked	
studied	
needed	

DRILL: Transformation Drill

Student changes a statement in the present tense into a statement in the past tense.

Be sure the student changes the time expressions as appropriate, for example, *every day* to *yesterday*, *every week* to *last week*, and so on.

Note: All the verbs used here have been introduced before.

Teacher	Student
I open this door every day.	I opened this door yesterday.
Ellen walks home on Monday.	
They study English every Tuesday.	
We need some new clothes.	
Jill jumps rope every day.	
Glenn hunts every week.	
Ann thanks Bob.	
They work every day.	
The children play every day.	
You cook dinner every night.	
The teacher helps me with my English.	

STRUCTURE FOCUS: Questions and Answers in the Past Tense

	You	studied	English	yesterday.	
Did	you	study	English	yesterday?	Yes, I did.
	Ellen	walked	home	yesterday.	
Did	Ellen	walk	home	yesterday?	No, she didn't.
	They	watched	television	last night.	
Did	they	watch	television	last night?	Yes, they did.

Teacher models the statement, question, and short answer, having the student repeat all three.

[Say: "Listen to *Did*."]

Note: We use *did* with the simple form of the verb (*study, walk*) to make questions in the past tense.

Listen carefully to be sure that the student is using the simple form of the verb and not the past tense form (*studied*) in the question.

We use a rising intonation pattern with this type of question.

DRILL: Transformation Drill

Student changes a past tense statement into a past tense question.

Teacher	Student
She opened the door.	Did she open the door?
Ellen looked at the book.	
We studied English yesterday.	
Kim played with her doll.	
Will had breakfast.	
Mrs. Hill cooked dinner.	
We signed the paper.	
You closed the windows.	
I brushed my teeth.	
The teacher helped Bob with his English.	

DRILL: Question and Answer Drill

Student gives a short affirmative or negative answer to the past tense questions.

Teacher	Student
Did she open the door?	Yes, she did.
Did the child cry?	No, he didn't.
Did you thank Bob?	
Did Jill play with the ball and bat?	
Did you study English yesterday?	
Did they sign the paper?	
Did your husband (wife) go shopping yesterday?	
Did Bob and Ann laugh?	
Did you watch television last night?	
Did your son need a coat?	
Did the teacher help you with your English?	

STRUCTURE FOCUS: *say* + a Direct Quotation

The teacher says, "Please open the door."
The student says, "OK."

Bob's friend says, "I'm going home."
Bob says, "Good-bye."

Teacher models the sentences, having the student repeat. [Say: "Listen to *says*."]

DRILL: Combining Sentences

1. Teacher gives two statements, which the student combines.

Teacher	Student
Please close the door. The teacher says.	The teacher says, "Please close the door."
Please open the door. The teacher says.	
I'm going home. Bob says.	
Please help me. Ann says.	
Don't go home. Fred says.	
This bread is stale. Mrs. Hill says.	
Please answer the phone. Mr. Hill says.	

2. Student makes statements using *say* plus a direct quotation which is a polite response or request.

Teacher	Student
Bob's friend gives him a cigarette. What does Bob say?	
Bob says, "Thank you."	Bob says, "Thank you."
The teacher helps Ann with her English. What does Ann say?	Ann says, "Thank you."
The boy kicked the girl. What does the boy say? (I'm sorry.)	
The girl wants the ball. What does the girl say?	The girl says, "Please give me the ball."
The waitress gives Bob a stale sandwich. What does the waitress say? (I'm sorry.)	
The little boy wants his toy. What does the little boy say?	
The girl picks up the paper for the teacher. What does the teacher say?	
[Repeat the drill.]	

STRUCTURE FOCUS: *a lot of* with Count and Non-count Nouns

He	has	a lot of eggs.
He doesn't	have	a lot of apples.
He	has	a lot of money.
She doesn't	have	a lot of money.

Teacher models sentences several times, having student repeat. Use pp. 36-37 of *ESOL Illustrations 2*.

[Say: "Listen to *a lot of*."]

Note: We use *a lot of* with plural count nouns and with non-count nouns, in either affirmative or negative sentences.

DRILL: Expansion Drill

Student adds *a lot of* to the sentence.

Teacher	Student
He has friends.	
He has a lot of friends.	He has a lot of friends.
He doesn't have friends.	He doesn't have a lot of friends.
He doesn't have apples.	
He has money.	
He has neighbors.	
He doesn't have bread.	
He has milk.	
He doesn't have money.	
He has eggs.	
He doesn't have books.	
He has children.	

STRUCTURE FOCUS: *a lot of* and *many/much*

He has	a lot of friends.
He has	many friends.
He doesn't have	a lot of money.
He doesn't have	much money.

Teacher models the sentences several times, having the student repeat.

[Say: "Listen to *a lot of* and *many*." Then model the first two sentences. Gesture for the student to repeat after each one.]

[Say: "Listen to *a lot of* and *much*," and continue in the same way.]

Note: *Many* is used only with plural count nouns. It may be used in either affirmative or negative statements.

Much is used only with non-count nouns. It is usually used only in negative statements.

DRILL: Replacement Drill

Student replaces *a lot of* with *many* or *much*.

Teacher	Student
He has a lot of friends.	He has many friends.
He has a lot of eggs.	He has many eggs.
He has a lot of neighbors.	He has many neighbors.
He doesn't have a lot of money.	He doesn't have much money.
He doesn't drink a lot of milk.	He doesn't drink much milk.
He doesn't drink a lot of coffee.	He doesn't drink much coffee.

STRUCTURE FOCUS: *many, a few / much, a little*

He has many eggs.	He has a few eggs.
We have many apples.	We have a few apples.
He doesn't drink much coffee.	He drinks a little coffee.
He doesn't have much money.	He has a little money.

Teacher models the sentences, having the student repeat.

Use *ESOL Illustrations 2*, pp. 36-37.

Note: *Many* and *a few* are used with plural count nouns. *Much* and *a little* are used with non-count nouns.

A few and *a little* are usually used only in affirmative statements.

The chart below summarizes the uses of all five of the expressions of quantity taught in this lesson. The chart is for your own use only.

[Say: "Listen to *many*," and model the sentences containing *many*.]

[Then do *a few, much,* and *a little*—in that order—in the same way.]

	Plural Count Nouns	Non-count Nouns	Affirmative Statements	Negative Statements
a lot of	X	X	X	X
many	X		X	X
much		X		X
a few	X		X	
a little		X	X	

DRILL: Expansion Drill

1. The student adds *many* or *much* to the sentence.

Teacher	Student
He has eggs.	He has many eggs.
He doesn't have money.	He doesn't have much money.
He has apples.	
He has children.	
He doesn't eat meat.	
He doesn't drink coffee.	
He doesn't have money.	

2. The student adds *a few* or *a little* to the sentence.

Teacher	Student
He has apples.	He has a few apples.
He has money.	He has a little money.
He has jackets.	
She has blouses.	
She drinks soda (pop).	
I drink coffee.	
Fred has cheese.	
Glenn has eggs.	
They have packages of cookies.	

STRUCTURE FOCUS: Questions with *How many* and *How much*

How many children do you have?	Four.
How many sisters does Liz have?	Two.
How much coffee do you drink?	A little.
How much is this blouse?	Twelve dollars.

Teacher models the questions and answers several times, having the student repeat both.

Note: *How many* is used to ask questions with plural count nouns; *how much*, with non-count nouns. When we ask about money, we use *how much* without a noun following it.

[Say: "Listen to *How many*," and model the questions and answers. Then do *How much*.]

DRILL: Transformation Drill

Student changes statements into questions with *How many* and *How much.*

Teacher	Student
He has six books.	How many books does he have?
He buys bread.	How much bread does he buy?
Ann has three children.	
I have two brothers.	
He works eight hours every day.	
She drinks water.	
She is buying a quart of milk.	
She drinks coffee.	
There are seven days in a week.	
There are twelve months in a year.	

DRILL: Producing Questions

Teacher gives count or non-count noun items, and student makes his own questions using *How many* and *How much.*

Teacher	Student
6 books	How many books do you have?
3 sisters	
4 blouses	
2 sandwiches	
milk	How much milk do you drink?
coffee	
paper	
bread	
soup	

DRILL: Question and Answer Drill

Review simple measurements by asking questions with *How much* and *How many.* Let the student refer to pp. 30-31 of *ESOL Illustrations 2.*

Teacher	Student
How many pints are there in a quart?	Two.
How many quarts are there in a half-gallon?	
How many quarts are there in a gallon?	
How much meat are you buying?	
How much does Jill weigh?	
How much milk are you buying?	
How much sugar are you buying?	
How many eggs are you buying?	

STRUCTURE FOCUS: The Future Tense with *will*

I	will	help Mr. Hunt tomorrow.	I'll	help Mr. Hunt tomorrow.
You	will	help Mr. Hunt tomorrow.	You'll	help Mr. Hunt tomorrow.
He	will	help Mr. Hunt tomorrow.	He'll	help Mr. Hunt tomorrow.
We	will	help Mr. Hunt tomorrow.	We'll	help Mr. Hunt tomorrow.
They	will	help Mr. Hunt tomorrow.	They'll	help Mr. Hunt tomorrow.

Teacher models each pair of sentences, having the student repeat both.

Explain the meaning of *tomorrow* by using a calendar.

Note: Be sure that the student understands that *I will* and *I'll* are two ways of saying the same thing.

Use the contracted forms, since they are common in conversational English.

Notice that *will* does not change its form: *I will, he will,* and so on.

Since the contracted form is in such common use, do not introduce *shall* at this time.

[Before you begin modeling the sentences, say:
"I'm helping Mr. Hunt today." Pause.
Say: "Listen to *I will* and *I'll*." Then model each sentence.]

[Continue in the same way with the remaining sentences.]

DRILL: Transformation Drill

The student changes a statement in the present progressive tense with *now* into a future tense statement using *will* (contracted) and *tomorrow.*

Teacher	Student
I'm helping Mr. Hunt now.	I'll help Mr. Hunt tomorrow.
He's eating an apple now.	He'll eat an apple tomorrow.
They're playing ball now.	They'll play ball tomorrow.
Glenn's going home now.	
Ann's buying a ring now.	
Ted's watching television now.	
She's cooking dinner now.	
I'm studying English now.	
Bob's helping him now.	
They're going to the supermarket now.	

STRUCTURE FOCUS: Questions with *will*

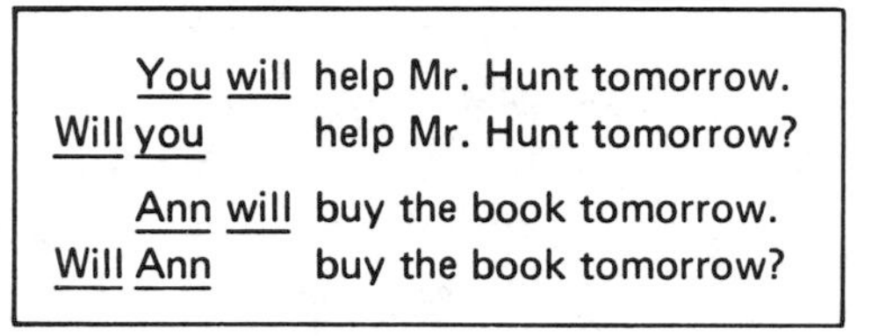
You will help Mr. Hunt tomorrow.
Will you help Mr. Hunt tomorrow?
Ann will buy the book tomorrow.
Will Ann buy the book tomorrow?

Teacher models the statement and its corresponding question several times, having the student repeat.

[Say: "Listen to *will*."]

Note: Questions with *will* are made by reversing the word order, that is, *You will* becomes *Will you.*

DRILL: Transformation Drill

Student transforms a statement into a question.

Note: The drill statements contain proper names plus *will*. These are written in contracted form (*Ann'll*) to remind you to use contractions with nouns as well as pronouns.

Teacher	Student
He'll drink the milk.	Will he drink the milk?
She'll eat the apple.	Will she eat the apple?
They'll go home at 9 o'clock.	
Ann'll cook dinner tomorrow.	
They'll like these cookies.	
You'll help me.	
Mr. Hunt'll get well.	
We'll study with the teacher.	
My sister'll come here tomorrow.	

STRUCTURE FOCUS: Negative Statements with *will not/won't*

He will not get sick.	He won't get sick.
They will not buy the ring.	They won't buy the ring.

Teacher models the sentences with *will not* and *won't* several times, having the student repeat.

[Say: "Listen to *will not* and *won't*." Shake your head to indicate the negative.]

Be sure the student understands that *will not* and *won't* are both negative forms for *will.*

DRILL: Transformation Drill

Student transforms an affirmative statement with *will* into a negative statement with *won't.*

Teacher	Student
She'll go to the store.	She won't go to the store.
He'll go to the store.	
We'll watch television.	
Kitty'll live in this building.	
Kim'll sit with Ed.	
They'll sit and talk.	
The man'll laugh.	
You'll thank her.	

STRUCTURE FOCUS: Short Answers with *will/won't*

Will you come here?	Yes, I will.
Will Ann give the money to him?	No, she won't.

Teacher models the question and its short answer several times, having the student repeat.

[Say: "Listen to *will* and *won't.*"]

DRILL: Short Answers

Teacher asks questions with *will* which elicit affirmative and negative short answers.

[Ask the question and indicate by shaking or nodding your head whether you want an affirmative or a negative reply. After giving one or two examples, do not prompt your student.]

Teacher	Student
Will Glenn go home?	Yes, he will.
Will you go downtown?	No, I won't.
Will Jill brush her teeth?	
Will Kim wash her hands?	
Will Mr. Hunt get well?	
Will Ann get sick?	
Will Ted run fast?	
Will you buy a jacket?	
Will we stand here?	
Will they watch television with us?	
Will you help me?	

PRONUNCIATION: /ā/ and /e/

See the Pronunciation section in Lesson 1 for the steps to follow in teaching the vowel sounds /ā/ and /e/ as in *gate* and *get*.

This is review, so it should be drilled quickly.

[Say: "Listen to /ā/ and /e/."]

/ā/	/e/	Sentences
gate	get	The men rang the bell.
laid	led	Taste the tea.
bail	bell	He has a pain.
main	men	It's gray.
taste	test	The lady is late.
		Did you get a letter?

PRONUNCIATION: Sounds of the Regular Past Tense Verb Endings

Note: All the sounds of English can be divided into voiced and unvoiced sounds.
Voiced sounds are produced with vibration of the vocal cords.
Unvoiced sounds are produced without vibration of the vocal cords.
The unvoiced sounds are /f/, /h/, /k/, /p/, /s/, /t/, /ch/, /sh/, /wh/, and /th/ as in *thank*.
All the rest, including the vowels, are voiced, as is /th/ as in *this*.

1. When the final *sound* of a regular verb is an unvoiced sound, we form the past tense by adding the unvoiced sound /t/.
   Examples: *fished, jumped, looked, passed.*
2. When the final *sound* of a regular verb is a voiced sound, we form the past tense by adding the voiced sound /d/.
   Examples: *closed, opened, sailed, showed.*
3. When the final sound of a regular verb is /t/ or /d/, we form the past tense by adding a separate syllable, /ud/.
   Examples: *hunted, patted, needed, added.*

Procedure:

1. Teacher models the pronunciation of the past tense form of verbs, focusing on the unvoiced ending, /t/. The student repeats.

[Say: "Listen to the /t/." Pause. *"Walked."* Emphasize the /t/ sound.]

[Say each word twice, having the student repeat twice.]

Teacher: walked, walked
Student: walked, walked

[Continue with *fished, jumped, kicked, looked, passed.*]

2. Teacher models the pronunciation of the past tense form of verbs, focusing on the voiced ending, /d/. The student repeats.

[Say: "Listen to the /d/." Pause. *"Closed."* Prolong the vowel sound.]

Teacher: closed, closed
Student: closed, closed

[Continue with *opened, sailed, studied, showed, yelled.*]

3. Teacher models the pronunciation of the past tense form of verbs ending with /t/ or /d/, focusing on the /ud/ as a separate syllable.

[Say: "Listen to the /ud/." Pause. *"Wanted."* Pronounce the /ud/ syllable clearly.]

Teacher: wanted, wanted
Student: wanted, wanted

[Continue with *hunted, patted, repeated, needed, added.*]

4. Teacher gives the present tense of known verbs as a vocal cue. The student gives the past tense form.

   Listen carefully to the student's pronunciation of the final sound or combination of sounds. Correct him if necessary.

[Give the present tense form of the verbs already taught. Ask the student for the past tense form. Use the lists below, choosing a verb from a different column each time.]

Teacher: want
Student: wanted

/t/	/d/	/ud/
like	close	add
cook	cry	hunt
fish	live	need
help	open	pat
jump	play	repeat
kick	sail	want
look	show	
pass	sign	
pick	study	
walk	yell	
wash		
watch		

ORAL EVALUATION

1. Review food in containers. Student should be able to name seven of these.

   [Using pp. 28-29 of *ESOL Illustrations 2*, ask: "What's this?" The expected answer form is: "It's a quart of milk."]

2. Review the words *fresh* and *stale*, both of which the student should be able to use with ease.

   [Do the Statement and Rejoinder Drill following Vocabulary: *fresh* and *stale*.]

3. Review the chart and story words *hens* and *nest*, both of which the student needs to know.

   [Do the Expansion Drill following Vocabulary: Chart and Story Words *hens, nest*.]

4. Review *very* plus adjectives. Student should know all four adjectives.

   [Do the Expansion Drill with *very*.]

5. Review the past tense of regular verbs. Student should be able to do all of these quickly since none of the verbs are new vocabulary items and since making questions in the past tense has been practiced before.

   [Do the Transformation Drill and the Question and Answer Drill following Structure Focus: Questions and Answers in the Past Tense.]

6. Review the use of *a lot of* with plural count nouns and non-count nouns.

   This is a useful modifier, so the student should be able to use it correctly.

   [Do the Expansion Drill following Vocabulary: *a lot of* with Count and Non-count Nouns.]

7. Review *many, much, a little,* and *a few* with count and non-count nouns. Student should be able to do all of these fairly quickly.

   [Do the Expansion Drills following Structure Focus: *many, a few/much, a little.*]

8. Review making questions with *How many* and *How much*. Student should be able to do these quickly since information questions have been practiced before. These drills will review simple measurements as well.

   [Do the Drills following Structure Focus: Questions with *How many* and *How much*.]

9. Review making questions with *will* and giving short affirmative and negative answers. If the student cannot do this pattern fairly quickly, review it at the next class.

   [Do the Transformation Drill with *will* and ask the student to answer the question as well.]

   Teacher: He will drink the milk.
   Student: Will he drink the milk?
   Yes, he will.

   [Be sure some answers are negative.]

II. Reading

Check your student's homework for Lesson 5 before beginning the chart.

CHART 6: Page 26

Teach this chart in the same way you taught the chart for Lesson 1. ("Read. What is the sound? What is the vowel sound? Read.")

Point out these things about the new chart words:

hens: [Point to *s*.] The sound is /z/, but you write *s*.

cents: The *c* has the sound /s/.

twelve: [Point to *tw*.] Say these two sounds together very quickly: *twelve.* [Point to the final *e*.] This *e* is silent.

STORY: Eggs to Sell

Teach the story according to the seven steps oulined in Lesson 1.
The new story words are: *Fred, fresh, Ellen, will, very, many.*

Use the following comprehension questions. Either short or long answers are acceptable.

	Teacher	Student
Paragraph 1	Who has many hens?	Ellen Bell does.
	Does Ellen sell many hens and eggs?	Yes, she does.
Paragraph 2	Who helps Ellen?	Her son does.
	Does he help her sell the eggs and hens?	Yes, he does.
Paragraph 3	Are the eggs fresh?	Yes, they are.
	How much are twelve eggs?	Seventy cents.
	How many eggs does Ms. Bell sell for seventy cents?	Twelve.
Paragraphs 4-5	Who is looking at the eggs?	Fred King is.
	What does Fred King say?	"Are the eggs fresh?"
	What does Ellen Bell say?	"Yes, the eggs are very fresh."
Paragraph 6	How many eggs does Fred get?	Twelve.
	Who sells the eggs to Fred?	Ellen does.
	How much money does Fred give to Ellen?	Seventy cents.
Paragraphs 7-8	What does Fred say?	"Do you sell hens?"
	What does Ellen say?	"Yes, my son will help you. He will get a hen for you."
	Who will get a hen for Fred?	Ellen's son will.

SKILLS PRACTICE: Contrasting the Short Vowels *i* and *u*

Step 1: Write the following headings and words on the blackboard. Line up the vowels in the words under the headings, as shown:

i	u
him	hum

Step 2: Model the minimal pair several times as the student listens.
Say: *"him, hum,"* pointing to each word as you say it.

Step 3: Have the student repeat after you several times.
Say: *"him, hum,"* pointing to the word as you say it.

Step 4: Say the words in random order.
Have the student point to the word you are saying.

Step 5: Point to the words in random order.
Have the student say the word you are pointing to.

Step 6: Point to *i* in *him*.
Say: "What is the vowel sound?" [Student: /i/.]
Say: "What letter makes the sound /i/?" [Student: *i*.]

Step 7: Point to *u* in *hum*.
Say: "What is the vowel sound?" [Student: /u/.]
Say: "What letter makes the sound /u/?" [Student: *u*.]

Step 8: Erase *him* and *hum*, and write the next pair (*hill* and *hull*) under the headings *i* and *u*.

Repeat the seven steps above with each of the following minimal pairs. Be sure to have only one minimal pair showing at a time.

i	u	i	u
hill	hull	hint	hunt
sin	sun	ring	rung
pick	puck	sing	sung
big	bug	trick	truck
hit	hut	stick	stuck

Step 9: Erase the last minimal pair, but leave the headings *i* and *u* on the board.

Review by reading words from the minimal pairs in random order and asking the student to point to the letter that makes the vowel sound. (If you read *big*, for example, the student should point to *i*.)

SKILLS PRACTICE: Contrasting the Short Vowels *e* and *u*

Following the same nine steps, contrast the short vowel sounds /e/ and /u/, using the minimal pairs shown here. Work with only one pair at a time.

e	u	e	u
get	gut	fen	fun
deck	duck	pep	pup
bed	bud	pen	pun

SKILLS PRACTICE: Review of Words with *br-*, *pr-*, *tr-*, *st-*, *str-*

Step 1: Write the following consonant blends and words as shown. Then have your student read each word.

br	pr	tr	st	str
brick	pretty	truck	stuck	street
bring			study	
brother				

Step 2: Write the following consonant blends and words as shown. Then ask your student to read each word. Prompt him only if necessary.

br	pr	tr	st
brick	prick	trick	stick

III. Writing

CHECKUP: Page 28

Ask your student to read this page silently and write the answers. When he has finished, ask him to read aloud everything on the page, including the heading and instructions.

WRITING LESSON: Page 29

Study

Help your student study the chart and story words shown below. He may copy them directly from the chart or story onto page 29, if necessary.

1. twelve
2. cents
3. very
4. many

Listen and write

Dictate the following words for the student to write.

1. egg
2. bell
3. hens
4. help
5. yes
6. fresh

Check the student's work carefully. Then, cover the top two-thirds of the page and dictate the following sentences for the student to write. Check the student's spelling very carefully. Correct any mistakes in a positive way.

1. Ellen Bell sells eggs.
2. Her son helps her.
3. Fred gets twelve eggs.
4. Ellen gets seventy cents.

WRITING LESSON: Page 30

This exercise is a written transformation drill, in which the student changes a statement to a question. The first question is written for him to show him what to do.

Have the student read aloud the statement and question in number 1. Show him how to write a question mark, and have him practice writing question marks on the guidelines after the question in number 1.

For each of the remaining items, have the student read the statement, say the question, and then write the question. If he cannot say the question correctly, say it for him and have him repeat it after you before he writes it. Be sure that he uses a question mark after each question.

HOMEWORK: Page 31

Ask your student to do this page at home.

READING AND WRITING EVALUATION

1. Ask your student to write the following words. He should be able to write at least four correctly.

very	seventy	twelve
many	cents	yes

2. Write the following words, and ask your student to read them. He should be able to read at least eight correctly.

him	bud	hunt	truck	says
hum	bed	hint	trick	very

3. Write the following paragraph, and ask your student to read it. (To save lesson time, write it beforehand. But do not let the student see it until now.) Your student should make no more than eight mistakes.

Ellen Bell gets many eggs from her hens.
Ellen sells twelve big eggs for seventy cents.
Ellen's mother comes from the city to get some eggs.
Her sisters come from the city to get eggs from Ellen.
Her eggs are very fresh.

MORE READING

In the supplementary reader *More Stories 2,* the stories for Lesson 6 may be read in class or suggested for reading at home.

Lesson 7

OBJECTIVES

When a student completes this unit, he should be able to:

1. Say and respond to a new dialog.
2. Say the chart and story words.
3. Use *before* and *after* with noun objects; use *first* and *last* to modify nouns.
4. Use some vocabulary concerning health; use *take* and *put* with kinds of medicine.
5. Use some adverbs, such as *quickly, loudly,* and so on.
6. Make questions with *How* and give adverbs as answers.
7. Use *one* and *it* as substitute words.
8. Use the past tense of regular verbs in negative statements.
9. Use *tell* plus a clause.
10. Pronounce the consonant sounds /s/, /t/, and /th/ as in *thank*.
11. Read the following new words:
    Chart words: *men, bed, red, send, friends, letter*
    Story words: *them, well, sick, sits, quickly, women.*
12. Read a simple story, using the new chart and story words.
13. Read some words beginning with the consonant blend *fr-*.
14. Read some words contrasting the short vowels *e* and *i*.
15. Write the new chart and story words.
16. Identify a written verb root or *-s* form with the verb heard in a spoken sentence.
17. Read and write *man/men, woman/women* and use these words correctly in written sentences.
18. Address an envelope correctly.

VISUAL AIDS

1. *ESOL Illustrations 2*, p. 38.
2. Bring to class a letter in a stamped, addressed envelope; a calendar which contains all 12 months; and as many of the following items as possible:

some aspirin tablets	a teaspoon	a Band-Aid
a liquid medicine	nose drops	a fever thermometer

3. You will need one postage stamp for a first class letter and several blank envelopes for the Skills Practice on addressing an envelope.

REVIEW

Review any items your student had difficulty with when doing the Oral Evaluation in Lesson 6.

I. Conversation Skills

DIALOG

Doctor:	Hello, Mr. Hunt. Come in.
Mr. Hunt:	Hello, Doctor.
Doctor:	What can I do for you?
Mr. Hunt:	I don't feel well. I have a fever and a sore throat.
Doctor:	Let me look. Yes, your throat is very red.
Mr. Hunt:	Will you give me something for it?
Doctor:	Yes, here's a prescription. Take two pills every four hours.
Mr. Hunt:	Thank you, Doctor. Good-bye.
Doctor:	Good-bye, Mr. Hunt.

Teacher models the dialog, using the procedure outlined in Lesson 1.

VOCABULARY: Some Chart and Story Words

> Mr. Hunt and Mr. Hill are friends.
> Mr. Hill gives Mr. Hunt a box of red apples.
> Mr. Hunt writes a letter and sends it to his friend.

Teacher models the sentences several times, having the student repeat.

Most of these words are needed to read the story.

Use the visual aids you have brought with you, or open to *Skill Book 2,* p. 32, if necessary. The last picture on this page is especially helpful for showing the meaning of *send a letter*. Be sure to cover everything on this page except the illustrations.

[As you model the sentences, demonstrate the meanings as much as possible. For example, show your student a letter, and so on.]

DRILL: Question and Answer Drill

Teacher asks questions which elicit the vocabulary being taught.

Teach your student the difference between *What are Mr. Hunt and Mr. Hill?* (Friends.) and *Who are friends?* (Mr. Hunt and Mr. Hill).

Teacher	Student
Who are friends?	Mr. Hunt and Mr. Hill.
What does Mr. Hill give to Mr. Hunt?	A box of red apples.
What does Mr. Hunt write to his friend?	A letter.
What are Mr. Hunt and Mr. Hill?	(They're) friends.
Who gives Mr. Hunt a box of apples?	Mr. Hill does.
Who writes a letter to his friend?	Mr. Hunt does.
Who are you?	[Student gives his name.]
What are you?	[Student gives his occupation.]
Who am I?	You're ___________.
What am I?	You're a teacher.

VOCABULARY: *before* and *after, first* and *last*

B comes before C.
B comes after A.
Tuesday comes after Monday.
Wednesday comes before Thursday.

January is the first month of the year.
December is the last month of the year.
Sunday is the first day of the week.
Saturday is the last day of the week.

Teacher models the sentences several times, having the student repeat.

[Write the letters *A B C D* on the blackboard. Point to *B* as you say: "*B* comes before *C*."]

Demonstrate the meanings. Use a calendar to explain *year* and *week.*

[Use a calendar to explain the last six sentences.]

DRILL: Question and Answer Drill

Teacher asks questions which elicit answers containing *before, after, first,* and *last*.

[On the blackboard, write: 1 2 3 4 5.
Then ask the following questions.]

Teacher	Student
What comes before 2?	1.
What comes after 4?	
What comes before 3?	
What number is first?	
What number is last?	

[Write *A B C D E F* on the blackboard, and ask the following questions.]

Teacher	Student
What comes before *D*?	*C.*
What letter is first?	
[And so on.]	

VOCABULARY: Aches and Pains

Mr. Hunt's head	hurts.	He has a	headache.
Mr. Hunt's ear	hurts.	He has an	earache.
His tooth	hurts.	He has a	toothache.
His back	hurts.	He has a	backache.
Mr. Hunt's throat	hurts.	He has a	sore throat.
His shoulder	hurts.	He has a	sore shoulder.
His elbow	hurts.	He has a	sore elbow.
His foot	hurts.	He has a	sore foot.

Teacher models the sentences several times, having the student repeat.

Explain the meaning by demonstration.

[Say: "Listen to *hurt* and *ache*." Model the sentence, grimacing with pain and pointing to the appropriate part of the body.]

[Say: "Listen to *hurt* and *sore*." Continue as above.]

DRILL: Transformation Drill

Teacher gives the student a sentence with *hurt.* Student responds with a statement using *ache* or *sore.*

Teacher	Student
My head hurts.	I have a headache.
His throat hurts.	He has a sore throat.
His ear hurts.	
His shoulder hurts.	
Your tooth hurts.	
My back hurts.	
His elbow hurts.	
Her foot hurts.	

VOCABULARY: *take* and *put* + Medicine

Mr. Hunt	takes	his temperature with a thermometer.
Mr. Hunt	takes	a teaspoon of medicine for his sore throat.
He	takes	aspirin for his headache.
He	takes	pills for his earache.
He	puts	nosedrops in his nose.
He	puts	a Band-Aid on his arm.
The medicine will help him get well.		

Teacher models sentences, having the student repeat.

[Say: "Listen to *take*."]

Explain the meaning by showing the objects or by using p. 38 of *ESOL Illustrations 2.*

DRILL: Question and Answer Drill

Teacher asks a question about aches and pains. Student answers by naming the medicine which will be taken.

Teacher	**Student**
What does Mr. Hunt take for his sore throat?	He takes two teaspoons of medicine.
What does Mr. Hunt take for his headache?	He takes aspirin.
What does Mr. Hunt take for his earache?	
What does he put in his nose?	
What will the medicine do for Mr. Hunt?	
Where does Mr. Hunt put the Band-Aid?	

VOCABULARY and STRUCTURE FOCUS: Adverbs

Mary	is a slow	walker.	She walks	slowly.
Ed	is a quick	worker.	He works	quickly.
Ned	is a loud	speaker.	He speaks	loudly.
The child	is a soft	speaker.	He speaks	softly.
Mary	is a careful	worker.	She works	carefully.
Ann	is a bad	singer.	She sings	badly.
Ed	is a good	student.	He works	well.
The girl	is a fast	worker.	She works	fast.
Glenn	is a hard	worker.	He works	hard.

Teacher models the sentences several times, having the student repeat.

[Say: "Listen to *quick* and *quickly*," and model the sentences.]

[Continue with the remaining sentences given.]

Explain the meanings by demonstration as much as possible.

Note: Adverbs of manner usually end in *-ly. Well, fast,* and *hard* are exceptions.

DRILL: Transformation Drill

Teacher gives the student a sentence with an adjective, and the student responds with a sentence containing an adverb.

Teacher	Student
Ed is a quick worker.	He works quickly.
Ned is a loud speaker.	
The child is a soft speaker.	
Bob is a bad singer.	
Ann is a careful worker.	
Ed is a good student.	
The girl is a fast worker.	
Glenn is a hard worker.	
Mr. Hill is a slow walker.	

DRILL: Expansion Drill

Teacher gives a statement with an adverb; student adds *very* to the statement.

Teacher	Student
He works quickly.	He works very quickly.
Ed works well.	
Glenn works hard.	
Glenn speaks slowly.	
Ann speaks quickly.	
Mr. Hunt gets well quickly.	
Bob speaks softly.	
The child speaks loudly.	

STRUCTURE FOCUS: Questions with *How* and Answers with Adverbs

How does Ed work?	Quickly.
How do you work?	Carefully.
How does the baby cry?	Loudly.
How does Glenn run?	Fast.

Teacher models the questions and answers several times, having the student repeat.

Note: Information questions with *How* elicit adverbs of manner (*quickly*) or answers with *By* (taught in Lesson 5).

[Say: "Listen to *How*."
Say: "How does Will work?" Pause. "Quickly."]

[Continue with the remaining questions and answers.]

DRILL: Question and Answer Drill

Teacher asks questions which can be answered with an adverb or a *By* phrase.

1. Answers with adverbs.

Teacher	Student
How does Ed work?	Quickly.
How do you work?	Carefully.
How does the baby cry?	
How does Glenn walk?	
How does Ann laugh?	
How does Jill play?	
How does Mrs. Hill work?	

2. Answers with *By* phrases.

Teacher	Student
How do you come to class?	By bus.
How do you go downtown?	
How do you come here?	
How do the women go to Puerto Rico?	
How do you go to your sister's house?	

STRUCTURE FOCUS: The Noun Substitutes *one* and *it*

My pencil is on the table.
Do you see it?

I have a black dress.
Do you have one?

Teacher models the sentences several times, having the student repeat. Do not emphasize the underlined words.

[Say: "Listen to *it*." Model the two sentences. Then say: "Listen to *one*," and model the next two sentences.]

Note: Both *it* and *one* can be substituted for a noun or noun phrase already mentioned.

It refers to the specific item mentioned. *One* refers to *any* item like the one mentioned, not to a specific item.

One cannot be used to refer to a non-count noun like *water*, but it can be used to refer to the noun in a phrase like *a glass of*, that modifies a non-count noun.

DRILL: Question and Answer Drill

Teachers asks questions which elicit answers with *it* or *one* used as a noun substitute.

Teacher	Student
Would you like an apple?	Yes, I'd like one.
Would you like this apple?	Yes, I'd like it..
Would you like a cup of coffee?	
Would you like this sandwich?	
Would you like this glass of milk?	
Would you like a glass of water?	
Are you buying this can of coffee?	No, I'm not buying it.
Are you buying an apple?	
Do you drink milk?	
Do you eat meat?	
Do you have a watch?	
Do you have a bicycle?	

STRUCTURE FOCUS: Negative Statements in the Past Tense

They		camp<u>ed</u>	in the valley
They	<u>didn't</u>	<u>camp</u>	in the valley.
She		kick<u>ed</u>	the ball.
She	<u>didn't</u>	<u>kick</u>	the ball.
He		fish<u>ed</u>	in the river.
He	<u>didn't</u>	<u>fish</u>	in the river

Teacher models each pair of affirmative and negative statements. Have the student repeat.

[Say: "Listen to *didn't*."]

Note: In the past tense, the negative is formed with *did not* plus the simple form of the verb.

DRILL: Transformation Drill

Student changes an affirmative statement in the past tense into a negative statement in the past tense.

Teacher	Student
She passed the butter.	She didn't pass the butter.
She passed the ball.	
Ed kicked the ball.	
We sailed the boat.	
They fished in the river.	
We looked at the book.	
She studied Spanish.	
The girl jumped rope.	
The teacher repeated her name.	

STRUCTURE FOCUS: *tell* + a Clause

His boss	tells him	the letter is on the desk.
Her neighbor	tells her	the coffee is good.
Ann	tells her mother	the baby is crying.

Teacher models the sentences several times, having the student repeat.

[Say: "Listen to *tell*."]

DRILL: Combining Sentences

Teacher says two sentences, which the student combines into one.

Teacher	Student
The letter is on the desk. His boss tells him.	His boss tells him the letter is on the desk.
The money is on the table. Her boss tells her.	
The coffee is hot. Her neighbor tells her.	
Dinner is on the table. His wife will tell him.	
He needs a new shirt. His mother tells him.	
The television is very loud. His friend tells him.	
The baby is crying. Ann tells her mother.	
Mr. Hunt is well. The letters will tell them.	

PRONUNCIATION: /s/ and /th/, /t/ and /th/ as in *thank*

1. See the Pronunciation section in Lesson 1 for the steps to follow in teaching the consonant sounds /s/ and /th/ as in *sink* and *think*.

   Both /s/ and this /th/ are unvoiced. Be sure that the student's tongue is between his teeth when he makes the /th/ sound.

[Say: "Listen to /s/ and /th/."]

/s/	/th/	Sentences
sink	think	Sing a sad song.
seem	theme	She's very thin.
sank	thank	He passed me on the path.
sin	thin	She's faithful.
pass	path	It's a sad theme.
face	faith	Thank you for the suit.

2. Following the same procedure, teach the consonant sounds /t/ and /th/ as in *tank* and *thank*.

   Both are unvoiced sounds.

[Say: "Listen to /t/ and /th/."]

/t/	/th/	Sentences
tank	thank	I see three trees.
tick	thick	She carried three trays.
taught	thought	Thanks, Tom.
bat	bath	He's taking a bath.
tree	three	She's thinking about Tony.
		He taught me something.

ORAL EVALUATION

1. Review the words *before, after, first,* and *last.* Student should be able to use all four words. [Do the Question and Answer Drill following Vocabulary: *before* and *after*, *first* and *last.*]

2. Review vocabulary on aches and pains. Student should be able to answer seven of these fairly quickly. [Do the Drill after Vocabulary: Aches and Pains.]

3. Review the use of *take* and *put* plus medicine. Student should be able to answer three of these fairly quickly. [Do the Question and Answer Drill following Vocabulary: *take* and *put* + Medicine.]

4. Review questions with *How* and answers with adverbs (*slowly*) and *By* phrases (*by bus*). Student should be able to do this pattern fairly quickly. [Do the Question and Short Answer Drills following Questions with *How* and Answers with Adverbs.]

5. Review the noun substitutes *one* and *it*. Student should be able to use these with ease. [Do the Question and Answer Drill following Structure Focus: The Noun Substitutes *one* and *it*.]

6. Review negative statements in the past tense. Student should be able to do this entire drill, since no new vocabulary is presented. [Do the Transformation Drill following Structure Focus: Negative Statements in the Past Tense.]

7. Review the use of *tell* plus a clause. This structure is necessary for the story, so the student should be able to use it with ease. [Do the Drill on Combining Sentences following Structure Focus: *tell* + a Clause.]

II. Reading

Check your student's homework from Lesson 6, page 31, before beginning the chart.

CHART 7: Page 32

Teach this chart in the same way you taught the chart for Lesson 1.
("Read. What is the sound? What is the vowel sound? Read.") Be sure the student reads everything on the page.

Point out these things about the new chart words:

bed/red: [After teaching both lines on the chart, point out the similarity.]

[Cover the *b*.] *Bed* ends with *e, d.*
[Cover the *r*.] *Red* ends with *e, d.*

friends: [Point to *fr*.] Say these two sounds together very quickly: *friends.*
[Point to *i*.] The *i* is silent: *friends.*
[Point to *s*.] *Friends* ends with the sound /z/, but you write *s.*

[Cover the *s*.] *Friend.*
[Uncover the *s*.] *Friends.*

letter: The letters *tt* make one sound: /t/. You write two *t's*.
The letters *er* make the sound /er/.

STORY: Get Well Quickly!

Teach the story according to the seven steps outlined in Lesson 1.
The new story words are: *them, well, sick, sits, quickly, women.*

Use the following comprehension questions. Either short or long answers are acceptable.

	Teacher	Student
Paragraph 1	Where is Fred?	In bed.
	Why is he in bed?	He's sick.
	Who is visiting Fred?	Two men and two women are visiting him.
	Are the men and women his friends?	Yes, they are.
Paragraph 2	Why does Fred sit up in bed?	He sits up to visit with his friends.
Paragraph 3	What do the men bring to Fred?	They bring some apples.
	What color are the apples?	They're red.
Paragraph 4	What do the women bring to Fred?	They bring some eggs.
	Are the eggs fresh?	Yes, they are.
Paragraph 5	Does Fred thank his friends?	Yes, he does.
	What does he thank the men for?	He thanks them for the apples.
	What does he thank the women for?	He thanks them for the eggs.
Paragraph 6	What do Fred's friends say?	"Get well quickly!"
Paragraph 7	Is Fred very sick?	No, he isn't.
	Will he get well quickly?	Yes, he will.
Paragraph 8	What will Fred send to his friends?	He will send letters to them.
	Will he send a letter to the men?	Yes, he will.
	Will he send a letter to the women?	Yes, he will.
	Will the letters thank them for their visit?	Yes, they will.
	What will the letters tell them?	Fred is well.

SKILLS PRACTICE: Beginning Consonant Blend *fr*-

Step 1: Write *red* and *Fred* as shown below. Be careful to line up the words and to underline the *r* and *Fr* as shown.

red
Fred

Step 2: Point to and pronounce each word, first *red*, then *Fred*. Repeat a few times. The student listens.

Step 3: Point to and pronounce each word, having the student repeat. Do *red,* then *Fred*. Repeat a few times.

Step 4: Point to each word, beckoning for the student to say it. Do *red,* then *Fred.*

Repeat these four steps with the following pairs, one pair at a time. (You may leave all the pairs showing on the blackboard.) Be sure to line up the words and underline the letters as shown.

rat	rill	rock	rank
frat	frill	frock	frank

Step 5: Write the following chart and story words from the skill book under the heading *fr* as shown. Underline the *fr* in each word. Ask the student to read each word.

fr
from
fresh
friend

SKILLS PRACTICE: Contrasting the Short Vowels *e* and *i*

Contrast the short vowel sounds /e/ and /i/, using the minimal pairs shown here. Follow the nine steps in the Skills Practice on contrasting short vowel sounds in Lesson 6.

Note: The student has learned to read at least one of the words in each of the minimal pairs given here.

e	i	e	i	e	i
bed	bid	sell	sill	bell	bill
red	rid	ten	tin	pet	pit
hem	him	set	sit	neck	nick
peck	pick	well	will	tent	tint

III. Writing

WRITING LESSON: Page 34

Study

Help your student study the spelling of the following words before writing them. Point out silent letters and all other differences between the way the words are pronounced and the way they are written.

1. letter
2. friends
3. quickly
4. women

Listen and write

Dictate the following words for the student to write.

1. men
2. bed
3. red
4. send
5. them
6. well
7. sell
8. tell

Write

Dictate the following sentences for the student to write. Check the student's work for spelling and punctuation. If he did not write the question mark, have him write it.

1. Fred is sick in bed.
2. Is Fred very sick?
3. Get well quickly.

SKILLS PRACTICE: Adding *-s* to Verbs

Step 1: Write the following 10 verbs in a column on the blackboard. Have the student read each verb, write it with *-s*, and then read the *-s* form he has written. Write the first *-s* word yourself as a cue to the student.

visit visits
get
sit
tell
send
help
thank
come
give
write

Step 2: Leave the two columns of words on the blackboard. Now, read the sentences below to the student, one at a time. Have the student point to the *-s* or non *-s* form of the verb that he hears in the sentence. Indicate to the student which pair of verbs you want him to choose from with each sentence you read.

Do not emphasize the verb as you say the sentence. You may repeat the whole sentence, but do not prompt the student by saying the verb alone.

1. Indicate *visit/visits.* Read: Jimmy visits his mother every Sunday.
2. Indicate *get/gets.* Read: Kitty gets some eggs.
3. Indicate *sit/sits.* Read: Please sit down.
4. Indicate *tell/tells.* Read: Bob tells his friend, "Get well."
5. Indicate *send/sends.* Read: We send her a letter every day.
6. Indicate *help/helps.* Read: He doesn't help his mother.
7. Indicate *thank/thanks.* Read: Dan thanks his boss.
8. Indicate *come/comes.* Read: Does Ann come to class with Bob?
9. Indicate *give/gives.* Read: Give me some paper.
10. Indicate *write/writes.* Read: Will you write a letter?

SKILLS PRACTICE: *man/men, woman/women*

Step 1: Write the following words and headings on the blackboard, lined up as shown here.

one	**some**
man	men
woman	women

Step 2: Point to *man.* Say: "a man, one man."
Point to *men.* Say: "some men, two men, three men, four men."

Step 3: Point to *woman.* Say: "a woman, one woman."
Point to *women.* Say: "some women, two women, three women, four women."

Step 4: Say: "Please read," pointing to *man, men; woman, women.*
The student reads the words.

Step 5: Write the following exercise on the blackboard. Have the student choose the correct word (*man* or *men*), write it in the blank, and then read the complete sentence.

man **men**

1. Some ________ are coming.
2. A ________ is in the truck.
3. Fred is a big ________.
4. The two ________ are brothers.

Step 6: Have the student do the next exercise in the same way, choosing between *woman* and *women*.

woman **women**

1. The two ____________ are friends.
2. Kitty is a pretty ____________.
3. Three ____________ are sitting in the kitchen.
4. A ____________ is in the shop.

SKILLS PRACTICE: Addressing an Envelope

You will need to have some blank envelopes for this exercise. Use the large business size if your student's writing is rather large. Also, have a postage stamp for a first class letter.

Before class, you should address an envelope to show the correct placement of the address and return address. Use manuscript writing (printing). On this model envelope, use your own name and address as the return address. Address the letter to:

Miss Ann Hunt
425 Hill Street
Sun City, New York 11234

Do this:	**Say this:**
Point to *Miss Ann Hunt.*	Teacher: I'm sending a letter to Miss Ann Hunt.
Point to the rest of the address.	Teacher: This is her address: four-twenty-five Hill Street, Sun City, New York one-one-two-three-four. [The word *New* is a new reading word for the student although he has learned it orally.]
Point to *New.*	Teacher: This word is *New.* Read: *New.* Student: New.
Point to *New York.*	Teacher: Please read. Student: New York.

Point to the return address.

Teacher: This is my name and address.
[Read the return address.]

Give the student a blank envelope.
Point to the place for the address.

Teacher: You are sending a letter to Miss Ann Hunt.
Write her name and address here.
Student: [Writes the name and address, copying from the model envelope.]

Point to the place for the return address.

Teacher: Write your name and address here.
Student: [Writes own name and address.]

[The student learned to write his name and full address—including zip code—in Lesson 11 of *Skill Book 1*, so this is review. Help him with the spelling or numbers if he has forgotten.]

Give the student the postage stamp.
Point to the upper righthand corner of the envelope.

Teacher: Put the stamp here.
Student: [Places stamp on envelope.]

Next, have the student address another envelope. Use the name Mr. Glenn Hill and a local address with the appropriate zip code. Write this name and address on the blackboard for the student to copy. Again, the student should use his own name and address for the return address.

If your student is advanced and indicates that he would like to address an envelope to a particular person in another area, help him to do that, also.

HOMEWORK: Page 35

Ask your student to do this page at home. In addition, ask him to address an envelope to you. Give him a blank envelope and the model envelope from the previous exercise so that he has the correct spelling of your name and your full address.

READING AND WRITING EVALUATION

1. Write the following sentences. Have your student circle the correct answer and then read the complete sentence. The student should be able to complete three sentences correctly.

	woman.			give	
Mr. Hill is a			Ellen		the eggs to Fred.
	man.			gives	
	men			gets	
Two		are in the truck.	Fred		well quickly.
	man			get	

2. Dictate the following words. The student should be able to write five of the six words correctly.

friend	letter	sick
quickly	send	them

MORE READING

In the supplementary reader *More Stories 2,* the stories for Lesson 7 may be read in class or suggested for reading at home.

Lesson 8

OBJECTIVES

When a student completes this lesson, he should be able to:

1. Say and respond to a new dialog.
2. Say the chart and story words.
3. Use the word *carry* with different objects one carries.
4. Use the prepositions *beside, between, over, under, in back of, in front of,* and *on top of.*
5. Use *a/an* and *the* (contrasted with one another).
6. Make statements and questions with *can*.
7. Use *can* and *can't* in short answers.
8. Use some irregular verbs in past tense statements and questions.
9. Use a *that* clause following an adjective, as in: "Sam is happy that Ann will marry Jack."
10. Make introductions which contain appositives ("Jill, this is my boss, Mr. Smith."), and give a polite reply ("How do you do, Mr. Smith.")
11. Pronounce the consonant sounds /d/, voiced /th/, and unvoiced /th/.
12. Read the following new words, in two charts and stories:
    Chart words: *cat, rat, bat, back, black, standing*
    Story words: *that, Smith, quick, kill, cannot, can*

    Chart words: *bag, basket, carrying, family, marry, happy*
    Story words: *Jack.*
13. Read two simple stories, using the new chart and story words.
14. Read some words beginning with the consonant blend *bl-*.
15. Read some words contrasting the beginning consonant blends *bl-* and *br-*.
16. Read some words contrasting the short vowels *a* and *e.*
17. Write the new chart and story words.
18. Write the *-ing* forms of new and old verbs. (This is partly review.)

VISUAL AIDS

1. *ESOL Illustrations 2*, pp. 39-40 and pp. 4-6.
2. Before your class session, color in all the items on p. 40 of *ESOL Illustrations 2.* This is necessary for drills in this lesson.
3. Bring as many of the following items as possible:

a wallet	a basket	a lunch box	a suitcase
a purse	a shopping bag	a briefcase	

REVIEW

Review any items that your student had difficulty with when doing the Oral Evaluation in Lesson 7.

I. Conversation Skills

DIALOG

Bob:	Hello, Operator. This is an emergency. I need an ambulance for my father. Right away.
Operator:	What's your name and address?
Bob:	This is Bob Samson. I live at 908 Main Street. Please hurry.
Operator:	I'll get an ambulance there right away.
Bob:	Thank you.

Teacher models the dialog, using the procedure outlined in Lesson 1. Dramatize the telephone call.

Note: Substitute your student's name and address for those above. In a class, substitute a suitable local address.

[If you use the number 908, say: "nine-oh-eight."]

[Write the street number that you use on the board.]

VOCABULARY: Some Chart and Story Words

This is a rat.
The black cat kills the rat.
The rat dies. The rat is dead.
The cat lives. The cat is alive.

Teacher models the sentences, having the student repeat. Use p. 39 of *ESOL Illustrations 2.*

DRILL: Question and Answer Drill

Teacher asks questions which elicit the vocabulary being taught.

Point to items in the pictures on p. 39 of *ESOL Illustrations 2*, as appropriate.

Teacher	**Student**
What is this?	A cat.
What is this?	A rat.
What kills the rat?	
What dies?	
What lives?	
What is alive?	
What does the cat do?	
What is dead?	

VOCABULARY: Containers for Carrying Things

Jack is carrying a wallet.	Ann is carrying a purse.
He's carrying a basket.	She's carrying a shopping bag.
He's carrying a lunch box.	She's carrying a briefcase.
He's carrying a bag.	She's carrying a suitcase.

Teacher models the sentences several times, having the student repeat.

Use the objects you have brought to class or p. 40 of *ESOL Illustrations 2*. Act out *carrying*, and have the student do likewise.

Note: The word *bag* is a chart word with a suitcase as its illustration. Refer to the picture of a suitcase as you teach both *bag* and *suitcase.*

[Say: "Listen to *carrying*," and hold up or indicate the objects as you say each sentence. Act out *carrying*.]

DRILL: Identification Drill

Student identifies the items on p. 40 of *ESOL Illustrations 2.*

[Using the appropriate objects or illustrations, ask: "What is Jack carrying?" and "What is Ann carrying?"]

VOCABULARY: Chart and Story Words

Ann is Jack's girl friend.
Ann and Jack will marry in June.
They will be husband and wife.
They will be Mr. and Mrs. Black.
They will be happy.

Teacher models the sentences several times, having the student repeat.

Demonstrate *happy* with a broad smile.

[Say: "Listen," and then model each sentence.]

DRILL: Question and Answer Drill

Teacher asks questions which elicit answers containing the vocabulary items being taught.

Teacher	**Student**
Who is Ann?	Ann is Jack's girl friend.
What will Ann and Jack do in June?	
Who will be Jack's wife?	
Who will be Ann's husband?	
When will Ann and Jack marry?	
Will they be happy?	

VOCABULARY: Prepositions of Location

I'm beside you.
I'm in front of you.
I'm in back of you.
I'm between you and the door.

The light is over the desk.
The book is under the desk.
The pencil is on top of the desk.

Teacher models the sentences several times, having the student repeat.

Demonstrate the meaning of the first four sentences by positioning yourself appropriately.

Use classroom objects, placed appropriately, for the last three sentences.

[Stand or sit beside the student as you say: "I'm sitting beside you."]

[Move to the correct positions and use gestures as you say the rest of the sentences.]

DRILL: Question and Answer Drill

Prepare for the drill by placing classroom objects in these positions:

– a pen between two books
– a pencil on top of a book
– a chair beside a desk or table
– a lunch box or book under the desk
– a chair in front of the student
– a chair behind the student.

Class: In a class situation, ask:
"Who is sitting beside you? Who is sitting behind you?" and so on.

Teacher	**Student**
[Point to the item.]	
Where is the pen?	It's between two books.
Where is the chair?	It's beside the desk.
Where is the lunch box (book)?	It's under the desk.
Where is the pencil?	It's on top of the book.
Where am I standing? [in front of] [in back of] [beside]	
Where are you sitting?	

VOCABULARY: Story Words

I'm standing with my back to you.
She's standing with her back to the wall.

Teacher models the sentences several times, having the student repeat.

[Say: "Listen to *with my back to*," and then actually stand with your back to the student as you model the first sentence.]

DRILL: Question and Answer Drill

1. Teacher performs actions and asks questions which elicit answers containing *with your back to.*

[Stand with your back to the wall, the window, the door, the blackboard, and other items in the room. Ask: "Where am I standing?"

The student answers:
"You're standing with your back to the wall," and so on. Prompt him only if necessary.]

2. Teacher has the student perform the same actions, that is, stand with his back to the wall, the window, and so on. Student describes what he is doing.

Teacher	**Student**
Stand with your back to the wall.	[Performs the action.]
Where are you standing?	I'm standing with my back to the wall.

[Continue with other locations.]

STRUCTURE FOCUS: The Definite and Indefinite Articles *the* and *a*

> I have a book in my hand.
> The book is my English book.
>
> I have a pen in my hand.
> The pen is black.
>
> I have a purse.
> The purse is brown.

Teacher models the sentences in pairs, having the student repeat both. Do not emphasize *a* and *the* as you pronounce the sentences.

[Say: "Listen to *a* and *the*."]

Note: The indefinite article *a* is used before a singular count noun to indicate one of something.

The definite article *the* is used before singular and plural count nouns and non-count nouns. It indicates something already referred to, that is, something specific.

(Only count nouns are used in this lesson.)

DRILL: Statement and Rejoinder

Teacher gives a sentence with *a*, such as *I have a pen.* Indicate the color of the item by using objects in the classroom or the pictures on pp. 4-6 of *ESOL Illustrations 2.*

Student makes a more specific sentence about the item, using *the*, such as, *The pen is black*

You may add to the list given here other items that you have brought with you, such as shopping bag, lunch box, suitcase, and so on. Or, refer to p. 40 of *ESOL Illustrations 2.*

Teacher	**Student**
I have a pen.	
The pen is black.	The pen is black.
I have a pencil.	
The pencil is yellow.	The pencil is yellow.
I have a coat.	
I have a sweater.	
I have a jacket.	
I have a belt.	
I have a dress.	
I have a blouse.	
I have a skirt.	
I have a suit.	
I have a shirt.	
I have a tie.	
I have a wallet.	
I have a purse.	

VOCABULARY: The Modal *can*

He was sick. He's well now.	He can go to work.
Dinner is on the table.	We can eat now.
I'm teaching you English.	You can speak English now.
I'm teaching you English.	You can read English now.

Teacher models each set of sentences several times, having the student repeat only the sentence with *can.*

[Say: "Listen to *can.*"]

Do not emphasize *can* as you pronounce the sentences.

Note: *Can* is one of several modals, or modal auxiliaries, in English. Some others are *could, should, would, may, might,* and *must.* Modals are used to indicate such ideas as possibility, necessity, obligation, and the like. The modal *can* means *be able.*

The modal *can* is followed by the simple form of the verb.

STRUCTURE FOCUS: Statements and Questions with *can*

	I	can	teach English.
Can	I		teach English?
	She	can	jump rope.
Can	she		jump rope?
	We	can	speak English.
Can	we		speak English?

Teacher models each statement and question several times, having the student repeat both.

[Say: "Listen to *can*."]

Note: Notice that *can,* like *will,* does not change form: *I can, he can,* and so on.

There is a similar reversal in word order in questions, that is, *I can* becomes *Can I.*

We use a rising intonation pattern with these questions.

DRILL: Transformation Drill

Student changes a statement into a question.

Teacher	**Student**
You can speak English.	Can you speak English?
I can help you.	
He can come with us.	
She can jump rope.	
The cat can kill the rat.	
Jill can study with Kim.	
We can swim here.	
They can play ball.	
She can carry the bag.	

STRUCTURE FOCUS: Short Answers with *can/can't*

Can you speak English?	Yes, I can.
Can Kim play ball?	Yes, she can.
Can you speak Chinese?	No, I can't.
Can Ted jump rope?	No, he can't.

Teacher models the question and short answer, having the student repeat both.

[Say: "Listen to *Yes, I can,*" and model the questions and answers.]

[Do the negative (*can't*) in the same way.]

DRILL: Free Reply

Teacher asks questions which elicit short affirmative and negative replies.

Teacher	Student
Can you speak English?	Yes, I can.
Can you speak Chinese?	(No, I can't.)
Can you speak Spanish?	
Can you speak Polish?	
Can you speak German?	
Can you speak Korean?	
Can you play ball?	
Can you jump rope?	
Can you carry the suitcase?	

STRUCTURE FOCUS: Affirmative Past Tense Statements with Irregular Verbs

I	go	shopping every day.
I	went	shopping yesterday.
I	do	my homework every day.
I	did	my homework yesterday.
You	drink	a glass of water every day.
You	drank	a glass of water yesterday.
He	sits	in the living room every day.
He	sat	in the living room yesterday.
She	gives	the money to Glenn.
She	gave	the money to Glenn.
We	buy	some food every day.
We	bought	some food yesterday.
They	teach	English every day.
They	taught	English yesterday.

Teacher models in pairs the present and past tense sentences for each verb. Have the student repeat both.

[Say: "Listen to *go* and *went*."]

[Continue in the same way with the remaining verbs.]

Note: All these verbs have been introduced previously.

DRILL: Transformation Drill

1. Student changes a present tense statement into a past tense statement.

Teacher	Student
I drink two cups of coffee every day.	I drank two cups of coffee yesterday.
Ann drinks a glass of water every day.	
He sits in the classroom every day.	
I buy some books.	
We give the book to Ann.	
We do our homework every day.	
I go shopping every day.	

2. Student changes a past tense statement into a present tense statement.

Teacher	Student
We bought some books.	We buy some books.
We did our homework.	
I went shopping.	
I sat in the living room.	
I drank a glass of milk.	
Ann taught English.	
She gave the book to Glenn.	

STRUCTURE FOCUS: Past Tense Questions with Irregular Verbs

She	went	shopping yesterday.
Did she	go	shopping yesterday?
You	did	your homework yesterday.
Did you	do	your homework yesterday?
We	drank	some coffee yesterday.
Did we	drink	any coffee yesterday?
They	bought	some food yesterday?
Did they	buy	any food yesterday?

Teacher models the statements and questions in pairs. Have the student repeat both.

[Say: "Listen to *Did*."]

Note: Use *did* and the simple form of the verb to make questions in the past tense. Students may have difficulty remembering to use *go* (not *went*) in the question.

DRILL: Transformation Drill

Student changes a past tense statement into a past tense question.

Teacher	Student
She went shopping yesterday.	Did she go shopping yesterday?
Ann went shopping yesterday.	
We did our homework.	
Ann drank some coffee.	
We bought some meat.	
Glenn sat in the living room.	
You gave the money to Bob.	
They bought some food.	
Mrs. Hill taught English.	
She drank a glass of water.	
Bob went downtown.	
Jack bought a wallet.	

STRUCTURE FOCUS: Adjective + *that* Clause

Sam	is	happy	that	Ann will marry Jack.
I	am	happy	that	Bob will buy the house.
We	are	sad	that	you are sick.

Teacher models the sentences, having the student repeat.

[Say: "Listen to *happy that*."]

DRILL: Combining Sentences

Teacher gives two statements, which the student combines, using *that*.

Teacher	Student
Ann will marry Jack. I'm happy.	I'm happy that Ann will marry Jack.
Liz will marry Dan. I'm happy.	I'm happy that Liz will marry Dan.
Ann will marry Jack. Bob's sad.	
She will study English. We're happy.	
Ann will sing. Jack's happy.	
It's sunny. I'm happy.	
You are learning English. I'm happy.	
My sister will go shopping with me. I'm happy.	

VOCABULARY and STRUCTURE FOCUS: Making Introductions with Appositives

Introduction (Containing Appositive)	**Polite Reply**
Jill, this is my friend Sam.	It's nice to meet you, Sam.
Bob, this is my wife, Ann.	It's nice to meet you, Ann.
Fred, this is my boss, Mr. Smith.	How do you do, Mr. Smith.
Betty, this is my neighbor Mrs. Hill.	How do you do, Mrs. Hill.

Teacher models the introduction and its polite reply several times, having the student repeat both.

Indicate by using gestures and shifting your body that you are introducing one person to another.

Class: In a class situation, introduce students to each other. Have the men shake hands.

Note: The comma in *my wife, Ann* means that Ann is my one and only wife. The lack of a comma in *my friend Sam* means that I have several friends and Sam is one of them.

[Say: "Listen," then model the introduction and its polite reply. Have the student repeat both.]

DRILL: Making Introductions

Teacher gives the names of two persons being introduced. Student makes the introduction.

Teacher	**Student**
Jill—my friend Sam. Jill, this is my friend Sam.	Jill, this is my friend Sam.
Linda—my friend Dan.	
Bob—my girl friend, Ann	
Kathy—my boy friend, Jack	
Cindy—my neighbor Mrs. Bell	
Dan—my boss, Mr. Smith	
Jack—my mother, Mrs. Hill	

DRILL: Polite Replies

Teacher introduces a "person" to the student. Student gives the polite reply.

Use your student's name instead of *Linda.*

Note: In a more informal situation, we have given *It's nice to meet you* as the expected polite reply. In a slightly more formal situation, we have given *How do you do.*

Teacher	**Student**
Linda, this is my friend Ann. It's nice to meet you, Ann.	It's nice to meet you, Ann.
Linda, this is my friend Jack.	It's nice to meet you, Jack.
Linda, this is my boss, Mr. Smith.	How do you do, Mr. Smith.
Linda, this is my neighbor Mrs. Hill.	How do you do, Mrs. Hill.
Linda, this is my boy friend, Sam.	
Linda, this is my father, Mr. Bell.	
Linda, this is my friend Kathy.	
Linda, this is my mother, Mrs. Bell.	
Linda, this is my sister Cindy.	
Linda, this is my son Dan.	

PRONUNCIATION: /d/, voiced /t̲h̲/, unvoiced /th/

1. See the Pronunciation section in Lesson 1 for the steps to follow in teaching the consonant sounds /d/ as in *dare* and voiced /t̲h̲/ as in *there.*

   Both are voiced sounds. Be sure the student's tongue is between his teeth when he makes the voiced /t̲h̲/ sound.

[Say: "Listen to /d/ and /t̲h̲/."]

/d/	/t̲h̲/	Sentences
dare	there	It's a nice day.
Dan	than	I need the other one.
day	they	His father is doing well.
wordy	worthy	They're loading the truck.
sued	soothe	I went there yesterday.
		Dan's in the dining room.

2. Following the same procedure, teach the consonant sounds in *thigh* and *thy*. The /th/ in *thigh* is unvoiced; the /t̲h̲/ in *thy* is voiced.

[Say: "Listen to /th/ and /t̲h̲/."]

/th/	/t̲h̲/	Sentences
thigh	thy	He hurt his thigh.
ether	either	They gave him ether.
teeth	teethe	He opened his mouth.
mouth (n.)	mouth (v.)	I'll take either one.
wreath	wreathe	Thy will be done.

ORAL EVALUATION

1. Review the chart and story words. Student should be able to say all of these, since they are necessary for the story.

   [Do the Question and Answer Drills following Vocabulary: Some Chart and Story Words and Vocabulary: Chart and Story Words.]

2. Review the verb *carry* plus the objects. Since much of this is review, student should be able to say all of these.

   [Do the Identification Drill following Vocabulary: Containers for Carrying Things.]

3. Review the prepositions of location. These words are essential for indicating location correctly, so it is important that your student know them.

   [Do the Question and Answer Drill following Vocabulary: Prepositions of Location.]

4. Review the use of the definite article (*the*) and the indefinite article (*a*).

   [Do the Drill following Structure Focus: The Definite and Indefinite Articles *the* and *a.]*

5. Review questions and short answers with *can*. The student must learn this question pattern, since it is a very necessary one in English.

   [Do the Transformation Drill following Structure Focus: Statements and Questions with *can*. Have the student answer the questions, too.]

   Teacher: You can speak English.
   Student: Can you speak English? Yes, I can.

   [Be sure that some answers are negative.]

6. Review the past tense of the irregular verbs in this lesson. The student should know all of these.

   [Do the Transformation Drill following Structure Focus: Affirmative Past Tense Statements with Irregular Verbs.]

7. Review the use of a *that* clause following an adjective. This structure is necessary for the story.

   [Do the Combining Sentences Drill following Structure Focus: Adjective + *that* Clause.]

8. Review making introductions. Student should be able to introduce two people to each other and should know the expected polite reply.

   [Do both Drills following Vocabulary and Structure Focus: Making Introductions with Appositives.]

II. Reading

Check your student's homework from Lesson 7, including the envelope addressed to you. If the student did not finish his homework, ask him to do so now. Be sure that he knows how to address an envelope correctly.

CHART 8-A: Page 36

Teach this chart in the same way you taught the chart for Lesson 1.
("Read. What is the sound? What is the vowel sound? Read.")

Point out these things about the new chart words.

back: In *back*, the letters *ck* make one sound: /k/.

black: [Point to *bl*.] Say these two sounds together very quickly: *black*.
In *black*, the letters *ck* make one sound: /k/.

standing: [Point to *st*.] Say these two sounds together very quickly: *standing*.

Cover the *-ing*, and say: "Stand up."
Uncover the *-ing*, and say: "I'm standing up."

After teaching the entire chart, point out the similarities in *cat, rat, bat,* and in *back, black*.

Pointing to *at* in each word, say: "*Cat* ends with *a, t; rat* ends with *a, t; bat* ends with *a, t*."

Pointing to *ack* in each word, say: "*Back* ends with *a, c, k; black* ends with *a, c, k*."

STORY: The Rat

Teach the story according to the seven steps outlined in Lesson 1.
The new story words are: *that, can, cannot, kill, Smith, quick*.

Use the following comprehension questions. Either short or long answers are acceptable.

	Teacher	Student
Paragraph 1	Who is that woman?	She's Ann Smith.
	Who is Sam Smith?	He's Ann's brother.
	Who is Ann's little brother?	He's Dan Smith.
Paragraph 2	Where is Ann standing?	She's standing in the kitchen.
	Who is in the kitchen with Ann?	Sam and Dan are.
	Is Ann standing with her back to the boys?	Yes, she is.
Paragraph 3	Who hits Ann on the back?	Dan does.
	What does Dan yell?	He yells, "A rat! A rat! A rat is in back of that black box."
	Where is the rat?	It's in back of the black box.
Paragraph 4	What does Ann yell?	She yells, "Quick, Sam, bring a bat! I can kill the rat."
Paragraph 5	What does Sam bring?	He brings a bat.
	What does Ann say?	She says, "I will kill that rat. Quick, Sam, pick up that black box."
Paragraph 6	What does Sam do?	He picks up the black box.
	What does the rat do?	It runs quickly.
	Can Ann hit the rat?	No, she can't.

Paragraph 7	What will Ann get? Why does she want to get a cat?	She'll get a cat. A cat can kill the rat.
Paragraphs 8-9	Does Sam think a cat can kill a rat? What does Sam say?	No, he doesn't. He says, "A cat cannot kill a rat."
	Does Ann think a cat can kill a rat? What does Ann say?	Yes, she does. She says, "That is a little rat. A big cat can kill a little rat."

After finishing the story, ask the student: "What do you think? Can a cat kill a rat?"

CHART 8-B: Page 38

Teach this chart in the same way you taught the chart for Lesson 1.
("Read. What is this sound? What is the vowel sound? Read.")

Point out these things about the new chart words.

happy: The letters *pp* make one sound: /p/. You write two *p's*.
In *happy, y* has the vowel sound /y/.

marry: The letters *rr* make one sound: /r/. You write two *r's*.
In *marry, y* has the vowel sound /y/.

carrying: The letters *rr* make one sound: /r/. You write two *r's*.
In *carrying, y* has the vowel sound /y/.

Cover the *-ing,* and say: "Carry the basket."
Uncover the *-ing,* and say: "He's carrying the basket."

family: In *family, y* has the vowel sound /y/.

STORY: Jack and Ann Will Marry

Teach the story according to the seven steps outlined in Lesson 1. The only new story word is *Jack.*
Use the following comprehension questions. Either short or long answers are acceptable.

	Teacher	**Student**
Paragraph 1	Where does the Smith family live?	The Smith family lives in the city. [The student is not prepared to use the pronoun *They* to stand for *the Smith family.* If he tries to use another pronoun—such as *He* or *It*—in his answer, prompt him to say *They.* Do not try to explain why.]
Paragraph 2	Where does Jack Black live? What is Jack doing?	He lives in the valley. He's visiting the Smith family.
Paragraph 3	What is Sam Smith carrying for Jack?	He's carrying Jack's bag.
Paragraph 4	What is Jack carrying? What's in the basket? Who is Jack bringing the apples to?	He's carrying a basket. Apples. He's bringing them to the Smith family.
Paragraph 5	Who will Jack marry? Who will Ann marry?	He'll marry Ann Smith. She'll marry Jack Black.
Paragraph 6	Are Jack and Ann happy or sad? Are Mr. and Mrs. Smith happy or sad? Are Ann's brothers happy that Ann will marry Jack? Is the Smith family happy or sad?	They're happy. They're happy. Yes, they are. The Smith family is happy. [The previous note about *the Smith family* applies here, too.]

SKILLS PRACTICE: Beginning Consonant Blend *bl-*

Step 1: Write *lack* and *black* as shown below. Be careful to line up the words and to underline the *l* and *bl* as shown.

lack
black

Step 2: Point to and pronounce each word, first *lack*, then *black*. Repeat a few times. The student listens.

Step 3: Point to and pronounce each word, having the student repeat. Do *lack*, then *black*. Repeat a few times.

Step 4: Point to each word, beckoning for the student to say it. Do *lack*, then *black*.

Repeat these four steps with the following pairs, one pair at a time. (You may leave all the pairs showing on the blackboard.) Be sure to line up the words and underline the letters as shown.

lot	less	lock	lip
blot	bless	block	blip

SKILLS PRACTICE: Contrasting *bl-* and *br-*

Do not write any words for the student in this exercise. Many of the minimal pairs have spellings the student is not yet equipped to read.

Step 1: Write *bl* and *br* on the blackboard.

Sept 2: Model a minimal pair, *black* and *brack*, several times as the student listens.
Say: *"black, brack,"* pointing to *bl*, then *br*.

Step 3: Have the student repeat after you several times.
Say: *"black, brack,"* pointing to *bl*, then *br*.

Step 4: Say the words in random order.
Have the student point to the correct symbol (*bl* or *br*) for the word you are saying.

Step 5: Point to the symbols *bl* and *br* in random order. Have the student say the word.

Continue in the same way with the following minimal pairs. Do ***not*** write the words nor explain what they mean.

bl	**br**	**bl**	**br**	**bl**	**br**
bled	bread	bloom	broom	bloke	broke
blue	brew	bland	brand	blight	bright
blush	brush	bleach	breach	blink	brink

SKILLS PRACTICE: Contrasting the Short Vowels *a* and *e*

Contrast the short vowel sounds /a/ and /e/, using the minimal pairs shown here. Follow the nine steps in the Skills Practice on contrasting short vowel sounds in Lesson 6.

Note: The student has learned to read at least one of the words in each of the minimal pairs given here.

a	e	a	e	a	e
bat	bet	pat	pet	pan	pen
man	men	tan	ten	sand	send
and	end	bad	bed	latter	letter

III. Writing

WRITING LESSON: Page 40

Listen and write

Dictate the following words and sentences for the student to write.

1. cat
2. Jack
3. back
4. black
5. that
6. rat
7. standing
8. basket

1. That is a little rat.
2. Dan is standing with Sam.
3. Sam is carrying Jack's bag.
4. Ann will marry Jack Black.
5. The Smith family is happy.

SKILLS PRACTICE: Review Adding *-ing* to Verbs

Step 1: Write the following verbs, in two columns, lined up as shown.
Write the *-ing* form of the first verb in each column, as shown.

sell	selling	get	getting
tell		hit	
help		sit	
send		run	
stand		cut	
think		put	

Step 2: Point to *sell*, and say: "Please read."
Point to *selling,* and say: "Please read."

Step 3: Point to *tell*, and say: "Please read."
Point to the space to the right of *tell*, and say: "Write *telling.*"

Continue the same way with the rest of the words in the first column.

Then do the second column of words, following steps 2 and 3. If the student has any difficulty doubling the final consonant, review the chart with *CVC + C + ing* that you used in Lesson 4.

HOMEWORK: Page 41

Ask your student to write this page at home and to review this lesson's charts and stories.

READING AND WRITING EVALUATION

1. Write the following sentences. Have your student circle the correct answer and then read the complete sentence. The student should be able to complete all three sentences.

    The man / men is in the kitchen.

    Jack hits his brother on the black. / back.

    Sam is carrying Jack's bag. / back.

2. Dictate the following words. The student should be able to write eight out of 10 correctly.

marry	carrying	cannot	black	that
family	happy	back	quick	cat

3. Write the following paragraphs beforehand, and have the student read them now. The student should make no more than five errors. (These paragraphs review words from Lessons 1-8.)

    Jack is visiting the Smith family.
    Jack is carrying a big black bag.

    Jack is bringing gifts for the Smith family.
    The gifts are in his bag.

    Jack has a bat for Sam.
    Jack has a little truck for Dan.
    Jack has some apples for Mr. Smith.
    Jack has a pretty dish for Mrs. Smith.
    Jack has a pretty ring for Ann.

MORE READING

In the supplementary reader *More Stories 2,* the stories for Lesson 8 may be read in class or suggested for reading at home.

Lesson 9

OBJECTIVES

When a student completes this unit, he should be able to:

1. Say and respond to a new dialog.
2. Say the chart and story words, for example: *glass, factory, path.*
3. Say some words describing items for seating with the verb *sit*.
4. Use the simple fractions *a half* and *a quarter.*
5. Use *another, the other,* and *the others.*
6. Use *very, too,* and *enough.*
7. Say some future time expressions.
8. Use *be + going to* to express future time.
9. Use more irregular verbs in the past tense, in both affirmative and negative statements.
10. Pronounce the vowel sounds /o/ and /uu/ as in *pot* and *put* and the consonant sounds /n/ and /ng/ as in *ban* and *bang.*
11. Read the following new words:
    Chart words: *path, grass, glass, half, laugh, factory*
    Story words: *after, lunch.*
12. Read a simple story, using the new chart and story words.
13. Read some words beginning with the consonant blends *gl-* and *gr-* and read some words contrasting these two blends.
14. Read some words contrasting the short vowels *a* and *u*.
15. Write the new chart and story words.
16. Write the *-ing* form of verbs, dropping the final silent *e*. (This is review.)

VISUAL AIDS

1. *ESOL Illustrations 2*, p. 8 and pp. 41-43.
2. A dollar bill, a half dollar, and four quarters.
3. A calendar for the full year.

REVIEW

Review any items your student had difficulty with when doing the Oral Evaluation in Lesson 8.

I. Conversation Skills

DIALOG

Jack: What did you do yesterday?
Ann: We went to the park.

Jack: Did you have a picnic?
Ann: Yes, we sat on the grass and ate our lunch.

Teacher models the dialog, using the procedure outlined in Lesson 1.

VOCABULARY: Chart and Story Words (Factories)

This is a car	factory.	The workers make cars.
This is a toy	factory.	The workers make toys.
This is a glass	factory.	The workers make glass.
This is a paper	factory.	The workers make paper.
This is a candy	factory.	The workers make candy.

Teacher models the sentences in pairs, having the student repeat both.

Use pp. 42-43 of *ESOL Illustrations 2.*

[Say: "Listen to *car factory*."]

[Continue in the same way with the remaining items.]

DRILL: Question and Answer Drill

Teacher asks questions eliciting identification of the factory and what is done in it.

Point to pictures on pp. 42-43 of *ESOL Illustrations 2.*

Teacher	Student
What's this?	It's a glass factory.
What do the workers make there?	They make glass.

VOCABULARY: The Story Word *path*

There's a path in back of the house.
There's a path in back of the toy factory.
There's a path in back of the glass factory.

Teacher models the sentences several times, having the student repeat.

Use p. 8 of *ESOL Illustrations 2* to show the meaning of *path* and *in back of.*

[Say: "Listen to *a path in back of*."]

VOCABULARY: Seating

She's sitting on the grass.
He's sitting on the rock.

The woman's sitting on the bench.
The children are sitting on the stairs.

The boys are sitting on the floor.
The man's sitting on the chair.

The friends are sitting on the sofa.

Teacher models the sentences several times, having the student repeat. Use *ESOL Illustrations 2*, p. 41.

The words *floor* and *chair* have already been taught.

[Say: "Listen to *grass*," and point to the appropriate picture as you say the sentence.]

[Continue in the same way with the remaining items.]

DRILL: Question and Answer Drill

Teacher asks questions eliciting the names of the seating items.

[Pointing to pictures on p. 41 of *ESOL Illustrations 2*, ask: "Where is she sitting?" and so on.]

VOCABULARY: The Simple Fractions *half* and *a quarter*

This is a circle.
This is half of the circle.
This is a quarter of the circle.

Teacher models the sentences several times, having the student repeat.

[Say: "Listen to *circle*."
Draw a circle on the board as you say the word.]

Draw a circle on the board, dividing it into halves and dividing one half into two quarters.

[As you divide the circle in half, say: "Listen to *half of*." Point to half of the circle.]

[Teach *a quarter of* the same way.]

DRILL: Question and Answer Drill

1. Teacher asks questions eliciting the words *circle, half,* and *quarter.*

Teacher	Student
[Point to item.]	
What's this?	It's a circle.
What's this?	It's half of the circle.
What's this?	It's a quarter of the circle.

2. Teacher asks questions about money, using the words *half* and *quarter.*

   Place on the table a dollar bill, two half dollars, and four quarters.

Teacher	Student
[Point to item.]	
What's this?	It's a dollar.
What's this?	It's a half dollar.
What's this?	It's a quarter.
[Do not point.]	
How many half dollars are there in a dollar?	
How many quarters are there in a dollar?	
How many quarters are there in a half dollar?	
How many cents are there in a dollar?	
How many cents are there in a half dollar?	
How many cents are there in a quarter?	

DRILL: Expansion Drill

1. Teacher makes a statement; student adds *half* to the statement.

   Note: Before the indefinite article *a* or *an* plus a singular count noun, we often use the word *half* by itself (*half an apple*).

   When we speak of a non-count noun, *half* modifies the noun that indicates the quantity (*half a cup of coffee*).

Teacher	Student
I'd like a cup of coffee.	
I'd like half a cup of coffee.	I'd like half a cup of coffee.
I'd like an apple.	I'd like half an apple.
Please give me a glass of water.	Please give me half a glass of water.
I bought a pound of meat.	I bought half a pound of meat.
I had a sandwich for lunch.	I had half a sandwich for lunch.
We have a loaf of bread.	
He drank a bottle of soda.	
I need a cup of sugar.	

2. Teacher says a sentence; student adds *half of* to the sentence.

   Note: With the definite article *the* or other modifiers that indicate a specific item, we often use the words *half of.*

   Half of may be used with both singular and plural count nouns and with non-count nouns.

Teacher	Student
Give me that apple.	
Give me half of that apple.	Give me half of that apple.
Give me that orange.	
Do you want my sandwich?	
Give me that piece of paper.	
Jill drank her milk.	
I did my homework yesterday.	
Put the olives in this dish.	
You can eat these cookies now.	

STRUCTURE FOCUS: *another one, the other one,* and *the others*

I have a pen.	I	want	another	one.
She has a black dress.	She	wants	another	one.
One shoe is in the closet.	The	other	one	is under the bed.
One pen is on the table.	The	other	one	is in my hand.
Two cups are on the table.	The	others	are in the sink.	
Two dishes are on the table.	The	others	are in the cabinet.	

Teacher models the sentences several times, having the student repeat.

Note: Do not confuse the student by adding the expression *the other ones* at this time.

[Say: "Listen to *another one*," and model the two pairs of sentences.]

[Continue in the same way with *the other one* and *the others.*]

DRILL: Statement and Rejoinder

1. Teacher makes a statement. Student replies with a rejoinder (a question), using *another one.*

Teacher	Student
I have a pen.	Do you want another one?
I have a jacket.	
I have a wallet.	
I have a suitcase.	
I have a purse.	
I have a basket.	

2. Student replies, using *the other one.*

Teacher	Student
I have two sisters. One is at home.	Where is the other one?
I have two brothers. One is at work.	
I have two boots. One is in the closet.	
I have two shoes. One is under the bed.	
I have two books. One is on the desk.	
I have two pens. One is in my purse.	

3. Student replies, using *the others.*

Teacher	Student
I have three sisters. One is at home.	Where are the others?
Dan has three daughters. One is at school.	
I need six dishes. Three are on the table.	
I have four quarters. Two are in my wallet.	
I need four chairs. Two are in the room.	
I need six eggs. Two are on the table.	

STRUCTURE FOCUS: *very, too,* and *enough*

Jimmy is handsome.	Jimmy is very handsome.
The child is little.	The child is very little.
We can sit down.	There are enough chairs.
We can read.	There are enough books.
We can eat.	There is enough food.
I can't wear the dress.	It's too short.
I can't drink the coffee.	It's too sweet.
I can't carry the box.	It's too big.

Teacher models each pair of sentences—without and with *very*—several times, having the student repeat.

Do not emphasize *very* in the second sentence. Pronounce the sentence as you would if it occurred alone, with the emphasis on the adjective (*handsome, little*).

Do the pairs of sentences concerning *enough* and *too* in the same way.

Note: *Very* (introduced earlier) is used to intensify; *enough* indicates sufficiency; *too* indicates an inordinate degree.

[Say: "Listen to *very*.
Jimmy is handsome. Jimmy is very handsome."
Use gestures to indicate the meaning.]

[Do *enough* and *too* in the same way.]

DRILL: Expansion Drill

Student adds *very* to the statement.

Teacher	**Student**
He is little.	He is very little.
The child is big.	
The box is little.	
The girl is tall.	
The man is old.	
It's windy.	
It's sunny.	

DRILL: Question and Answer Drill

1. Teacher asks questions which elicit answers with *enough.*

   Give the noun the student will use in his answer as a verbal cue.

Teacher	Student
Can we sit down? chairs	Yes, there are enough chairs.
Can we drink? coffee	Yes, there is enough coffee.
Can we eat dinner? food	
Can you buy a jacket? money	
Can you buy shoes? money	
Can you buy a wallet? money	
Can you buy a car? money	No, I don't have enough money.
Can you buy a house?	
Can you buy a truck?	
Can you buy a bus?	

2. Teacher asks questions which elicit answers with *too.*

   Give the adjective the student will use in his answer as a verbal cue.

Teacher	Student
Can you wear the dress? short	No, it's too short.
Can you drink the coffee? cold	
Can you carry the suitcase? big	
Can you wear this ring? little	
Can you go swimming? cold	
Can you wear that coat? short	
Can you drink the coffee? sweet	
Can you carry the basket? big	

VOCABULARY: Future Time Expressions

I'm going	to the bank	today.	I will go	to the supermarket	tomorrow.
I'm making	dinner	this week.	Ann will make	dinner	next week.
I'm visiting	my mother	this month.	I will go	home	next month.
I'm going	to school	this year.	I will work		next year.

Teacher models each pair of sentences several times, having the student repeat.

Use a calendar to explain the meaning of the new vocabulary.

You may wish to write the numbers for *this year* and *next year* on the board as you say the sentences.

[Say: "Listen to *today* and *tomorrow*," and then model the first two sentences.]

[Continue in the same way with the remaining pairs of sentences.]

STRUCTURE FOCUS: The Use of *be + going to* to Indicate Future Time

I'm	going to buy	a coat	tomorrow.
She's	going to buy	a dress	next week.
We're	going to buy	a television	next month.
They're	going to buy	a house	next year.

Teacher models the sentences several times, having the student repeat.

Note: Future time is often indicated with the present tense of the verb *be* plus *going to* followed by the simple form of the verb.

[Say: "Listen to *I'm going to*."]

DRILL: Transformation Drill

1. Student transforms a present tense statement into a future tense statement using *going to.*

Teacher	Student
I'm buying the book now.	I'm going to buy the book tomorrow.
I'm reading the book now.	
We're speaking English now.	
He's signing the paper now.	
Dan's helping his mother now.	
You're studying English now.	
Jill's playing with her doll now.	

2. Student transforms a statement into a question. (This is not a new pattern.)

   Be sure the student uses a rising intonation pattern when making the question.

Teacher	Student
He's going to buy a wallet.	Is he going to buy a wallet?
She's going to send the letter.	
They're going to sit on the bench.	
Jack's going to marry Ann.	
Bob's going to help her.	
Ann's going to take the money.	

DRILL: Short Answer Drill

Teacher asks student a question in the future tense with *going to*. Student gives a short answer.

Teacher	Student
Are you going to buy a coat?	Yes, I am.
Are you going to buy a jacket?	No, I'm not.
Is Ann going to watch television?	
Are Mr. and Mrs. Hill going to sit in the living room?	
Are you going to wear your watch?	
Are they going to go shopping?	
Is Ann going to marry Jack?	
Are you going to carry the suitcase?	
Is Will going to put his clothes in the closet?	

STRUCTURE FOCUS: Past Tense of Irregular Verbs

The telephone	rings.		The telephone	rang.	
Ann	gives	the book to Bob.	Ann	gave	the book to Bob.
She	drinks	milk.	She	drank	milk.
Glenn	swims	in the river.	Glenn	swam	in the river.
Kitty	sits	on the bench.	Kitty	sat	on the bench.
The dog	runs	after the cat.	The dog	ran	after the cat.

Teacher models each pair of sentences—present and past—several times, having the student repeat.

Model and practice the past tense sentences more often.

[Say: "Listen to *rings* and *rang*." Have the student repeat both sentences and then do the past tense sentence again.]

[Continue in the same way with the remaining verbs.]

DRILL: Transformation Drill

Student changes a present tense statement into a past tense statement.

Prompt the student if he needs help.

Teacher	Student
The telephone rings.	The telephone rang.
She drinks a lot of milk.	
Glenn swims in the river.	
Kitty sits on the grass.	
Ann gives the book to Bob.	
The dog runs after the cat.	
The bell rings.	
Dan drinks a lot of coffee.	
Ann and Bob swim in the river.	
Kitty and Jimmy sit on the rock.	
The children run fast.	
Jimmy gives the money to his mother.	

STRUCTURE FOCUS: Negative Statements in the Past Tense

Kitty		sat on the bench.
Kitty	didn't	sit on the bench.
The dog		ran after the cat.
The dog	didn't	run after the cat.

Teacher models the sentences several times, having the student repeat.

[Say: "Listen to *didn't sit.*"]

Note: The negative form of the past tense is made with *didn't* plus the simple form of the verb.

DRILL: Answering Questions

Student answers past tense questions with a negative answer, using a complete sentence. Do not accept "No, I didn't," and the like.

Note: The student may say **didn't rang* at first.

Teacher	**Student**
Did the telephone ring?	No, the telephone didn't ring.
Did Ann drink milk?	
Did Bob sit on the bench?	
Did Glenn swim in the river?	
Did the dog run after the cat?	
Did the bell ring?	
Did Bob give the money to his mother?	
Did you give the book to your friend?	
Did you swim in the river?	
Did you sit on the rock?	
Did you run after the children?	
Did you drink a lot of milk?	

PRONUNCIATION: /o/ and /uu/, /n/ and /ng/

1. See the Pronunciation section in Lesson 1 for the steps to follow in teaching the vowel sounds /o/ and /uu/ as in *pot* and *put*.

[Say: "Listen to /o/ and /uu/."]

/o/	/uu/	**Sentences**
pot	put	This is a shock.
lock	look	Look it up.
knock	nook	I shook hands with him.
posh	push	It's good.
hockey	hooky	He's a crook.
god	good	

2. Following the same procedure teach the consonant sounds /n/ and /ng/ as in *ban* and *bang.*

   Note: Both the sounds /n/ and /ng/ are voiced nasal sounds. The tip of the tongue does not touch the teeth when making /n/. The back of the tongue is used in making the /ng/ sound.

[Say: "Listen to /n/ and /ng/."]

/n/	/ng/	**Sentences**
ban	bang	He's a good singer.
pin	ping	She ran fast.
sun	sung	He banged his head.
sinner	singer	He's the king.
tons	tongue	She's too thin.
clan	clang	

ORAL EVALUATION

1. Review the chart and story words (factories). Student should know all of the factory names.

   [Do the Question and Answer Drill following Vocabulary: Chart and Story Words (Factories).]

2. Review the vocabulary on seating. Student should be able to answer all of these items since some items are review.

   [Using p. 41 of *ESOL Illustrations 2*, ask: "Where is she sitting?" as you point to the various items of seating.]

3. Review the simple fractions *half* and *a quarter.* Student should be able to use both with ease.

   [Do the Question and Answer Drill and the Expansion Drill following Vocabulary: The Simple Fractions *half* and *a quarter*.]

4. Review the use of *another one, the other one,* and *the others*. Student should be able to make sentences using these expressions with some ease since they are important substitute words.

   [Do the Statement and Rejoinder Drill following Structure Focus: *another one, the other one,* and *the others.*]

5. Review the use of *very, too,* and *enough.* Concentrate on *too* and *enough*, which are the new items being taught.

   [Do the Question and Answer Drill following Structure Focus: *very, too,* and *enough*.]

6. Review the use of *be + going to* to indicate future time. This is an important basic structure in English so it must be drilled carefully.

   [Do the Transformation Drill which follows Structure Focus: The Use of *be + going to* to Indicate Future Time.]

7. Review the past tense form of the irregular verbs taught in this lesson. Student must know all of these.

   [Do the Transformation Drill which follows Structure Focus: Past Tense of Irregular Verbs.]

8. Review negative statements in the past tense with irregular verbs. Student should be able to make negative statements with ease.

   [Do the Drill on Answer Questions following Structure Focus: Negative Statements in the Past Tense.]

II. Reading

Check your student's homework from Lesson 8. If he has not done it, have him do it now. Be sure your student understands any corrections you make.

CHART 9: Page 42

Teach this chart in the same way you taught the chart for Lesson 1. ("Read. What is the sound? What is the vowel sound? Read.")

Point out these things about the new chart words.

grass: [Point to *gr.*] Say these two sounds together very quickly: *grass.* The letters *ss* make one sound: /s/. You write two *s's*.

glass: [Point to *gl.*] Say these two sounds together very quickly: *glass.* The letters *ss* make one sound: /s/. You write two *s's*.

half: In *half,* the *l* is silent.

laugh: In *laugh,* the *u* is silent. [Point to *gh.*] The sound is /f/. You write *g, h.*

factory: In *factory,* the letters *or* make the sound /er/. You write *o, r.* In *factory, y* has the vowel sound /y/.

STORY: Lunch on the Grass

Teach the story according to the seven steps outlined in Lesson 1. The new story words are: *after, lunch.* Use the following comprehension questions.

	Teacher	Student
Paragraph 1	What do Jack and Ann visit?	They visit the glass factory.
	What do they look at in the factory?	They look at the glass.
Paragraph 2	What do Jack and Ann do after the visit?	They have lunch.
	Where do they have lunch?	In back of the glass factory.
Paragraph 3	Do they sit on the grass or on a bench?	They sit on the grass.
Paragraph 4	What does Ann have?	She has an apple.
	What does Ann give to Jack?	She gives half of the apple to Jack.
Paragraph 5	What do Jack and Ann do after lunch?	They run up the path.
	Where is the path?	In back of the glass factory.
	Where does the path go?	It goes to the river.
Paragraph 6	What do Ann and Jack do?	They run and laugh.

SKILLS PRACTICE: Beginning Consonant Blend *gl-*

Step 1: Write *lass* and *glass* as shown below. Be careful to line up the words and to underline the *l* and *gl* as shown.

lass
glass

Step 2: Point to and pronounce each word, first *lass*, then *glass*. Repeat a few times. The student listens.

Step 3: Point to and pronounce each word, having the student repeat. Do *lass,* then *glass.* Repeat a few times.

Step 4: Point to each word, beckoning for the student to say it. Do *lass,* then *glass.*

Repeat these four steps with the following pairs, one pair at a time. (You may leave all the pairs showing on the blackboard.) Be sure to line up the words and underline the letters as shown.

lad	lib	lop
glad	glib	glop

SKILLS PRACTICE: Beginning Consonant Blend *gr-*

Following the four steps in the previous Skills Practice, work with these pairs of words, one pair at a time. Finally, have the student read the word *grass* by itself.

rip	rub	ram	
grip	grub	gram	grass

SKILLS PRACTICE: Contrasting *gl*- and *gr*-

Do not write any of the words for the student in this exercise. Many of the minimal pairs have spellings the student is not yet equipped to read.

Step 1: Write *gl* and *gr* on the blackboard.

Step 2: Model a minimal pair, *glass* and *grass*, several times as the student listens.
Say: *"glass, grass,"* pointing to *gl*, then *gr*.

Step 3: Have the student repeat after you several times.
Say: *"glass, grass,"* pointing to *gl*, then *gr*.

Step 4: Say the words in random order. Have the student point to the correct symbol (*gl* or *gr*) for the word you are saying.

Step 5: Point to the symbols *gl* and *gr* in random order. Have the student say the word.

Continue in the same way with the following minimal pairs. Do *not* write the words nor explain what they mean.

gl	gr	gl	gr
glad	grad	gland	grand
glow	grow	glue	grew
gloom	groom	glaze	graze
glade	grade	gloats	groats

SKILLS PRACTICE: Contrasting the Short Vowels *a* and *u*

Contrast the short vowel sounds /a/ and /u/, using the minimal pairs shown here. Follow the nine steps in the Skills Practice on contrasting short vowel sounds in Lesson 6.

Note: The student has learned to read at least one of the words in each of the minimal pairs given here.

a	u	a	u	a	u	a	u
bad	bud	pan	pun	bat	but	back	buck
mad	mud	fan	fun	cat	cut	track	truck
		ran	run	rat	rut	stack	stuck

III. Writing

CHECKUP: Page 44

Ask your student to read the directions aloud. Have him complete the whole page. Check his work, and refer him back to the appropriate chart or story for any words he has missed. Then have him read the entire page aloud.

WRITING LESSON: Page 45

Study

Help the student to study the spelling of the following words before he writes them.

1. half	3. factory
2. laughs	4. have

Listen and write

Dictate the following words and sentences for the student to write.

1. glass	3. grass
2. path	4. after

1. Ann sits on the grass.
2. This is the glass factory.
3. That is the path.
4. Jack has half an apple.
5. Ann laughs and laughs.

SKILLS PRACTICE: Review Dropping Final Silent *e* Before Adding *-ing*

Step 1: Write the following exercise on the blackboard, as shown.

give	come
giving	____________
live	whistle
____________	____________

Step 2: Point to *give,* and say: "Please read."
Point to *giving,* and say: "Please read."

Step 3: Point to *live,* and say: "Please read."
Point to the blank, and say: "Write *living.*"

Do the same with *come/coming* and *whistle/whistling.*

If the student has any difficulty writing the *-ing* form, cross out the final silent *e* in the root word.

HOMEWORK: Pages 46-47

Ask your student to complete both pages and to read the charts and stories in Lessons 8 and 9 at home.

READING AND WRITING EVALUATION

1. Write the following sentences. Have the student circle the correct word and then read the complete sentences. The student should be able to complete all three sentences correctly.

The girl laughs. The girl is happy. / not happy.

The number 61 comes after 62. / 60.

Ann sits on the glass. / grass.

2. Write the following letters, then ask the student to say the sound of each. The student should be able to say the correct sound for at least four items.

ss *th* *f* *rr* *pp*

3. Write the following paragraphs beforehand, and ask the student to read them now. The student should make no more than five errors.

Dan is sitting in back of the glass factory.
Dan is sitting on the grass.
Dan is sitting with his friend Cal.

Dan has a big red apple.
Dan gives half of the apple to Cal.

A cat is running on the path.
A pup is running after the cat.
Dan and Cal laugh at the pup.

MORE READING

In the supplementary reader *More Stories 2,* the stories for Lesson 9 may be read in class or suggested for reading at home.

Lesson 10

OBJECTIVES

When a student completes this unit, he should be able to:

1. Say and respond to a new dialog.
2. Say the names of various public rooms and some medical terms.
3. Use the verbs *do, fix, stop,* and *drop.*
4. Use the ordinal numbers from *first* to *thirty-first* with the names of months to express dates.
5. Say the names of holidays in the United States.
6. Use some more irregular verbs in the past tense.
7. Use the past tense expression *ago.*
8. Use sentences with *and...too* and with *not...and...not either.*
9. Use the structure *It's a little job to fix* ______.
10. Use *help* with an object + verb, as in *Don helps Bob do his homework.*
11. Pronounce the consonant sounds /g/ and /ng/ as in *bag* and *bang* and /r/ after vowels.
12. Read the following new words, in two charts and stories:
    Chart words: *doctor, Dr., office, hot, shot, doll, Molly*
    Story words: *got, Chan, head*

    Chart words: *rock, lock, clock, top, stops, stopped, dollar*
    Story words: *Don, Tom, job, fix, John, dropped.*
13. Read two simple stories, using the new chart and story words.
14. Read some words beginning with the consonant blends *cl-*, *dr-*, and *sp-*.
15. Read some words contrasting the short vowels *a* and *o, o* and *u.*
16. Recognize the words *MEN* and *WOMEN* written in capital letters.
17. Write the new chart and story words.
18. Use the root form, *-s* form, and *-ing* form of the verb correctly in written sentences.

VISUAL AIDS

1. *ESOL Illustrations 2*, pp. 44-49.
2. Bring a comb, a cardboard clock, and a calendar for the full year.
   You may want to circle with colored pen the holidays taught in Vocabulary: Holidays in the United States.
3. Bring any of the following items that you can. It is not absolutely necessary to have them, but it would be helpful.
   a. A toy, preferably one with a part that you can take off and put back easily to show both that the toy needs to be fixed and that it is easy to fix.
   b. A wind-up clock. If you can bring this item, arrange to have it stopped for your class session.
   c. A padlock, either one that opens with a key or a combination lock.

REVIEW

Review any items that your student had difficulty with when doing the Oral Evaluation in Lesson 9.

I. Conversation Skills

DIALOG

Nurse:	Dr. Chan's office.
Ann Hill:	Hello. This is Ann Hill. I'd like to make an appointment with the doctor.
Nurse:	Is this for a checkup?
Ann Hill:	Yes, it is.
Nurse:	Can you come on Friday at 3 o'clock?
Ann Hill:	Yes, I can. Thank you.

Teacher models the dialog, using the procedure outlined in Lesson 1.

Use your student's name instead of Ann Hill.

Pantomime talking on the telephone.

VOCABULARY: Public Rooms

The teacher works in a classroom.
Dr. Chan works in an office.

The patient sits in the doctor's waiting room.

He's washing his hands in the men's room.
She's combing her hair in the ladies' room.

Teacher models the sentences several times, having the student repeat.

Use pp. 44-45 of *ESOL Illustrations 2.* Teach *combing hair* by demonstration.

[Say: "Listen to *classroom*," and indicate the classroom as you say: "The teacher works in a classroom."]

[Continue in the same way with the remaining items.]

DRILL: Question and Answer Drill

Teacher asks questions which elicit the names of public rooms in the answers.

Use pp. 44-45 of *ESOL Illustrations 2.* If the student has difficulty, point to the illustration and ask: "What's this?"

Teacher	Student
Where does a teacher work?	She works in a classroom.
Where does a doctor work?	
Where does a patient sit?	
Where does a man wash his hands?	
Where does a woman comb her hair?	

VOCABULARY: Some Medical Terms

The baby	is getting a checkup.
Molly	is getting a shot in her arm.
Mrs. Roberts	is getting a chest x-ray.

Teacher models the sentences several times, having the student repeat. Use p. 46 of *ESOL Illustrations 2.*

[Say: "Listen to *a checkup*," and model the sentence, pointing to the appropriate picture.]

[Continue in the same way with the remaining items.]

VOCABULARY: The Verb *do*

The student	do	their	homework.
The worker	does	his	job.
He	does	his	work.
Tom and Don	do	the	dishes.
Mrs. Roberts	does	the	laundry.

Teacher models the sentences several times, having the student repeat.

Use p. 47 of *ESOL Illustrations 2.*

Note: .The words *job* and *laundry* are new vocabulary items here, also.

[Say: "Listen to *do* and *does*."]

DRILL: Question and Answer Drill

1. Teacher asks questions which elicit answers with *do* or *does.*

Teacher	Student
What does the student do?	He does his homework.
What does the worker do?	He does his job. *Or:* He does his work.
What do Tom and Don do?	
What does Mrs. Roberts do?	

2. Teacher asks student questions with *do*, eliciting *when* or *where* he does the activities named in the box.

Teacher	Student
When do you do your homework?	I do my homework at night.
Where do you do your homework?	
Where do you do your work?	
Where do you do the dishes?	
When do you do the dishes?	
When do you do the laundry?	

VOCABULARY: The Verbs *stop* and *drop*

The taxi driver	stops	the taxi. Tom gets in.
Don	stopped	at the supermarket to buy some bread.
Mrs. Miller	dropped	the clock. The clock stopped.

Teacher models the sentences several times, having the student repeat.

[Say: "Listen to *stops*."]

Demonstrate the meaning of *stop* by holding up your hand in a Stop gesture. (If you have brought a "stopped" clock, use it now, also.)

Demonstrate *drop* by actually dropping something.

DRILL: Substitution Drill

1. Student substitutes the names of vehicles in a request with *Stop*.

   The student must also use *get out* and *get off* appropriately. (This is review.)

Teacher	**Student**
Stop the car. I want to get out here.	Stop the car. I want to get out here.
bus	Stop the bus. I want to get off here.
taxi	
truck	
bicycle	
car	

2. Student substitutes the place and the item gotten there in a sentence with *stopped at*.

Teacher	**Student**
I stopped at the supermarket to get some milk.	I stopped at the supermarket to get some milk.
library, some books	I stopped at the library to get some books.
post office, some stamps	
bank, some money	
department store, some shoes	
office, that paper	
supermarket, some bread	

VOCABULARY: The Verb *fix*

The clock stopped.	Tom will fix the clock.
The lock won't open.	Tom will fix the lock.
The television won't work.	Tom will fix the television.
The top is broken.	Tom will fix the top.

Teacher models each pair of sentences several times, having the student repeat.

[Say: "Listen to *fix*."]

Use pp. 48-49 of *ESOL Illustrations 2.* (If you have brought a "stopped" clock and a padlock, use them now, also. Pretend that the lock won't open even though you are unlocking it correctly.)

[Point to the appropriate pictures on pp. 48-49 of *ESOL Illustrations 2* as you say each pair of sentences.]

Note: The words *lock* and *broken* are new here also.

DRILL: Question and Answer Drill

Teacher asks questions which the student answers using the verb *fix.*

Teacher	Student
The clock stopped. What will Tom do? Tom will fix the clock.	 Tom will fix the clock.
The lock won't open. What will Tom do?	
The television won't work. What will Tom do?	
The top is broken. What will Tom do?	
My watch stopped. What will Tom do?	
The whistle won't work. What will Tom do?	
The cup is broken. What will Tom do?	

VOCABULARY: Ordinal Numbers

first	eleventh	twenty-first
second	twelfth	twenty-second
third	thirteenth	twenty-third
fourth	fourteenth	twenty-fourth
fifth	fifteenth	twenty-fifth
sixth	sixteenth	twenty-sixth
seventh	seventeenth	twenty-seventh
eighth	eighteenth	twenty-eighth
ninth	nineteenth	twenty-ninth
tenth	twentieth	thirtieth
		thirty-first

Teacher models the ordinal numbers, using a calendar to illustrate "This is the first day," and so on.

Note: Listen carefully to the student's pronunciation of the endings of these words, especially those ending in /th/.

[Say: "Listen to the numbers: *first, second, third, fourth, fifth*." Have the student repeat. Use the calendar to explain if the student has difficulty.]

[Teach the numbers five at a time.]

DRILL: Question and Answer Drill

1. Teacher asks questions about the order of the months in the year.

Teacher	Student
What is the first month?	January is the first month.
[Continue with the rest of the months.]	

2. Teacher asks, "What's the date today?" pointing, in order, to the days in May on a current calendar. Student answers, "It's May first," and so on.

Teacher	Student
What's the date today?	It's May first.
[Continue with the rest of the month.]	It's May second.
	It's May third.

3. Teacher asks, "What's the date today?" pointing at random to different dates in different months.

Teacher	Student
What's the date today?	It's April first.
What's the date today?	It's June fifteenth.
[Continue in the same way.]	

VOCABULARY: Holidays in the United States

New Year's Day	is on January 1st.
Easter	is in March or April.
Memorial Day	is in May.
Independence Day	is on July 4th.
Labor Day	is in September.
Thanksgiving Day	is in November.
Christmas Day	is on December 25th.

These are holidays.

Teacher models the sentences several times, having the student repeat.

[Say: "Listen to the holidays."]

Use a calendar to show the holidays.

To teach the meaning of *holidays*, say: "We don't go to work on holidays." You may also indicate that the post office, banks, and some stores are closed on these holidays.

Note: Pronounce the dates "first," "fourth," and "twenty-fifth." Be sure the student hears and pronounces the ending sound /th/.

Note: If you live in Canada, substitute the appropriate holidays.

DRILL: Answering Questions

1. Teacher asks questions which elicit the dates when the holidays occur.

Teacher	Student
When is New Year's Day?	It's in January.
When is Easter?	
When is Memorial Day?	
When is Independence Day?	
When is Thanksgiving?	
When is Christmas?	

2. Teacher gives the date (or month) and asks the student to say which holiday occurs when.

Teacher	Student
January 1st	New Year's Day
March or April	Easter
May	
July 4th	
September	
November	
December 25th	

3. Teacher points on the calendar to each of the four holidays taught that occur on different dates each year, asking when each is this year. Student gives the date.

Teacher	Student
When is Easter this year?	It's (*date*).
When is Memorial Day this year?	
When is Labor Day this year?	
When is Thanksgiving Day this year?	

STRUCTURE FOCUS: Past Tense of Irregular Verbs

Present		Past	
I get	thirsty every day.	I got	thirsty yesterday.
I eat	meat every day.	I ate	meat yesterday.
I make	breakfast every day.	I made	breakfast this morning.
I wear	my watch every day.	I wore	my watch yesterday.
The pup tears	my clothes.	The pup tore	my pants yesterday.
He sells	clothes in a store.	He sold	some clothes yesterday.
He tells	Ann, "Sit down."	He told	Ann, "Sit down."

Teacher models each pair of sentences several times, having the student repeat.

Act out the meaning of the new verb, *tear*, by tearing a piece of paper.

[Say: "Listen to ***get*** and ***got***."]

[Continue in the same way with the remaining items.]

DRILL: Question and Answer Drill

Teacher asks questions which elicit affirmative answers in the past tense of irregular verbs.

The student should answer with complete sentences.

Teacher	Student
Did you get thirsty?	Yes, I got thirsty.
Did you wear your watch yesterday?	
Did you tear your coat?	
Did the man sell his car?	
Did Bob tell Ann, "Sit down"?	
Did you make dinner last night?	
Did you eat any bread yesterday?	
Did you get thirsty before lunch?	
Did you tear your shirt?	
Did you get a shot?	

VOCABULARY: The Use of *ago*

I ate breakfast at 7 o'clock. It is 10 o'clock now. I ate breakfast three hours ago.	I did my homework on Monday. It is Wednesday now. I did my homework two days ago.

Teacher models each group of sentences several times, having the student repeat only the sentence with *ago.*

Use a clock and a calendar to help explain the meaning of *ago* with the past tense.

[Say: "Listen to *ago*."]

DRILL: Statement and Rejoinder

Teacher tells when she did a certain activity and indicates the present time. Student indicates how much time has elapsed, using *ago.*

The teacher makes statements with *I,* the student, with *you.*

Use a calendar or a clock if necessary.

Give the student enough time to figure out the answer.

Teacher	Student
I ate breakfast at 7 o'clock. It's 10 o'clock now. You ate breakfast three hours ago.	You ate breakfast three hours ago.
I came here at 8 o'clock. It's 12 o'clock now.	You came here four hours ago.
I did my homework at 9 o'clock. It's 2 o'clock now.	You did your homework five hours ago.
I went to the supermarket on Friday. It's Tuesday now.	You went to the supermarket four days ago.
I bought this coat in 19___. It's 19___ now.	
I bought my car in January. It's ___________ now.	
I visited the candy factory in 1973. It's 19___ now.	
I wore my new dress on Monday. It's Friday now.	You wore your new dress four days ago.

STRUCTURE FOCUS: The Use of *and...too*

I am a teacher. Mary is a teacher.	I am a teacher, and Mary is too.
Bob is a doctor. Sue is a doctor.	Bob is a doctor, and Sue is too.
Helen was sick yesterday. Her son was sick yesterday.	Helen was sick yesterday, and her son was too.
Bob and Ann were tired. I was tired.	Bob and Ann were tired, and I was too.

Teacher models the two sentences on the left and then the sentence on the right with *and...too*. Have the student listen and repeat.

[Say: "Listen to *and...too*."]

Note: Sentences with *and...too* are combinations of two similar sentences. The same verb—in the same tense—must be in both parts of the combined sentence.

DRILL: Combining Sentences

Teacher gives the student two similar affirmative statements which the student combines into one, using *and...too.*

Teacher	Student
Maria is from Puerto Rico. Juan is from Puerto Rico.	Maria is from Puerto Rico, and Juan is too.
Anna is from Italy. Peter is from Italy.	
He's tired. I'm tired.	
She's getting hungry. I'm getting hungry.	
Glenn is going fishing. Ed is going fishing.	
I was tired yesterday. You were tired yesterday.	
Ann is in the car. Bob and Glenn are in the car.	
We were happy. They were happy.	

STRUCTURE FOCUS: The Use of *not...and...not either*

I'm not a doctor. Mary isn't a doctor.	I'm not a doctor, and Mary isn't either.
Bob isn't a teacher. Sue isn't a teacher.	Bob isn't a teacher, and Sue isn't either.
Helen wasn't here yesterday. Her son wasn't here yesterday.	Helen wasn't here yesterday, and her son wasn't either.
Bob and Ann weren't tired. I wasn't tired.	Bob and Ann weren't tired, and I wasn't either.

Teacher models the two sentences on the left and then the sentence on the right with *not...and...not either.*

[Say: "Listen to *not...and...not either.*"]

Have the student listen and repeat the *either* sentence several times.

Note: Sentences with *not...and...not either* are combinations of two similar negative sentences. The same verb—in the same tense—must be in both parts of the combined sentence.

DRILL: Combining Sentences

Teacher gives the student two similar negative statements, which the student combines into one, using *not...and... not either.*

Teacher	Student
I'm not from Puerto Rico. You're not from Puerto Rico.	I'm not from Puerto Rico, and you're not either.
Sue isn't tired. Bob isn't tired.	
Helen isn't a waitress. Anna isn't a waitress.	
John wasn't here yesterday. Glenn wasn't here yesterday.	
Bob wasn't happy. We weren't happy.	
He wasn't on the bus. Jill wasn't on the bus.	
We aren't hungry. She isn't hungry.	
My son isn't here. My daughter isn't here.	

DRILL: Combining Sentences

Teacher gives the student two similar negative statements or two similar affirmative statements. Student must combine the two, using either *and...too* or *not...and...not either.*

Teacher	Student
I'm a teacher. My husband is a teacher.	I'm a teacher, and my husband is too.
My daughter isn't here. My son isn't here.	My daughter isn't here, and my son isn't either.
My mother isn't sick. My father isn't sick.	
I am tired. She is tired.	
Anna isn't from Spain. Peter isn't from Spain.	
Helen isn't a taxi driver. John isn't a taxi driver.	
Bob was in the kitchen. Jill was in the kitchen.	
The cups are in the sink. The dishes are in the sink.	
We were in the car. Glenn was in the car.	
Sue wasn't sad. Bob wasn't sad.	

STRUCTURE FOCUS: The Use of *help* with Object + Verb

Dan	helps	Bob	do	his homework.
Ann	is helping	John	do	the dishes.
Tom	helped	Bob	fix	the toy.
The doctor	will help	Molly	get	well.

Teacher models the sentences several times, having the student repeat.

[Say: "Listen to *helps Bob do*."]

Note: The verb *help* is followed by an object and an infinitive without *to*.

Compare verbs which take an infinitive with *to*, for example: *I want him to go.*

DRILL: Combining Sentences

Teacher gives two statements, which the student combines into one. The student's sentence contains *help* with an object plus another verb.

Teacher	Student
Dan helps Bob. Bob does his homework. Dan helps Bob do his homework.	Dan helps Bob do his homework.
Molly helps Mrs. Roberts. Mrs. Roberts does the dishes.	
The boss helps the worker. The worker does his job.	
Ann is helping John. John is doing the dishes.	Ann is helping John do the dishes.
Tom is helping Don. Don is carrying the bags.	
Mrs. Roberts is helping Molly. Molly is getting dressed.	
Tom helped Bob. Bob fixed the toy.	Tom helped Bob fix the toy.
Jimmy helped Mr. Hill. Mr. Hill washed the car.	
The teacher helped the student. The student did his homework.	
The doctor will help Molly. Molly will get well.	The doctor will help Molly get well.
Kitty will help Ann. Ann will make dinner.	
Don will help Tom. Tom will fix the bicycle.	

PRONUNCIATION: /g/ and /ng/, Vowel + /r/

1. See the Pronunciation section in Lesson 1 for the steps to follow in teaching the consonant sounds /g/ and /ng/ as in *bag* and *bang.*

[Say: "Listen to /g/ and /ng/."]

/g/	/ng/	Sentences
bag	bang	It's a big bag.
big	bing	She sang a nice song.
tug	tongue	The rug is brown.
rag	rang	Please ring the bell.
log	long	It's spring.
gags	gangs	

2. Teacher models the words which contain /r/ after vowels. Have the student repeat each word after you three or four times.

   Practice the words in column 1 first, then the words in column 2.

   Practice the sentences in the same way.

   Note: When making /r/ after vowels, the tip of the tongue is raised slightly and curved toward the back of the mouth. At no time does the tongue touch the roof of the mouth.

[Say: "Listen to *ore.*" Pronounce *ore* several times, gesturing for the student to repeat. Correct his pronunciation if necessary.]

Vowel + /r/	Vowel + /r/	Sentences
		He's learning English.
ore	fern	She's from Turkey.
arm	farm	She burned her arm.
car	work	The letter is finished.
sir	girl	Remember Ernie.
burn	curl	He tore his shirt.

ORAL EVALUATION

1. Review the various public rooms taught. Student should be able to identify all of these.

   [Do the Question and Answer Drill following Vocabulary: Public Rooms.]

2. Review the verb *do*. The student should be able to answer all of the questions in the drill, using *do* correctly.

   [Do part 2 of the Question and Answer Drill following Vocabulary: The Verb *do*.]

3. Review the verb *stop*. The student needs this verb for the story.

   [Do part 2 of the Substitution Drill following Vocabulary: The Verbs *stop* and *drop.*]

4. Review the names and dates of the holidays in the United States. Student should be able to name six of these.

   [Using a calendar, do either part 1 or part 2 of the Answering Questions Drill following Vocabulary: Holidays in the United States.]

5. Review the past tense of the irregular verbs taught in this lesson. Student should know all of these.

   [Do the Question and Answer Drill following Structure Focus: Past Tense of Irregular Verbs.]

6. Review the use of *ago.* This is a useful past time expression.

   [Do the Statement and Rejoinder Drill following Vocabulary: The Use of *ago.*]

7. Review *and...too* and *not...and...not either.* The student must be able to use these important structures. Review them at the next session, as they contain useful review material.

   [Do the second Combining Sentences Drill following Structure Focus: The Use of *not...and...not either*.]

8. Review the structure *It's a little job to fix the toy.* This structure is necessary for the story.

   [Do the Substitution Drill with Vocal Cues following Structure Focus: *It's a little job to fix the toy.*]

9. Review the use of *help* with object + verb. This is an important structure, and it is necessary for the story.

   [Do the Combining Sentences Drill following Structure Focus: The Use of *help* with Object + Verb.]

II. Reading

Check your student's homework from Lesson 9 carefully. Make sure that he understands any corrections that you make. On p. 46, accept either *Ann* or *She* in number 3, and either *Jack* or *He* in number 5.

CHART 10-A: Page 48

Teach this chart in the same way you taught the chart for Lesson 1.
("Read. What is the sound? What is the vowel sound? Read.")

Point out these things about the new chart words:

doctor: In *doctor, c* has the sound /k/. You write *c.*
The letters *or* make the sound /er/. You write *o, r.*

Dr.: Point to *Dr.*, and say: "This means *doctor.* You write this with the doctor's name: *Dr. John.*"
Point to *doctor,* and say: "This is a doctor."
Point to *D* in *Dr.* and say: "Write this with a *capital D.*"
Point to the period at the end of *Dr.*, and say: "Put a period at the end."

office: The letters *ff* make one sound: /f/. You write two *f*'s.
In *office, c* has the sound /s/. You write *c.*
In *office*, the *e* is silent.

shot: The letters *sh* make the sound /sh/.

doll: The letters *ll* make one sound: /l/. You write two *l*'s.

Molly: The letters *ll* make one sound: /l/. You write two *l*'s.
In *Molly, y* has the vowel sound /y/.

STORY: At the Doctor's Office

Teach the story according to the seven steps outlined in Lesson 1. The new story words are: *got, Chan, head.* Note, also, that the name *Robert,* which the student has learned, appears here as a last name with *-s: Roberts.* Use the following comprehension questions.

	Teacher	Student
Paragraph 1	What is the doctor's name?	Her name is Dr. Chan.
	Is the doctor's office big or little?	It's big.
Paragraphs 2-4	Who brings Molly to the doctor?	Mrs. Roberts does. (Her mother does.)
	Is Mrs. Roberts Molly's mother?	Yes, she is.
	Why does Mrs. Roberts bring Molly to the doctor?	Molly is sick.
	Why is Molly's head hot?	She is sick.
Paragraphs 5-7	What does Molly have with her?	Her doll.
	Does Molly say that the doll is sick?	Yes, she does.
	Does Dr. Chan give a shot to the doll and to Molly?	Yes, she does.
	Does Molly yell?	No, she doesn't.
Paragraph 8	What does Mrs. Roberts thank Dr. Chan for?	The shots.
Paragraph 9	Did Molly get well?	Yes, she did.

After finishing the story, ask the student: "Does Dr. Chan like children?"

CHART 10-B: Page 50

Teach this chart in the same way, pointing out these things about the new words.

rock: The letters *ck* make the sound /k/. You write *c, k.*

lock: The letters *ck* make the sound /k/. You write *c, k.*

clock: [Point to *cl.*] Say these two sounds together very quickly: *clock.*
The letters *ck* make the sound /k/. You write *c, k.*

stops: [Point to *st.*] Say these two sounds together very quickly: *stops.*

stopped: The letters *pp* make one sound: /p/. You write *stopped* with two *p's*.
Stopped ends with the sound /t/. You write *e, d.* In *stopped,* the letters *ed* make the sound /t/.

stops, Point to *stops,* and say: "He stops at the supermarket every day."
stopped: Point to *stopped,* and say: He stopped at the supermarket yesterday."

dollar: The letters *ll* make one sound: /l/. You write two *l's*.
The letters *ar* make the sound /er/. You write *a, r.*

STORY: John Oliver's Shop

Teach the story according to the seven steps outlined in Lesson 1.
The new story words are: *Don, Tom, job, fix, John, dropped.*
Use the following comprehension questions.

	Teacher	Student
Paragraph 1	Who has a shop?	John Oliver does.
	What does John do in his shop?	He does many jobs.
Paragraphs 2-3	What does Tom Bell bring to John's shop?	He brings a clock.
	What did Tom do to the clock?	He dropped it.
	Did the clock stop?	Yes, it did.
	Can John fix the clock?	Yes, he can.
	How much money will John get for fixing the clock?	Five dollars.
Paragraphs 4-5	What does Don Roberts bring to John's shop?	He brings a lock.
	What did Don do to the lock?	He dropped it (on a rock).
	Can John fix the lock?	Yes, he can.
	Is it a big job?	No, it isn't.
	How much money will John get for fixing the lock?	One dollar.
Paragraphs 6-9	What does Ann Smith bring to John's shop?	She brings a box.
	What did Ann do to the box?	She dropped it (on a rock).
	Can Ann open the box?	No, she can't.
	Why can't she open the box?	The top (of the box) is stuck.
	Can John fix the box?	Yes, he can.
	How much money will John get for fixing the box?	Two dollars.

If the student asks why John says, "That is funny," in paragraph 7, explain as follows:
"Ann dropped her box on a rock. It's funny that Don dropped his lock on a rock, too."

If you have a very able student, you might, after finishing the story, want to ask:
"How much money will John get for the three jobs?" The answer is "Eight dollars."

SKILLS PRACTICE: Beginning Consonant Blend *cl-*

Step 1: Write *lock* and *clock* as shown below. Be careful to line up the words and to underline the *l* and *cl* as shown.

lock
clock

Step 2: Point to and pronounce each word, first *lock,* then *clock.* Do *lock,* then *clock.* Repeat a few times. The student listens.

Step 3: Point to and pronounce each word, having the student repeat. Do *lock,* then *clock.* Repeat a few times.

Step 4: Point to each word, beckoning the student to say it. Do *lock,* then *clock.*

Repeat these four steps with the following pairs, one pair at a time. (You may leave all the pairs showing on the blackboard.) Be sure to line up the words and underline the letters as shown.

lap	lass	lip	lot
clap	class	clip	clot

SKILLS PRACTICE: Beginning Consonant Blend *dr-*

Following the four steps in the previous Skills Practice, work with these pairs of words, one pair at a time. Finally, have the student read the word *drop* by itself.

rug	rip	rag	rum	
drug	drip	drag	drum	drop

SKILLS PRACTICE: Beginning Consonant Blend *sp-*

Following the same four steps, work with these pairs of words, one pair at a time. If the student has difficulty pronouncing the *sp-* words, have him prolong the /s/ sound: *sssspot.*

pot	pan	pin	pit	pun
spot	span	spin	spit	spun

SKILLS PRACTICE: Contrasting the Short Vowels *a* and *o*

Contrast the short vowel sounds /a/ and /o/, using the minimal pairs shown here. Follow the nine steps in the Skills Practice on contrasting short vowels in Lesson 6.

a	o	a	o	a	o
tap	top	cat	cot	rack	rock
jab	job	pat	pot	lack	lock
can	con	rat	rot	black	block
Dan	Don			clack	clock

SKILLS PRACTICE: Contrasting the Short Vowels *o* and *u*

Contrast the short vowel sounds /o/ and /u/, using the minimal pairs shown here and following the nine steps outlined in Lesson 6.

o	u	o	u	o	u
cop	cup	cot	cut	dock	duck
pop	pup	got	gut	lock	luck
mod	mud	hot	hut	clock	cluck
doll	dull	not	nut	stock	stuck
		shot	shut		

SKILLS PRACTICE: Review *MEN* and *WOMEN*

On the blackboard, draw two doors. Label one door *MEN* and the other *WOMEN*. Write these words in capital letters as they are usually written on actual restroom doors.

Point to *MEN*, and say: "Read this word." Point to *WOMEN*, and say: "Read this word."

Ask: "Which is the men's room?" and gesture for the student to point to the correct door. Then ask, "Which is the ladies' room?"

III. Writing

WRITING LESSON: Page 52

Study

Help your student study these words before writing them. Point out any differences between how they are written and how they are pronounced.

1. doctor
2. John
3. office
4. head
5. stopped
6. dollar

Listen and write

Dictate the following words and sentences for the student to write. Then check his work carefully.

1. doll
2. hot
3. got
4. shot
5. top
6. stop
7. rock
8. clock

1. Can John fix the lock?
2. Tom's clock stopped.

SKILLS PRACTICE: Review *-s* and *-ing* Verb Endings

To save class time, write out the exercise below on a sheet of paper before class. (Make individual copies for a class.)

Have the student read aloud the three verb forms in the first group. Then have the student choose the correct verb form to complete the sentence and write it in the blank. Finally, have the student read the completed sentence aloud. If the student cannot choose the correct verb form, read the sentence aloud for him.

Continue in the same way with each group of verb forms.

stand
stands 1. _______ up.
standing 2. Ann is _______ in the kitchen.

come
comes 1. Jack is _______ to visit Ann.
coming 2. Bud _______ to the city in his truck.

stop
stops 1. Bob _______ at Tom's shop.
stopping 2. Kim and Jill _______ at a gift shop.

laugh
laughs 1. Jack _______ at Sam.
laughing 2. The children are _______ at the pup.

help
helps 1. Ann _______ her mother with dinner.
helping 2. The men are _______ Bob carry his bags.

put
puts 1. The doctor _______ his bag in his office.
putting 2. _______ the apples in the kitchen.

HOMEWORK: Page 53

Ask your student to do this page at home.

HOMEWORK: Singular and Plural Nouns

Prepare this homework sheet beforehand. Write the words below in *one* long column. Have the student write the plural form with *-s* next to each word. Have him do the first one or two items in class so you can be sure he understands what to do. Then let him complete the list at home.

1. truck	5. clock	9. friend	13. finger
2. cent	6. sister	10. letter	14. bed
3. cat	7. brother	11. dollar	15. bag
4. shot	8. son	12. job	16. lock

READING AND WRITING EVALUATION

1. Dictate the following names for your student to write. The student should be able to write correctly at least three titles and most of the names.

   Dr. John Hunt   Miss Ann Smith   Mr. Fred Hill   Mrs. Molly Black   Ms. Ellen Bell

2. Write the following words. (In each pair, the first word is one that the student has learned to read, but the second is one that he has learned to use orally only.) Ask the student to read the words. He should be able to read all of the known reading words and to sound out at least four of the new ones.

cat	men	will	hot	think	funny
fat	when	pill	lot	drink	sunny

3. Dictate the following words for the student to write. He should be able to write at least five correctly.

lock	fix	head	office
clock	job	stopped	dollar

MORE READING

In the supplementary reader *More Stories 2,* the stories for Lesson 10 may be read in class or suggested for reading at home.

Lesson 11

OBJECTIVES

When a student completes this unit, he should be able to:

1. Say and respond to a new dialog.
2. Say the names of articles of living room furniture.
3. Say the new chart and story words.
4. Use *first* and *then* with sequential actions.
5. Say the present and past forms of some new regular and irregular verbs.
6. Use the past of *be* + verb-*ing*, as: *I was sitting here yesterday.*
7. Use verb + object + infinitive, as: *I told John to listen to me,* and verb + object + *not* + infinitive, as: *I told Ann not to speak Spanish.*
8. Use verb + verb-*ing*, as: *The man started talking.*
9. Use verb + object + verb-*ing*, as: *I heard the baby crying.*
10. Use preposition + verb-*ing*, with some prepositions, as: *We stopped the curtains from burning.*
11. Use the passive voice, to a limited degree.
12. Use the comparative (*-er*) form of regular adjectives previously introduced.
13. Use the comparative forms *better* and *worse.*
14. Ask the question *How do you feel*? and give a variety of appropriate answers.
15. Pronounce the vowel sounds /ō/ and /oi/ as in *cone* and *coin* and /ou/ and /oi/ as in *cow* and *coy*.
16. Read the following new words, in two charts and stories:
    Chart words: *burn, fern, father, were, skirt, curtains, burning, burned*
    Story words: *rug, ran, match, was, heard, Miller, yelling, running, picked, yelled*

    Chart words: *hurry, hurried, nurse, person, cover, covered, better, first*
    Story words: *us, then, said, helping, burns, looked.*
17. Read two simple stories, using the new chart and story words.
18. Read with ease all known reading words containing *er, ir, ur,* and other spellings of /er/. (This is review.)
19. Write the new chart and story words.
20. Read and write the *-ed* form of all known (reading) regular verbs.

VISUAL AIDS

1. *ESOL Illustrations 2,* pp. 50-51.
2. Bring a book of matches, and, if easily available, a cigarette.
3. Prepare the chart and writing exercise on adding *-ed* and the homework worksheet described in this lesson.

REVIEW

Review any items that your student had difficulty with when doing the Oral Evaluation in Lesson 10.

I. Conversation Skills

DIALOG

A: What happened to Fern?
B: She burned her fingers.

A: Did she go to the doctor?
B: Yes, she did. She's feeling better now.

Teacher models the dialog, using the procedure outlined in Lesson 1.

VOCABULARY: Living Room Furniture

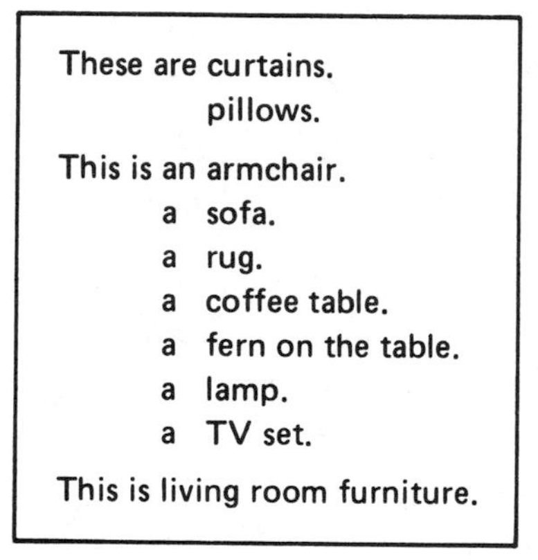

These are curtains.
pillows.

This is an armchair.
a sofa.
a rug.
a coffee table.
a fern on the table.
a lamp.
a TV set.

This is living room furniture.

Using the picture on p. 50 of *ESOL Illustrations 2*, teacher models the sentences several times, having the student repeat.

[Indicating the curtains in the picture, say: "Listen. These are curtains."]

[Continue in the same way with the remaining items, always reviewing the items previously taught. When you come to *TV set*, explain: "*TV* means *television*."]

[Finally, indicating all the items, say: "This is living room furniture."]

VOCABULARY: The Word *person*

One	person	can sit in the armchair.
Three	persons	can sit on the sofa.
Six	persons	can sit in my car.

Teacher models the sentences several times, having the student repeat.

[Say: "Listen to *person*."]

As you say the sentences, point to the persons sitting in the picture on p. 50 of *ESOL Illustrations 2.* Be sure the student understands that *person* refers to both male and female by pointing one by one to the male and female persons sitting on the sofa.

DRILL: Question and Answer Drill

1. Teacher asks questions which elicit the word *person* in the answer.

Teacher	Student
How many persons can sit in the armchair?	
One person can sit in the armchair.	One person can sit in the armchair.
How many persons can sit on the chair?	
How many persons can sit in a large car?	
How many persons can sit in a small car?	
How many persons can sit on a bus? (40)	
How many persons can sit on a bicycle?	
How many persons can sit in this room?	

2. Teacher gives a sentence with *some persons* and an adjective. Student replies with another sentence containing *other persons* and an adjective of the opposite meaning.

Teacher	Student
Some persons are tall. Other persons are short.	Other persons are short.
Some persons are fat.	
Some persons are young.	
Some persons are good.	
Some persons are sad.	
Some persons are sick.	
Some persons are pretty.	
Some persons are handsome.	

VOCABULARY: *match, fire, burning*

Ed dropped a match on the rug. The match started a fire. The rug is burning. Betty dropped a cigarette on the sofa. The cigarette started a fire. The sofa is burning.

Teacher models the sentences several times, having student repeat.

Hold up a match and strike it to illustrate *match, fire,* and *burn.*

Note: The verb *start* is new here, also. It will appear in other parts of this lesson.

[Holding up a single match, say: "Listen to *match.* Ed dropped a match on the rug. Please repeat."]

[Striking the match and indicating the flame, say: "Listen to *fire.*"]

[Continue in a similar way with the remaining sentences.]

DRILL: Question and Answer Drill

Teacher asks questions which elicit the new vocabulary.

Teacher	Student
What did Ed drop on the rug?	
He dropped a match on the rug.	He dropped a match on the rug.
What did the match start?	
What is burning?	
What did Betty drop on the sofa?	
What did the cigarette start?	
What is burning?	

VOCABULARY: Injuries

Fern's arms and legs hurt.
She has cuts on her leg. She has bruises on her arm. She has burns on her fingers.

Using the "before" picture of Fern on p. 51 of *ESOL Illustrations 2,* teacher models the sentences, having the student repeat.

[Indicating the appropriate parts of the picture, say: "Fern's arms and legs hurt."]

[Continue in the same way with the remaining items.]

DRILL: Question and Answer Drill

Pointing to the "before" picture of Fern on p. 51 of *ESOL Illustrations 2,* teacher asks questions which elicit the new vocabulary. Have the student answer with complete sentences.

Teacher	**Student**
What does Fern have on her leg?	
She has cuts on her leg.	She has cuts on her leg.
What does Fern have on her arm?	
What does Fern have on her fingers?	
Where does Fern have cuts?	She has cuts on her leg.
Where does Fern have bruises?	
Where does Fern have burns?	

VOCABULARY: *first* and *then*

First, I closed the door. Then, I walked to my desk.
First, I picked up the pencil. Then, I gave it to you.

Teacher models the first two sentences several times, having the student repeat.

Perform the action in both sentences first, and then say the pair of sentences.

Continue in the same way with the next pair.

[Without saying anything, close the door and then walk to your desk. Say: "Listen to *first* and *then.* First, I closed the door. Then, I walked to my desk."]

[Without saying anything, pick up a pencil and give it to the student. Continue with the second pair of sentences as above.]

DRILL: Question and Answer Drill

1. Teacher performs two sequential actions and asks a question which elicits answers containing *first* and *then.*

Teacher	Student
[Perform two actions in sequence: close the door, and walk to your desk.]	
What did I do?	First, you closed the door. Then, you walked to your desk.
[Prompt the student if he needs help at first. Continue with other actions below.]	
[Pick up a pencil. Give it to the student.]	
[Pick up your book. Open your book]	
[Walk to the door. Open the door.]	
[Pick up a piece of paper. Tear the paper.]	

2. Teacher tells the student to perform two actions. Student performs the actions.

   Teacher asks, "What did you do?" Student replies, using *first* and *then.*

Teacher	Student
First, pick up a pencil.	
Then, give it to me.	[Performs actions.]
What did you do?	First, I picked up the pencil. Then, I gave it to you.
First, pick up your book. Then, open your book. What did you do?	
First, walk to the door. Then, open the door. What did you do?	
First, get the paper. Then, tear the paper. What did you do?	
First, go to the blackboard. Then, look at the words. What did you do?	
First, drop your pencil. Then, pick it up. What did you do?	

VOCABULARY and STRUCTURE FOCUS: Regular Verbs, Present and Past Tenses

I watch TV every night.	I watched TV last night.
He hurries to school.	He hurried to school.
She covers her eyes.	She covered her eyes.
I yell, "Help!"	I yelled, "Help!"
She answers the telephone.	She answered the telephone.
I add the numbers.	I added the numbers.
I start the car.	I started the car.

Teacher models the sentences containing the present and past tense of each verb. Have the student repeat both.

[Say: "Listen to *watch, watched*."]

Demonstrate the meaning of the verbs, all of which are new except *yell* and *watch (TV).*

Listen carefully to the student's pronunciation of the past tense endings /t/, /d/, and /ud/.

DRILL: Transformation Drill

Teacher gives a present tense statement. Student changes it to a past tense statement.

Teacher	**Student**
The children watch TV every night.	The children watched TV last night.
The students hurry to school.	
He covers his eyes.	
I yell, "Help!"	
She answers the telephone.	
We add the numbers.	
We hurry to work.	
She covers the paper with her hands.	
Mother answers the doorbell.	
He yells, "Stop!"	
Ann starts the car.	

VOCABULARY and STRUCTURE FOCUS: Irregular Verbs, Present and Past Tenses

I see my neighbor every day.	I saw my neighbor yesterday.
I say, "Hello."	I said, "Hello."
I hear my name.	I heard my name.
I take off my clothes at night.	I took off my clothes last night.
I shake hands with my teacher.	I shook hands with my teacher.
He puts on his clothes in the morning.	He put on his clothes this morning.

Teacher models the sentences containing the present and past of each verb. Have the student repeat both.

[Say: "Listen to *see* and *saw*."]

Demonstrate the meaning of the new verbs: *see, hear,* and *shake* (*hands*).

DRILL: Transformation Drill

Teacher gives a negative past tense statement. Student changes it to an affirmative past tense statement.

Teacher	Student
I didn't see the building.	I saw the building.
I didn't say, "Good-bye."	
He didn't hear his name.	
I didn't take off my sweater.	
I didn't put on my ring.	
We didn't shake hands.	
They didn't put their coats in the closet.	
I didn't hear my name.	
We didn't see the car.	
She didn't shake hands with me.	

STRUCTURE FOCUS: Past of *be* + Verb-*ing*

> I was studying English yesterday.
> Then I stopped to eat lunch.
>
> We were watching TV last night.
> Then the Hills came to visit.

Teacher models the pairs of sentences, having the student repeat.

[Say: "Listen to *was studying*."]

Note: The past of *be* + verb-*ing* is used to indicate action that continued over a period of time in the past. (This is the past progressive tense.)

The sentence-pairs in the box contrast the past progressive tense with the simple past tense.

DRILL: Transformation Drill

Student changes a present progressive tense statement to a past progressive tense statement.

All verbs used here have been taught previously.

Teacher	Student
I'm sitting here now.	
I was sitting here yesterday.	I was sitting here yesterday.
She's studying English now.	
You're helping her.	
They're drinking milk.	
We're looking at the books now.	
Bob's going home.	
I'm teaching English.	
The telephone is ringing.	

STRUCTURE FOCUS: Verb + Object + Infinitive

Ann, wash the dishes.	I told Ann to wash the dishes.
Bob, do your homework.	I told Bob to do his homework.
John, listen to me.	I told John to listen to me.

Teacher models the sentences in pairs, having the student repeat only the sentence with *told*.

Turn your head to speak to the imaginary person (Ann, Bob, John). Face the student as you say the sentence with *I told*.

[Say: "Listen to *to wash*." Turn your head as if you were speaking to Ann, and say: "Ann, wash the dishes." Then face your student, and say:
"I told Ann to wash the dishes. Please repeat.
I told Ann to wash the dishes."]

DRILL: Transformation Drill

1. Teacher gives a command to an imaginary person. Student changes it to a sentence with *You told*.

   Help the student make the correct change of pronouns where needed.

Teacher	Student
John, listen to me. What did I tell John?	You told John to listen to you.
Ann, wash the dishes.	
Ed, wash your hands.	
Bob, do your homework.	
Sue, take off your coat.	
Ed, open the door.	
Dan, drink your milk.	
Jill, help me make lunch.	
Jack, answer the telephone.	
Dan, shake hands with Mr. Miller.	

2. Teacher tells student to tell someone to do something. Student gives the command to the imaginary person.

   Again, help the student with the change of pronouns where needed.

Teacher	Student
Tell Ann to wash the dishes. Ann, wash the dishes.	Ann, wash the dishes.
Tell Kim to wear her boots.	
Tell Jill to wear a sweater.	
Tell Ed to wash his hands.	
Tell Tom to hurry.	
Tell Bob to answer the telephone.	
Tell Kim to go to bed now.	
Tell Jill to help her mother.	
Tell Ed to put his suitcase in the car.	
Tell John to take his medicine.	

STRUCTURE FOCUS: Verb + Object + *not* + Infinitive

Ann, don't speak Spanish.	I told Ann not to speak Spanish.
Bob, don't buy any soda.	I told Bob not to buy any soda.

Teacher models the two sentences, having the student repeat only the sentence with *told...not to.*

[Say: "Listen to *not to speak*."]

DRILL: Transformation Drill

1. Student changes a sentence containing an infinitive to a negative.

   Be sure that the student uses *not* before the infinitive, not before the main verb.

Teacher	Student
I told Ann to speak Spanish.	
I told Ann not to speak Spanish.	I told Ann not to speak Spanish.
We told Sue to take off her coat.	
We told Dan to drink a glass of soda.	
They told Jack to answer the doorbell.	
I told Jill to eat the sandwiches.	
She told Ed to open the door.	
I told John to whistle.	
I told Kitty to say good-bye.	
I told Betty to cover her eyes.	

2. Teacher tells student to give a negative command. Student gives the negative command to the imaginary person.

Teacher	Student
Tell Bob not to yell.	
Bob, don't yell.	Bob, don't yell.
Tell Kitty not to buy any bread.	
Tell John not to buy that suit.	
Tell Ed not to sing at the table.	
Tell Kim not to jump on the sofa.	
Tell Dan not to run in the house.	
Tell Molly not to play with matches.	
Tell Jill not to eat those cookies.	
Tell Jimmy not to swim in the river.	

STRUCTURE FOCUS: Verb + Verb-*ing*

The man started talking.
The man stopped talking.

Teacher models the sentences several times, having the student repeat.

[Say: "Listen to *started talking.*"]

Note: Some verbs can be followed by verb-*ing*, as: *The man started talking.* Notice how this structure differs from verb + infinitive (*I want to go*) and verb + infinitive without *to* (*I helped Bob do his homework*).

DRILL: Completing Sentences Drill

Teacher gives the student a verb and the beginning of a sentence. Student puts the two together in a sentence containing verb + verb-*ing*.

Teacher	Student
talk The man started . . . The man started talking.	 The man started talking.
walk The man stopped . . .	
eat The man started . . .	
watch TV The woman stopped . . .	
run The boy started . . .	
whistle The boy stopped . . .	
ring The telephone stopped . . .	
cry The baby started . . .	

STRUCTURE FOCUS: Verb + Object + Verb-*ing*

Bob was talking.	Ann heard Bob talking.
Mother was cooking.	Ann watched Mother cooking.
Bob was running.	Ann saw Bob running.

Teacher models each pair of sentences, having the student repeat only the second sentence.

[Say: "Listen to *heard...talking.*"]

Note: Some verbs, such as *hear, see,* and *watch,* can take an object + verb-*ing*.

DRILL: Completing Sentences Drill

Teacher gives the student a verb and the beginning of a sentence. Student puts the two together in a sentence containing verb + object + verb-*ing.*

Teacher	Student
talk I heard Bob . . . I heard Bob talking.	 I heard Bob talking.
run Ann saw Bob . . .	
hunt Ed watched his father . . .	
sing We heard Jill . . .	
make lunch Jack watched Ann . . .	
walk to the bank Dan saw Betty . . .	
cry I heard the baby . . .	

STRUCTURE FOCUS: Prepositions + Verb-*ing*

> The curtains were burning.
> We stopped the curtains from burning.
>
> Mother was making lunch.
> Ann helped Mother by making sandwiches.
>
> Jack helped Ed.
> Ed thanked Jack for helping.

Teacher models each pair of sentences several times, having the student repeat only the sentence with the preposition.

[Say: "Listen to *from burning.*" Pause.
"The curtains were burning.
We stopped the curtains from burning." Pause.
"We stopped the curtains from burning. Please repeat."]

DRILL: Combining Sentences Drill

1. Teacher gives two sentences which the student combines into one, using *from* + verb-*ing*.

Teacher	Student
The children were playing with matches. We stopped the children.	
We stopped the children from playing with matches.	We stopped the children from playing with matches.
The curtains were burning. We stopped the curtains.	
The pup was jumping on the sofa. We stopped the pup.	
Our son was drinking beer. We stopped our son.	

2. Student combines two sentences, using *by* + verb-*ing.*

Teacher	Student
Tom helped his mother. Tom did the dishes.	
Tom helped his mother by doing the dishes.	Tom helped his mother by doing the dishes.
Ann helped her father. Ann washed the car.	
Betty helped her mother. Betty made lunch.	
Jack helped Ann. Jack carried the suitcase.	

3. Student combines two sentences, using *for* + verb-*ing.*

Teacher	Student
Betty helped John. John thanked Betty.	
John thanked Betty for helping.	John thanked Betty for helping.
Jack picked up the paper. Kitty thanked Jack.	
Don fixed the clock. Mr. Smith thanked Don.	
Jill did the laundry. Mrs. Hill thanked Jill.	

STRUCTURE FOCUS: Passive Voice (*be* + Verb-*ed*)

Her leg is burned.
She was burned.
Her hands are burned.
The doors were opened.

Teacher models the sentences several times, having the student repeat.

[Say: "Listen to *is burned*."]

Note: Sentences in the passive voice are formed with the verb *be* (any tense) plus the past participle, as: *burned, taken, drunk.* Only verbs that can take an object are used in the passive voice.

At this time, only regular verbs (with *-ed* past participle) are being taught in the passive.

DRILL: Multi-Slot Substitution Drill with Vocal Cues

Teacher models the key sentence, then says only the cues. Give the student the response only as long as needed.

Teacher	Student
Her leg is burned.	Her leg is burned.
was	Her leg was burned.
Her legs	Her legs were burned.
are	Her legs are burned.
Her fingers	Her fingers are burned.
were	Her fingers were burned.
Her hands	Her hands were burned.
Her foot	Her foot was burned.
is	Her foot is burned.
Her leg	Her leg is burned.
was	Her leg was burned.

DRILL: Transformation Drill

Teacher gives a sentence in the active voice which the student changes to the passive voice. Prompt the student if necessary.

Teacher	Student
He washed the car yesterday.	
The car was washed yesterday.	The car was washed yesterday.
He signed the paper yesterday.	
He fixed the stove last week.	
He opened the windows this morning.	
He closed the door last night.	
He carried the bags to the car.	
He dropped the clock.	

STRUCTURE FOCUS: The *-er* Comparative Form of Adjectives

Dan is 18. Ed is 15.	He's young. He's younger than Dan is.
Mr. Smith is 70. Mrs. Smith is 75.	He's old. She's older than Mr. Smith is.
Ann weighs 115 pounds. Jill weighs 95 pounds.	She's thin. She's thinner than Ann is.
Bob weighs 225 pounds. Sam weighs 250 pounds.	He's fat. He's fatter than Bob is.
Ann is pretty. Sue is very pretty.	Sue is prettier than Ann is.

Teacher models the set of four sentences beginning with *Dan is 18. He's young.* Continue with the second pair containing the comparative form (*younger than*). Have the student repeat only the sentences that contain the comparatives.

Note: When we compare two persons or things, we use the comparative form of the adjective. With short adjectives, this is formed by adding *-er*, as in *older, fatter, prettier.*

[Say: "Listen to *young, younger.* Dan is 18. He's young. Ed is 15." Pause. "He's younger than Dan is." Gesture for the student to repeat. "He's younger than Dan is."]

[Continue in the same way with each group of sentences.]

DRILL: Making Comparisons

Teacher makes statements about two persons or things. Student forms a comparison with the *-er* form of the adjective + *than.* Give the student the adjective to use.

Teacher	Student
Dan is 18. Ed is 15. young	Ed is younger than Dan is.
Mrs. Hunt is 80. Mr. Hunt is 85. old	
Sue weighs 100 pounds. Kim weighs 80 pounds. thin	
Sam weighs 225 pounds. Bob weighs 250 pounds. fat	
The cat weighs 15 pounds. The dog weighs 30 pounds. big	

STRUCTURE FOCUS: Comparative Form of *good* and *bad*

> That red apple is good.
> This yellow apple is very good.
> This yellow apple is better than this red one is.
>
> I had a bad headache yesterday.
> I have a very bad headache today.
> My headache is worse today than it was yesterday.

Teacher models each set of sentences several times, having the student repeat only the sentences with *better* and *worse.*

[Say: "Listen to *better than*."]

DRILL: Combining Sentences

Teacher makes statements about two persons or things. Student forms a comparison, using the *-er* form of the adjective or the irregular forms *better* and *worse.*

Teacher	Student
The white bread is good. The brown bread is very good.	The brown bread is better than the white bread is.
This lemon is bad. That lemon is very bad.	
Mary is fat. Helen is very fat.	
John is thin. Ed is very thin.	
Ann is pretty. Kitty is very pretty.	
Bob is funny. Ed is very funny.	
This apple is sweet. This orange is very sweet.	
Ann makes bad coffee. Jack makes very bad coffee.	
These cookies are good. Those cookies are very good.	
I am happy. Ann is very happy.	Ann is happier than I am.

VOCABULARY and STRUCTURE FOCUS: *How do you feel?* and Replies

How do you feel?	I was sick yesterday. I feel better today.
How do you feel?	I feel much better today.
You look sick. How do you feel?	I feel a little tired.
You don't look well. How do you feel?	I don't feel well. I have a cold.
You look good. How do you feel?	I feel fine. OK. Good.

Teacher models the question and answer several times, having the student repeat both.

Demonstrate *have a cold* by sniffling, blowing your nose, and so on.

[Say: "Listen to *How do you feel?*"]

DRILL: Question and Answer Drill

1. Teacher asks student, "How do you feel?" and prompts him to an answer, if necessary, to get a variety of replies.

Teacher	Student
How do you feel? (sick)	
I was sick yesterday. I feel better today.	I was sick yesterday. I feel better today.
How do you feel? (much better)	
You look sick. How do you feel? (tired)	
You don't look well. How do you feel? (a cold)	
You look good. How do you feel? (fine) (OK) (good)	

2. Teacher and student reverse roles. Prompt the student as long as necessary.

Teacher	Student
Please repeat. How do you feel?	How do you feel?
I feel fine.	
(sick)	You look sick. How do you feel?
I feel a little tired.	
[Continue with the items in the box.]	

PRONUNCIATION: /ō/ and /oi/, /ou/ and /oi/

1. See the Pronunciation section in Lesson 1 for the steps to follow in teaching the vowel sounds /ō/ and /oi/ as in *cone* and *coin.*

   Note: The new sound being taught is /oi/ as in *coin*. To make this sound, the lips are rounded at first, then unrounded.

/ō/	/oi/	**Sentences**
cone	coin	She soaks it in oil.
load	Lloyd	These coins are old.
row	Roy	The boy cut his toe.
nose	noise	Joan will join us.
coal	coil	Roy is the host.
		It's cold.

2. Following the same procedure, teach the vowel sounds /ou/ and /oi/ as in *cow* and *coy.*

   Note: The new sound being taught is /ou/ as in *cow.* To make this sound, the lips are unrounded at first, then rounded.

/ou/	/oi/	**Sentences**
cow	coy	Get out.
loud	Lloyd	It's a brown coat.
owl	oil	Roy is proud.
plow	ploy	The bough is broken.
foul	foil	His voice is loud.

ORAL EVALUATION

1. Review living room furniture. Student should be able to name four items, *furniture,* and *fern* (needed for the reading).

   [Using p. 50 of *ESOL Illustrations 2,* ask the student: "What's this?" and "What are these?"]

2. Review *match, fire,* and *burning.* Student must know *match* and *burning* for the reading.

   [Do the Question and Answer Drill following Vocabulary: *match, fire, burning.*]

3. Review the vocabulary on injuries. Student must know *cuts* and *burns* for the reading in this lesson and following lessons.

   [Do the Question and Answer Drill following Vocabulary: Injuries.]

4. Review *first* and *then.* Student should be able to use both of these with ease.

   [Do the Question and Answer Drill following Vocabulary: *first* and *then*.]

5. Review the regular and irregular verbs in the present and past tenses. Student should know all of these, some of which are review items.

   [Do the Transformation Drills following the two Vocabulary and Structure Focus sections on regular and irregular verbs.]

6. Review past of *be* + verb-*ing* (the past progressive tense). This is an important tense for the student to be able to use with ease.

   [Do the Transformation Drill following Structure Focus: Past of *be* + Verb-*ing*.]

7. Review verb + object + (*not*) + infinitive. Student should be able to use this pattern in both the affirmative and the negative.

   [Do part 1 of the Transformation Drill following Structure Focus: Verb + Object + Infinitive. Then do part 1 of the Transformation Drill following Structure Focus: Verb + Object + *not* + Infinitive.]

8. Review verb + object + verb-*ing.* Student should be able to form this pattern with all three verbs (*saw, heard, watched*).

   [Do the Completing Sentences Drill following Structure Focus: Verb + Object + Verb-*ing.*]

9. Review prepositions + verb-*ing*. Student must know *stop ... from* verb *-ing* for the story and should know at least one other preposition + verb-*ing.*

   [Do the Combining Sentences Drill following Structure Focus: Prepositions + Verb-*ing.*]

10. Review the passive voice. Student will get further practice with this structure in later lessons. He must be able to use *is/are, was/were burned* to read the story.

    [Do the Multi-Slot Substitution Drill following Structure Focus: Passive Voice.]

11. Review the comparative form of adjectives. Student should know *better, worse,* and at least three of the *-er* forms.

    [Do the Combining Sentences Drill following Structure Focus: Comparative Form of *good* and *bad*.]

12. Review *How do you feel?* and appropriate replies. Student should be able to ask and answer this question with ease as it is useful in everyday conversation.

    [Do the Question and Answer Drill following Vocabulary and Structure Focus: *How do you feel?* and Replies.]

II. Reading

Check your student's homework from Lesson 10, including the extra homework worksheet on singular and plural nouns. Have him read aloud each singular noun and the plural form that he has written. Correct his spelling if necessary. Also, check the student's homework on page 53, and have him read this page aloud.

CHART 11-A: Page 54

Teach this chart in the same way you taught the chart in Lesson 1.

To be sure that your student understands that *er, ur,* and *ir* have the same sound, /er/, teach the key words at the top of the page as below.

Do this:	**Say this:**
Point to key word *her*.	Teacher: Please read this word. Student: *Her*.
Point to red *er* after *her*.	Teacher: The letters *er* make the sound /er/.
Point to key word *burn.*	Teacher: This word is *burn.* Read: *burn.* Student: Burn.
Point to red *ur* after *burn.*	Teacher: The letters *ur* make the sound /er/.
Point to key word *girl.*	Teacher: Please read this word. Student: Girl.
Point to red *ir* after *girl*.	Teacher: The letters *ir* make the sound /er/.
Point one at a time, to the large red *er, ur, ir* at top right.	Teacher: The letters *er* make the sound /er/. The letters *ur* make the sound /er/. The letters *ir* make the sound /er/.
Point to *er*, then *ur,* then *ir.*	Teacher: What is the sound? Student: /er/.../er/.../er/.

Now teach the rest of the chart, pointing out these things about the new chart words.

fern: The letters *er* make the sound /er/.

father: [Point to red *o*.] This vowel sound is /o/.
But you write *a*. [Point to *a* in third column.]

The letters *th* make the sound /th/. [Pronounce the voiced sound.]
The letters *er* make the sound /er/.

were: The letters *er* make the sound /er/.
The last *e* is silent.

skirt: [Point to *sk*.] Say these two sounds together very quickly: *skirt.*
The letters *ir* make the sound /er/.

curtains: The letters *ur* make the sound /er/.
In *curtains,* the letters *ai* make the sound /u/. You write *a, i.*
Curtains ends with the sound /z/. You write *s.*

burning: The letters *ur* make the sound /er/.
The letters *ng* make the sound /ng/.

burned: The letters *ur* make the sound /er/.
Burned ends with the sound /d/. You write *e, d.*
In *burned,* the letters *ed* make the sound /d/.

burning, Point to *burning,* and say: "The curtains were burning."
burned, Point to *burned,* and say: "My hand was burned."
burn: Cover the *-ed*, and say: "I have a bad burn."

STORY: Fern Gets Burned

Teach the story according to the seven steps outlined in Lesson 1.
The new story words are: *rug, ran, match, was, heard, Miller, yelling, running.*
Also, review the word *under* in paragraph 1.

Use the following comprehension questions.

	Teacher	Student
Paragraph 1	Is Fern a big girl or a little girl?	She's a little girl.
	Where was Fern?	She was in the kitchen.
	Were Fern's mother and father in the kitchen?	No, they weren't.
	Where was Fern standing?	She was standing under the curtains.
Paragraph 2	What did Fern have in her hand?	She had a match in her hand.
	Was the match burning?	Yes, it was.
	What did the match burn?	It burned the curtains.
	What did the curtains burn?	They burned Fern's skirt.
Paragraph 3	What did Fern yell?	"Help! I am burning!"
	Did Fern run from the kitchen?	Yes, she did.
Paragraph 4	Who heard Fern yelling?	Her father did.
	What did her father do?	He ran to help her.
Paragraph 5	Is Mr. Miller Fern's father?	Yes, he is.
	What did Mr. Miller tell Mrs. Miller to do?	He told her to get a rug.
Paragraph 6	Did Mrs. Miller hear her husband?	Yes, she did.
	Did she bring a rug?	Yes, she did.
	Did she bring the rug quickly?	Yes, she did.
	Then what did Mrs. Miller do?	She put Fern in the rug.
	Did Fern's skirt stop burning?	Yes, it did.
	Whose leg was burned?	Fern's.
	Whose hands were burned?	Mrs. Miller's.
Paragraph 7	What did Mr. Miller do?	He stopped the curtains from burning.
	Were his fingers burned?	Yes, they were.

CHART 11-B: Page 56

Teach this chart in the same way you taught the chart in Lesson 1. Review the key words and sounds at the top of the chart as below.

Do this:	**Say this:**
Point to key word *her.*	Teacher: Please read this word. Student: *Her.*
Point to red *er* after *her.*	Teacher: What sound do the letters *er* make? Student: /er/.
Point to key word *burn.*	Teacher: Please read this word. Student: Burn.
Point to red *ur* after *burn.*	Teacher: What sound do the letters *ur* make? Student: /er/.
Point to key word *girl.*	Teacher: Please read this word. Student: Girl.
Point to red *ir* after girl.	Teacher: What sound do the letters *ir* make? Student: /er/.
Point, one at a time, to the large red *er, ur, ir* at top right.	Teacher: What is the sound? Student: /er/.../er/.../er/.

Now teach the rest of the chart, pointing out these things about the new chart words.

hurry: The letters *ur* make the sound /er/.
The letters *rr* make one sound /r/. You write *hurry* with two *r*'s.
In *hurry, y* has the vowel sound /i/.

hurried: Point to *hurry,* and say: "I hurry to work every day."
Point to *hurried,* say "yesterday," and beckon to student to say:
"I hurried to work yesterday." Prompt him if necessary.

Then write the formula below on paper or on the board.

hurry
↓
hurri + ed ⟶ hurried

Point to *y,* and say:	"Change *y*..."
Point to *i,* and say:	"to *i*..."
Point to *+ ed,* and say:	"and add *e, d.*"
Point to *hurried,* and say:	"*Hurried.*"

[There will be more work on changing *y* to *i* before adding endings in Lesson 15. Do not spend any more time on this point now.]

nurse: The letters *ur* make the sound /er/.
The *e* is silent.

person: The letters *er* make the sound /er/.
This vowel sound [pointing] is /u/: *person.* You write *o.*

cover: This vowel sound [pointing] is /u/. You write *o.*
The letters *er* make the sound /er/.

covered: *Covered* ends with the sound /d/. You write *e, d.*

cover, Point to *cover,* and say: "Cover your ears." Then perform the action.
covered: Point to *covered,* and say: "I covered my ears."

better: The letters *tt* make one sound: /t/. You write two *t's*.
The letters *er* make the sound /er/.

first: The letters *ir* make the sound /er/.

STORY: Fern Gets Burned (Continuation on Page 57)

Before beginning this continuation, review the events of the first part of the story. Have the student turn back to page 55 to find the answers as you ask these questions.

Review	Teacher	Student
	Who started the fire?	Fern did.
	Who was burned?	Mr. and Mrs. Miller and Fern.
		[If the student names only one or two of these persons, say: "Good! And?" until he names all of them. If necessary, point to the appropriate parts of the story to prompt him.]

Now teach the continuation of the story on page 57 according to the seven steps outlined in Lesson 1. The new story words are: *us, then, said, helping, burns, looked.*

Use the following comprehension questions.

	Teacher	Student
Paragraph 1	What did Mrs. Miller say?	She said, "Hurry! Hurry! Hurry to the doctor!"
Paragraph 2	Where did the Millers go?	They went to Dr. Chan's office.
	Who was in the office?	A nurse.
	What did Mr. Miller say to the nurse?	He said, "Help us!"
Paragraph 3	What did Mrs. Miller say to the nurse?	She said, "Hurry! Get the doctor for us. Tell her to look at my little girl first."
Paragraph 4	What did the nurse do?	She hurried to get the doctor.
	How many persons are hurt?	Three persons are hurt.
Paragraph 5	What did Dr. Chan do first?	She looked at Fern.
	What did the doctor do to Fern's burns?	She covered them.
Paragraph 6	Who covered Mrs. Miller's burns?	The nurse did.
	Who covered Mr. Miller's burns?	The nurse did.
	Who told the nurse to cover their burns?	Dr. Chan did.
	Did the nurse work quickly or slowly?	She worked quickly.
Paragraph 7	What did Mr. Miller say?	He said, "Thank you for helping us."
Paragraph 8	Were Fern's burns better?	Yes, they were.
	Were Mrs. Miller's hands better or worse?	They were better.
	How were Mr. Miller's fingers?	They were better.

Note: If the student uses the pronoun *He* for Dr. Chan, you may gently remind him that Dr. Chan is a woman by turning back to the story illustration in Lesson 10 on page 57 of the skill book. Also, the story contains this clue in paragraph 3: "Get the doctor.... Tell her...."

In answers about the nurse, you may accept either *He* or *She,* since there is no clue in the story and no illustration that indicates whether the nurse is a man or a woman.

SKILLS PRACTICE: Review Words with /er/

Write the following groups of words as shown, but without the headings. Be sure to write the words ending in *-er* so that the *-er* endings line up.

Have the student read the words in each group. After he reads each word, underline the vowel + *r* (as, *er*) and ask him: "What is the sound?"

1. Words ending in *-er*

father	dinner	finger	cover
mother	zipper	number	river
brother	letter	quarter	Oliver
sister	better		

2. Words containing *er*

her	were	person	Robert

3. Words containing *ir*

girl	first	skirt
bird		

4. Words containing *ur*

burn	nurse	hurry	curtains	picture

5. Words with other spellings of the sound /er/

doctor	dollar	heard
factory		

III. Writing

WRITING LESSON: Page 58

Study: Words ending in *-er*

Help your student study the following *er* words in both charts:
father, cover, better, finger (Chart 1, page 2).

Point out again the *a* in *father,* the *o* in *cover,* the two *t*'s in *better,* and the *ng* in *finger*.

Then dictate the following words for the student to write:

1. father
2. cover

Study: Words containing *er*

Help your student study the following *er* words in both charts: *her, were, person.*
Point out again the silent *e* at the end of *were* and the *o* in *person.*

Then dictate the following words for the student to write:

3. were
4. person

Study: Words containing *ur*

Help your student study the following *ur* words in both charts:
curtains, burning, hurry, nurse.

Point out again the *ai* and final *s* in *curtains,* the two *r*'s and final *y* in *hurry,* and the silent *e* in *nurse.*

Then dictate the following words for the student to write:

5. curtains
6. hurry
7. nurse

Study: Words containing *ir*

Help your student study the following *ir* words in both charts: *girl, skirt, first.*

Then dictate the last word for him to write in this section.

8. first

Listen and write

Cover the Study section and dictate the following words for the student to write.

1. burned
2. hurry
3. her
4. were
5. person
6. better
7. first
8. skirt

SKILLS PRACTICE: Adding *-ed* to Verbs

Before class, prepare the chart below on paper for the student. (For a class, make a large wall chart and individual copies.) Also, make a copy of the writing exercise that follows the chart for each student.

1. yell yelled	burn burned	cover covered				
2. kick kicked	pick picked	help helped	jump jumped	thank thanked	look looked	fix fixed
3. hunt hunted	visit visited					
4. live lived	whistle whistled	e + d live + d ——→ lived				
5. stop stopped	drop dropped	CVC + C + ed stop + p + ed ——→ stopped				

Rows 1–3: Point to and say first the root and then the *-ed* form, having the student repeat after you.

Teacher: *Yell, yelled.* [Pointing.]
Student: *Yell, yelled.*

Teacher: *Yell.* [Point to word.]
We add *e, d* to make *yelled.* [Point to *ed* in *yelled*.]

Continue in the same way with the rest of the words in the row.
Then have the student read all the *-ed* forms again.

Teacher: Please read [pointing].
Student: *Yelled, burned, covered.*

Teacher: The ending sound is /d/. [for Row 1]
/t/. [for Row 2]
/ud/. [for Row 3]
We write *e, d.* [for all three rows]

Do all three rows in the same way.

Row 4: Point to and say first the root and then the *-ed* form, having the student repeat after you.

Teacher: *Live, lived.* [Pointing.]
Student: *Live, lived.*

Teacher: *Whistle, whistled.* [Pointing.]
Student: *Whistle, whistled.*

Teacher: [Point to appropriate parts of formula on the right.]
Live ends with the letter *e*.
We add *d* to make *lived.*

Row 5: Point to and say first the root and then the *-ed* form, having the student repeat after you.

Teacher: *Stop, stopped.* [Pointing.]
Student: *Stop, stopped.*

Teacher: *Drop, dropped.* [Pointing.]
Student: *Drop, dropped.*

Teacher: *Stop* ends with consonant, vowel, consonant.
[Point to *CVC* in formula at right.]

To make *stopped,* we add another consonant. [Point to *+C.*]
We add another *p*. [Point to *+p.*]

Then we add *e, d.* [Point to *+ed.*]

Stopped. [Point to *stopped* after arrow.]

Note: The student learned the exception to this rule (*fix, fixed*) in Row 2.

Now give the student the following writing exercise. The student is to write the *-ed* form of the word at the left in the blank in the sentence and then read the completed sentence. Fill in the first blank as an example. Let the student refer to the chart if he needs to.

yell	1. Ann yelled at Jack.
burn	2. Jill ______ the fish.
help	3. Kim ______ her father.
fix	4. Tom ______ the clock.
visit	5. Kitty ______ her mother.
live	6. Mr. and Mrs. Hill ______ in the city.
drop	7. Dan ______ the glass.
look	8. The doctor ______ at Tom's burns.
whistle	9. Jack ______ at Ann.
stop	10. Jimmy ______ at Bob's shop.

HOMEWORK: Page 59 and Extra Worksheet

Ask your student to do page 59 at home. In addition, give him a worksheet with the following exercises to do at home.

In the first exercise, the student is to complete analogies, using the example of the headings *woman* and *man.*

In the second exercise, the student is to change a statement with *was* or *were* into a question. Write out the first question as an example.

woman	**man**
mother	______
sister	______
Mrs. Miller	______

1. The building was burning.	Was the building burning?
2. The curtains were burning.	______
3. Mother and Father were in the kitchen.	______
4. Fern's father was burned.	______
5. The nurse was helping that person.	______
6. The doctor was in the office.	______

READING AND WRITING EVALUATION

1. Write the following sentences. Have the student circle the correct word and then read aloud the completed sentences. The student should be able to complete four out of six correctly.

1. That woman is a cover. / doctor.	4. Father heard / burned the girl yelling.
2. Her sister is a nurse. / father.	5. Mrs. Miller put on her red fern. / skirt.
3. The nurse is helping that person. / were.	6. Mr. Miller is getting well. He is better. / first.

2. Before class, prepare the following story for the student to read at this time.

   (Notice that this story contains two new reading words, *other* and *had*, which the student must sound out as part of the exercise. This should not be too difficult. The student has had a lot of oral practice with both words; a phonetic re-spelling is given for *other*; and the student's knowledge of *mother* and *brother* should help him to make an analogy.)

   Have the student read aloud first the title, then the new words, then the whole story. Help him with the new words only if necessary.

   After the student has finished the story, ask the comprehension questions.

   The student should be able to sound out at least one of the new words, read the story with no more than five errors, and answer at least three of the comprehension questions. (Either short or long answers are acceptable.)

The Nurse Helped

other (uther), had

The doctor was not in her office.
The nurse was in the office.

Two persons hurried in.

One person had a big cut on his leg.
The other person had some burns.
The burns were on his hands.
The burns were not very big.

First, the nurse helped the person with the big cut.
Then, the nurse helped the person with the burns.

Teacher	Student
Was the doctor in her office?	No, she wasn't.
Who was in the office?	The nurse was.
How many persons came in?	Two persons.
Which was worse, the cut or the burns?	The cut was worse.
Which person did the nurse help first?	The person with the cut.

MORE READING

In the supplementary reader *More Stories 2,* the stories for Lesson 11 may be read in class or suggested for reading at home.

Lesson 12

OBJECTIVES

When a student completes this unit, he should be able to:

1. Say and respond to a new dialog.
2. Say the chart and story words.
3. Use some prepositions of direction: *up, down, into, out of, across.*
4. Use some words that indicate trouble with a car: *flat tire, dead battery,* and so on.
5. Use vocabulary connected with driving a car to work, downtown, and home.
6. Use some adjectives with opposite meanings: *near, far; small, large; cheap, expensive; light, dark; new, used.*
7. Use *It's* + distance *from ... to....*
8. Make requests with *Let's.*
9. Make negative requests with *Let's not.*
10. Pronounce the vowel sounds /ou/ and /ī/ as in *bough* and *buy* and /ou/ and /oi/ as in *bough* and *boy* (review).
11. Read the following new words, in two charts and stories:

    Chart words: *arms, farm, farmer, Carmen, barn, garden, jar*
    Story words: *Carl, hard, Arthur, large, jelly, work, working*

    Chart words: *car, far, dark, market, parking, start, starting*
    Story words: *let's.*
12. Read two simple stories, using the new chart and story words.
13. Read some agent nouns with *-er*, formed from known reading words.
14. Write the new chart and story words.

VISUAL AIDS

1. *ESOL Illustrations 2,* pp. 52-58. (On p. 56, color in the lights on the traffic light. Color the top light bright red to show that the red light is on. Color the yellow and green lights faintly.)
2. Bring to class a new book and a used book.
3. Bring to class two small toy cars or any two small objects that you can use as "pretend" cars (match boxes, large erasers, or the like). You will use these to demonstrate making right and left turns and passing another car.
4. Prepare the chart on agent nouns and the extra worksheet on the past tense described in the Reading and Writing sections of this lesson.

OTHER PREPARATION

Before class, figure out the following items, which you will need to know for the Producing Statements Drill on distances.

1. Find a local example of *one mile,* between two well-known local points.
2. Find the distance in miles from your student's home to school (or other place where you have class).
3. Find the distance in miles from your community to several cities in your area.

REVIEW

Review any items that your student had difficulty with when doing the Oral Evaluation in Lesson 11.

I. Conversation Skills

DIALOG

A: Let's go to a movie.
B: That's a good idea. What's playing?

A: A love story.
B: Oh, good! That's my favorite kind.

Teacher models the dialog, using the procedure outlined in Lesson 1.

VOCABULARY: Chart and Story Words

Carl Arthur works on a farm.
Mr. Arthur is a farmer.
There's a big red barn on his farm.

Carmen Arthur has a garden.
Mrs. Arthur is a gardener.
Her garden is between the house and the garage.

The Arthurs go to the farmers' market every week.
Mr. Arthur sells eggs and apples.
Mrs. Arthur sells bread and jars of jelly.

Using the pictures on pp. 52-53 of *ESOL Illustrations 2,* teacher models the sentences several times, having the student repeat.

[Indicating the picture of the farm, say: "Listen to *farm.* Carl Arthur works on a farm."]

[Continue in the same way with the remaining items, always reviewing the items previously taught.]

DRILL: Question and Answer Drill

Pointing to the pictures on pp. 52-53 of *ESOL Illustrations 2,* teacher asks questions which elicit the words being taught.

For practice, the student should answer with complete sentences.

Teacher	Student
Where does Mr. Arthur work?	He works on a farm.
What is Mr. Arthur?	He's a farmer.
Where is the big red barn?	
What does Mrs. Arthur have?	
What is Mrs. Arthur?	
Where is Mrs. Arthur's garden?	
Where do the Arthurs go every week?	
What does Mr. Arthur sell at the farmers' market?	
What does Mrs. Arthur sell at the farmers' market?	
Where does Mr. Arthur sell his eggs and apples?	
Where does Mrs. Arthur sell her bread and jelly?	

VOCABULARY: Prepositions of Direction

Mr. Smith went into the house. He went up the stairs.
Mrs. Smith went down the stairs. She went out of the house. She walked across the street.

Using pp. 54-55 of *ESOL Illustrations 2,* teacher models the sentences several times, having the student repeat.

[Say: "Listen to *into*."]

DRILL: Question and Answer Drill

1. Teacher asks questions to which the student gives answers containing *into, out of, up, down, across.*

   Be sure that the student answers in complete sentences.

Teacher	Student
Where did Mr. Smith go?	He went into the house.
Who went up the stairs?	
Who went down the stairs?	
Where did Mrs. Smith go?	
Who walked across the street?	

2. Ask similar questions about places near you. Use the questions here as suggestions.

Teacher	Student
Who is coming into the room?	[Gives free replies.]
Who is sitting across from you?	
Who is going up the stairs?	
Who is going down the stairs?	
Who is going out of the room?	

VOCABULARY: Verbal Phrases with *back*

I go to work at eight o'clock. I come back home at five o'clock.
I gave my book to Mary last week. She gave it back to me yesterday.

Teacher models each pair of sentences several times, having the student repeat.

Note: Used with certain verbs, *back* means to or toward a former position, location, or condition.

[Say: "Listen to *back.*"]

DRILL: Question Rejoinder Drill

1. Teacher makes a statement. The student replies with a question, using the same verb plus *back.*

Teacher	Student
Ann hurried to the store. Did she hurry back?	Did she hurry back?
Ed hurried to the supermarket.	Did he hurry back?
The boys ran across the street.	Did they run back?
I drive to work with Tom.	Do you drive back with him?
Jack walks to work with Ann.	Does he walk back with her?

2. Teacher makes a statement and gives the verbal phrase as a cue. The student replies with a question, using the verbal phrase.

   In this part of the drill, the verb in the student's rejoinder is sometimes different from the verb in the teacher's statement.

Teacher	Student
I gave my book to Mary. give it back Did she give it back?	Did she give it back?
Jack gave his sweater to Ann. give it back	Did she give it back?
I got a book from the library. take it back	Did you take it back?
Ed took his jacket out of the closet. put it back	Did he put it back?
Bob took his lunch box to work. bring it back	Did he bring it back?

VOCABULARY: Driving a Car to Work

> Bob drives his car to work in the morning.
>
> First, he makes a right turn.
> Then, he makes a left turn.
>
> He stops at the red light.
>
> He parks his car in the parking lot.

Teacher models the sentences several times, having the student repeat.

Demonstrate *driving a car, making a right turn,* and *making a left turn* with the toy or "pretend" cars you have brought.

Use the top two pictures on p. 56 of *ESOL Illustrations 2* for the last two sentences. (You should have colored in the traffic light.)

[Say: "Listen to *drives.*
Bob drives his car to work in the morning. Please repeat."]

[Continue in the same way with the remaining items, always reviewing items previously taught.]

VOCABULARY: Driving a Car Downtown

> After work, Bob drives downtown.
>
> He drives fast.
> He passes another car.
>
> Bob parks his car on the street.
> He puts a quarter in the parking meter.

Teacher models the sentences several times, having the student repeat.

Demonstrate *driving, driving fast,* and *passing another car.*

Use the bottom picture on p. 56 of *ESOL Illustrations 2* for the last two sentences.

[Say: "Listen to *drives.*
After work, Bob drives downtown. Please repeat."]

[Continue in the same way with the remaining items, always reviewing items previously taught.]

VOCABULARY: Driving Home

Bob drives home. He stops at a gas station to buy gas for his car. Bob parks his car in the driveway. His wife's car is in the garage.

Teacher models the sentences several times, having the student repeat.

Use the pictures on p. 57 of *ESOL Illustrations 2* for the last three sentences.

[Say: "Listen to *gas station* and *gas.* Bob drives home. He stops at a gas station to buy gas for his car. Please repeat."]

[Continue in the same way with the remaining items, always reviewing items previously taught.]

DRILL: Question and Answer Drill

Teacher asks questions which elicit vocabulary from the three sections on driving.

Have the student answer with complete sentences.

Use the pictures on pp. 56-57 of *ESOL Illustrations 2* to prompt the student if necessary.

Teacher	**Student**
Where does Bob drive in the morning?	He drives to work in the morning.
[Indicate picture with the red light.] Where does he stop?	He stops at the red light.
Where does Bob drive after work?	
Does Bob drive fast or slow?	
Where does Bob buy gas?	
Where does Bob park at work?	
Where does he park downtown?	
What does Bob put in the parking meter?	
Where does Bob park at home?	
Where is his wife's car?	
[Use the toy or "pretend" cars to demonstrate the following actions as you ask the questions.]	
(making a right turn) What is Bob doing?	He's making a right turn.
(making a left turn) What is Bob doing?	He's making a left turn.
(passing another car) What is Bob doing?	He's passing another car.
[Review any vocabulary the student had difficulty with. Model the sentences again if necessary.]	

VOCABULARY: Car Trouble

Jimmy's car is at the repair shop. It has a flat tire. The trunk won't open. The door on the passenger's side won't close. The door on the driver's side is OK. The hood won't close. The battery is dead. The windshield is broken. The windshield wipers don't work. The brakes don't work. They don't stop the car.

Using p. 58 of *ESOL Illustrations 2,* teacher models the sentences several times, having the student repeat.

Point to every vocabulary item in the picture except *brakes,* which are explained in context.

[Say: "Listen to *repair shop.*
Jimmy's car is at the repair shop."]

[Continue in the same way with the remaining items, always reviewing items previously taught.]

DRILL: Question and Answer Drill

Teacher asks questions to which the student replies by naming the car part and telling what is wrong with it.

Use p. 58 of *ESOL Illustrations 2.*

Teacher	Student
[Point to the appropriate part of the illustration as you ask the questions.]	
Where is Jimmy's car?	It's at the repair shop.
What's this? What's wrong with the tire?	It's a tire. It's flat.
What's this? What's wrong with the trunk?	It's the trunk. It won't open.
Which door is this? Will it open?	It's the door on the driver's side. Yes, it will. It's OK.
Which door is this? Will it close?	It's the door on the passenger side. No, it won't.
What's this? What's wrong with the hood?	It's the hood. It won't close.
What's this? What's wrong with the battery?	It's the battery. It's dead.
What's this? Is the windshield broken?	It's the windshield. Yes, it is.
What are these? Do the windshield wipers work?	They're the windshield wipers. No, they don't.
Do the brakes work? Will the brakes stop the car?	No, they don't. No, they won't.

VOCABULARY: Adjectives with Opposite Meanings

Japan is far.	My house is near.
A bus is large.	A bicycle is small.
A car is expensive.	A pencil is cheap.
The night is dark.	The day is light.
This book is new.	This book is used.

Teacher models the contrasting sentences several times, having the student repeat both. Model first the sentence with *far,* then with *near,* and so on.

[Say: "Listen to *far, near.*"]

Write the prices $5,000 and 15¢ as you say *expensive* and *cheap.*

Show a new book and a used one as you model those two sentences.

DRILL: Question and Answer Drill

Teacher asks a question containing an adjective. Student answers with a negative sentence containing an adjective that is opposite in meaning.

Teacher	Student
Is your house far?	
No, it's near.	No, it's near.
Is Japan near?	No, it's far.
Is a bus small?	
Is a bicycle large?	
Is a car cheap?	
Is a pencil expensive?	
Is the night light?	
Is the day dark?	
Is this book new?	
Is this book used?	
Is China near?	
Is a pencil large?	
Is a gold ring cheap?	
Is New York small?	

STRUCTURE FOCUS: *It's* + Distance *from...to....*

It's far	from (Syracuse)	to	San Francisco.
It's not far	from my house	to	school.
It's 10 miles	from the city	to	the farm.

Teacher models the sentences several times, having the student repeat.

[Say: "Listen to *from...to.*"]

Substitute the name of your city for Syracuse, and, if necessary, another faraway city for San Francisco.

Note: Your student will understand *mile* if you tell him that one mile is 1.6 kilometers. It will help, also, to give an example of two well-known local points that are one mile apart.

DRILL: Producing Statements

Teacher gives two locations, and student makes a statement, using either the frame
It's far from_______ to_______, or
It's not far from_______ to_______.

Teacher	Student
(name of your city), Japan	It's far from_______ to Japan.
my house, the post office	
the post office, the bank	
New York, China	
my house, school	
Puerto Rico, Germany	
my house, work	
the bank, the supermarket	
the United States, Italy	

DRILL: Question and Answer Drill

Teacher asks a question about the distance in miles from one place to another.

Give the distance (shown in parentheses) as a vocal cue.

Teacher	Student
How many miles is it from the city to the farm? (10 miles)	It's 10 miles from the city to the farm.
How many miles is it from your house to school? (_____ miles)	It's_____ miles.

[Continue with similar questions, using local cities and towns. Give the student the distance in miles as a vocal cue.]

How far is it
from_____ to_____?
(_____ miles)

STRUCTURE FOCUS: Requests with *Let's*

Open your book.	
Let us close our books.	Let's close our books.
Let us speak English.	Let's speak English.
Let us go.	Let's go.

Teacher models each pair of sentences several times, having the student repeat only the contracted form.

Note: *Let's* is used to make a request that includes the speaker.

[Begin by saying: "Open your book." Have the student perform the action.]

[Then say: "Listen to *Let us* and *Let's*." Both you and the student should close your books as you say the sentences: "Let us close our books. Let's close our books." Pause. "Let's close our books. Please repeat. Let's close our books."]

DRILL: Transformation Drill

Student transforms an imperative into a request with *Let's*.

Teacher	Student
Open your book.	
Let's open our books.	Let's open our books.
Close your book.	
Speak English.	
Go.	
Sit down.	
Eat lunch.	
Study English.	
Speak English.	
Thank Bob.	

STRUCTURE FOCUS: Negative Requests with *Let's*

Let's not go.
Let's not speak Spanish here.
Let's not open the window.

Teacher models the sentences several times, having the student repeat.

[Say: "Listen to *Let's not.*"]

Note: The negative with *Let's* uses *not.* The student may tend to use *Don't.*

DRILL: Transformation Drill

Teacher makes an affirmative request with *Let's,* which the student changes to the negative.

Student must also change *some* to *any* in the negative.

Teacher	Student
Let's go.	
Let's not go.	Let's not go.
Let's speak Chinese.	Let's not speak Chinese.
Let's sell the books.	
Let's drink some soda.	
Let's study Spanish.	
Let's stand up.	
Let's make dinner now.	
Let's throw away this paper.	
Let's buy some new clothes.	

PRONUNCIATION: /ou/ and /ī/, /ou/ and /oi/

1. See the Pronunciation section in Lesson 1 for the steps to follow in teaching the vowel sounds /ou/ and /ī/ as in *bough* and *buy*.

   Note: The new sound being taught is /ī/ as in *buy.* The lips are unrounded when making this sound.

/ou/	/ī/
bough	buy
mouse	mice
vow	vie
crowd	cried
how	hi

Sentences

The sky is cloudy.
She cried and cried.
How did he die?
She signed her name.
She fried two eggs.

2. Following the same procedure, teach the vowel sounds /ou/ and /oi/ as in *bough* and *boy.*

   These are both review items, so they should be drilled quickly.

/ou/	/oi/
bough	boy
cloud	cloyed
owl	oil
loud	Lloyd
cow	coy

Sentences

Roy is wearing a tie.
There are clouds in the sky.
I saw the owl.
Where is the boy?
It's a nice sound.
She boiled the eggs.

ORAL EVALUATION

1. Review the chart and story words. Student should know all of these. [Do the Question and Answer Drill following Vocabulary: Chart and Story Words.]

2. Review prepositions of direction. Student should know all of these. [Do the Question and Answer Drill following Vocabulary: Prepositions of Direction.]

3. Review the vocabulary about car parts and car trouble. Student should know *battery* (needed for reading later on), plus six other new items. [Do the Question and Answer Drill following Vocabulary: Car Trouble.]

4. Review the vocabulary about driving a car. Student should know *drive, pass, park,* and *parking lot,* plus five other new items. [Do the Question and Answer Drill following Vocabulary: Driving Home.]

5. Review the new adjectives. Student should know *far* and *near,* plus four others. [Do the Question and Answer Drill following Vocabulary: Adjectives with Opposite Meanings.]

6. Review the structure *It's* + distance *from...to....* This pattern is needed for the story. [Do part 1 of the Question and Answer Drill following Structure Focus: *It's* + Distance *from...to....*]

7. Review affirmative and negative requests with *Let's* and *Let's not.* Student should know both of these. [Do the Transformation Drills following the Structure Focus sections on Requests with *Let's* and Negative Requests with *Let's not.*]

II. Reading

Check your student's homework from Lesson 11, both page 59 and the extra worksheet. Have the student read aloud all of page 59, including the heading, instructions, and page number. Check the extra worksheet to be sure that the student has written the correct "man" equivalents for the "woman" words and has spelled them correctly. Check the questions he formed from the statements for correct word order, spelling, and punctuation. Then have the student read aloud each statement and its question form.

CHART 12-A: Page 60

The key word for this chart, *arms,* is a new reading word. Teach the top of the chart as below.

Do this:	**Say this:**
Point to *arms* picture at top.	Teacher: These are the man's arms.
Point to the key word *arms.*	Teacher: This word is *arms.* Read: *arms.* Student: Arms.
Point to red *ar* under *arms.*	Teacher: The letters *ar* make the sound /ar/.
Point to large red *ar* at top right.	Teacher: What is the sound? Student: /ar/.

Teach the rest of the chart in the same way you taught the chart in Lesson 1.

For each new chart word, point out that "The letters *ar* make the sound /ar/."
Point out these other things, also:

farmer: The letters *er* make the sound /er/.

Carmen: *Carmen* is a woman's name.

When reviewing the chart words, be sure to review the new key word *arms.*

Note: If your student is still having difficulty with the sound /j/ as in *jar,* you may want to repeat two exercises in the *ESOL Manual for Skill Book 1:* the Pronunciation in Lesson 5 and the Skills Practice in Lesson 7. If so, do this review after reading the next story on page 61.

STORY: The Arthurs' Farm

Begin by saying: "Let's read the story," indicating the whole story on page 61.

Teach the story according to the seven steps outlined in Lesson 1.
The new story words are: *Carl, hard, Arthur, large, jelly, work, working.*

Use the following comprehension questions.

	Teacher	Student
Paragraph 1	Is Mr. Arthur's name Carl?	Yes, it is.
	Is Mrs. Arthur's name Carmen?	Yes, it is.
	What is Carl?	He's a farmer.
	What is Carmen?	She's a farmer.
Paragraph 2	What do the Arthurs have?	They have a farm.
	Is their farm large or small?	It's large.
	Do the Arthurs work hard on their farm?	Yes, they do.
Paragraph 3	Are Carl's arms hard or soft?	They're hard.
	Are his arms hard from working?	Yes, they are.
	Are Carmen's arms hard or soft?	They're hard.
	Are her arms hard from working?	Yes, they are.
Paragraph 4	What is the big building on the Arthurs' farm?	It's the barn.
Paragraph 5	Do the Arthurs have a large garden or a small garden?	They have a large garden.
	Do they work hard in the garden?	Yes, they do.
Paragraph 6	What's in the jars?	Jelly.
	Do the Arthurs have many jars of jelly?	Yes, they do.
	Do they have any jars of apple jelly?	Yes, they do.
	Will the Arthurs sell their jelly?	Yes, they will.

Finally, ask these questions about the story as a whole:

Teacher	Student
Do Carl and Carmen live on a farm or in a city?	On a farm.
Whose farm is it?	The Arthurs'.
Are the Arthurs hard workers?	Yes, they are.
The Arthurs are going to sell some jars of jelly. Do you think they made the jelly?	Yes, I do.
Did you like this story?	(Free reply.)

CHART 12-B: Page 62

Teach the chart in the usual way, pointing out the *ar* in each word: "The letters *ar* make the sound /ar/."

Give examples of the root and the *-ing* form for *park* (v.) and *start:*

park, parking: Cover the *ing* and say: "Park your car there."
Uncover the *ing* and say: "I'm parking my car."

start, starting: Point to *start* and say: "Start the car."
Point to *starting* and say: "I'm starting the car."

STORY: At the Farmers' Market

Again, begin by saying: "Let's read the story," indicating the whole story on page 63.
Follow the seven steps outlined in Lesson 1. The only new story word is *let's.*

Use the following comprehension questions.

	Teacher	Student
Paragraph 1	Where are the Arthurs?	They're in the car.
	Where are the Arthurs going?	They're going to the (farmers') market.
	Where is the farmers' market?	It's in the city.
Paragraph 2	Is the market far from the Arthurs' farm?	No, it isn't.
	Do the Arthurs get to the market quickly?	Yes, they do.
Paragraph 3	Are there many farmers at the market?	Yes, there are.
	Who parks the Arthurs' car?	Carl does.
Paragraphs 4-5	What do the Arthurs sell at the market?	Apples, eggs, hens, and jars of jelly.
	Do the Arthurs visit with friends?	Yes, they do.
Paragraph 6	Is it getting dark?	Yes, it is.
	Will the farmers sell after dark?	No, they won't.
	Where does Carmen want to go?	She wants to go back to the farm. *or* She wants to go home.
Paragraph 7	What does Carl say?	He says, "Yes, it is getting dark. Let's start back to the farm."
Paragraph 8	Who starts the car?	Carmen does.
	Where are the Arthurs going?	They're going back to the farm. *or* They're going home.
	Is it far from the market to their farm?	No, it isn't.

Relating the story to everyday life

Before class, find out if there is a farmers' market in your area. If so, find out where it is and when it is open.

Model the following group of sentences, substituting local information for the items in parentheses. Then model the sentences one at a time, having the student repeat. Finally, ask the student the questions, prompting him in his answer only if necessary.

Sentences

There's a farmers' market in (Syracuse).
It's (on Park Street).
It's open (on Saturday).
It's open (from five o'clock in the morning to one o'clock
in the afternoon).

Questions

Is there a farmers' market in__________?
Where is it?
What day(s) is it open?

SKILLS PRACTICE: Review Words with *ar*

Write the following words and sentences on the board or on paper. Line up the words as shown. Have the student read first the words, then the sentences.

car	barn	arm	hard	dark	start	large	Arthur
far		farm	garden	park			
jar				market			

1. The car will not start
2. Mr. and Mrs. Arthur have a hard bed.
3. The farm has a large red barn.
4. Kitty parked her car on a dark street.
   It is not far from her building.
5. Mrs. Smith is shopping at the farmers' market.
   Mrs. Arthur sells her a jar of apple jelly.
6. Ann is carrying a large black cat in her arms.

SKILLS PRACTICE: Agent Nouns with *-er*

Note: An agent noun indicates a person or thing that does something.

Agent nouns can be formed by adding the sound /er/ to many verb roots, as: *teach, teacher.* Often, the sound /er/ is spelled *-er*; sometimes, it is spelled *-or*, as: *collector*. Some agent nouns are formed in other ways, as: *study, student.*

In this exercise, all the agent nouns are persons and all are spelled with *-er.*

Notice that the student has learned two of the root forms here, *farm* and *garden*, as nouns rather than as verbs. This should not cause any difficulty, as the meanings are closely related.

Before class, write the following words and sentences, as shown, on paper for the student to read at this time.

Mr. Hill works.
Mr. Hill is a worker.

work	help	hunt	sing	farm	garden	listen
worker	helper	hunter	singer	farmer	gardener	listener

1. Mr. Hill works at a factory.
   Mr. Hill is a factory worker.
2. Bob helps Mr. Hill.
   Bob is Mr. Hill's helper.
3. Mr. Smith hunts ducks.
   Mr. Smith is a hunter.
4. Mr. Arthur has a farm.
   Mr. Arthur is a farmer.
5. Mrs. Arthur has a garden.
   Mrs. Arthur is a gardener.
6. Jack works hard.
   Jack is a hard worker.
7. Bob sings well.
   Bob is a good singer.
8. Ann helps her mother.
   Ann is a good helper.
9. Kitty listens very well.
   Kitty is a good listener.

Step 1: Teacher: [Run your finger under the sentence as you read it.]
Mr. Hill works. Please read.
Student: Mr. Hill works.

Teacher: Mr. Hill is a worker. Please read.
Student: Mr. Hill is a worker.

Step 2: Teacher: *Work, worker.* [Point to each word as you say it.]
A worker is a person who works.

Please read. [Point to the words.]

Student: *Work, worker.*

Continue in the same way with the rest of the words.

Step 3: Teacher: [Run your finger under the first sentence in number 1.]
Mr. Hill works at a factory.

[Run your finger under the second sentence in number 1.]
Please read.

Student: Mr. Hill is a factory worker.

Continue in the same way with the rest of the sentence pairs. You read the first sentence in the pair, and the student reads the second sentence.

Before you begin number 7, point to *good* and say: "This word is *good*."

III. Writing

WRITING LESSON: Page 64

Study

Help your student study the words below. Point out that (in three words) the letters *ar* make the sound /ar/, that *large* ends with a silent *e*, that the letters *or* in *work* make the sound /er/. Then dictate the words for the student to write.

1. large
2. work
3. garden
4. Arthur

Listen and write

Dictate the following words and sentences for the student to write.

1. farm
2. barn
3. arms
4. jar
5. hard
6. car
7. far
8. dark

1. The market is not far.
2. Mr. Arthur parked his car.
3. The farmer worked in his garden.

HOMEWORK: Page 65 and Extra Worksheet on Past Tense

Ask your student to do page 65 at home. In addition, have prepared before class the extra worksheet shown below.

On this worksheet, the student transforms present tense statements to past tense statements. The first exercise is on the *-ed* simple past tense; the second is on the past progressive tense (*was/were* + verb-*ing*). The second exercise also contains many agent nouns with *-er*.

Write out the first answer in each exercise as an example for the student to follow.

Have the student read aloud the example pair of sentences in the first exercise. Then have him read aloud the next sentence, say it in the past tense, and then write it in the past tense. Continue in the same way.

Have the student do two or three sentences of each exercise in class and complete the rest as part of his homework. Be sure that the student reads aloud all the present tense statements in class with you.

1. Tom thanks Ann. — Tom thanked Ann.
2. Kitty parks her car.
3. Bob and Don fix the clock.
4. Ed helps his mother.
5. Kim drops the dish.
6. Mrs. Smith stops the car.
7. The Birds visit the Hunts.
8. Jimmy works in a car factory.
9. The doctor looks at John's cuts.
10. Mr. and Mrs. Black live in River City.

1. Kitty and Jimmy are laughing. — Kitty and Jimmy were laughing.
2. The farmer is picking apples.
3. The gardener is working hard.
4. The hunter is carrying a gun.
5. The factory workers are cutting glass.
6. Kitty is listening to the singer.
7. Tom and Don are helping that worker.
8. That building is burning.
9. Mr. Hill's helper is carrying the box.
10. The man and the woman are looking at rings.

READING AND WRITING EVALUATION

1. Write the following sentences, as shown. Ask your student to circle the right word, then read the sentence. He should answer at least three correctly.

1. A barn is a building. / a person.

2. The car will not farm. / start.

3. The Arthurs work hard. / dark.

4. Mrs. Arthur sells jelly at the farmers' garden. / market.

2. Write the following sentences, and have the student read them aloud. He should not make more than three errors.

    1. Let's start back to the city.
    2. It is not far from the farm to the market.
    3. Mrs. Arthur will not work in her garden after dark.

3. Write the following sentences, as shown. Have the student fill in the blank, then read both sentences aloud. The student should write at least two words correctly and make no more than two errors in reading. (You may prompt him on the word *good.*)

1. Mr. Arthur has a farm.	Mr. Arthur is a ________ .
2. Don works at a factory.	Don is a factory ________ .
3. Kitty sings very well.	Kitty is a good ________ .

4. Dictate these sentences for the student to write. The student should make no more than two spelling errors and one error in capitalization and punctuation. The word order should be correct in all three sentences.

    1. Bob has a large car.
    2. Mrs. Arthur worked in her garden.
    3. Was it getting dark?

MORE READING

In the supplementary reader *More Stories 2,* the stories for Lesson 12 may be read in class or suggested for reading at home.

Lesson 13

OBJECTIVES

When a student completes this unit, he should be able to:

1. Say and respond to a new dialog.
2. Say the names of some recreation places, and give some replies to requests with *Let's go....*
3. Use questions with *What time.*
4. Use the verb *find out.*
5. Use some frequency adverbs in the correct word order in sentences.
6. Use *ever* in Yes/No questions.
7. Use *the same* and *different* with colors.
8. Make comparisons using *as...as.*
9. Use the simple present form of *see, hear, want, need, like,* and *know* for all present tense statements, recognizing that these verbs have no *-ing* form in the present tense.
10. Give short answers to Yes/No questions in all the verb tenses that have been taught (review).
11. Say statements, information questions, and Yes/No questions with the correct intonation (review).
12. Identify the short vowel sounds in words with the correct letters (review).
13. Use the correct short vowel in written words with regular spellings (review).
14. Read with ease words ending with *consonant* + *y* (review).
15. Identify the sounds /wh/ and /ng/ in words with their symbols (review).
16. Write *What* questions with *is/are* + verb-*ing.*
17. Read and write *-er* forms of some known adjectives.

VISUAL AIDS

1. *ESOL Illustrations 2,* pp. 59-61.
2. Prepare the exercise on forming *What* questions and the chart and exercise on forming the *-er* comparative of adjectives, as described in the Writing section of this lesson.

REVIEW

Review any items that your student had difficulty with when doing the Oral Evaluation in Lesson 12.

I. Conversation Skills

DIALOG

A:	Do you always take the bus to work?
B:	No, not always. I often walk. What about you?
A:	I usually drive to work.
B:	Where do you park your car?
A:	I park it in the parking lot in back of the factory.

Teacher models the dialog, using the procedure outlined in Lesson 1.

VOCABULARY: Recreation Places

Let's go to the movies.	That's a good idea.
Let's go to the party.	OK.
Let's go to a restaurant.	That's a good idea.
Let's go to a concert.	That's a good idea.
Let's go on a picnic.	I'd like to.
Let's go for a walk.	Sure.

Teacher models each request and reply several times, having the student repeat both.

Use pp. 59-61 of *ESOL Illustrations 2.*

[Say: "Listen to *to the movies.*"]

DRILL: Making Requests and Replies

1. Student makes a request to go to a recreation place; teacher replies.

   Use the pictures on pp. 59-61 of *ESOL Illustrations 2* as visual cues for the student.

   Vary your replies to include all of those in the box.

Teacher	**Student**
[Point to picture of recreation place.]	Let's go to the movies.
[Reply.] That's a good idea.	
[Continue with the remaining items and then repeat in random order.]	

2. Teacher and student reverse roles. Teacher makes request; student replies.

Class: In a class situation, you can combine steps 1 and 2. Have one student make the request and another answer it.

Teacher	**Student**
Let's go to the movies.	[Replies.]
[Continue with the remaining items.]	

STRUCTURE FOCUS: Questions with *What time*

What time does the class start?	It starts at 8 o'clock.
What time does the bank open?	It opens at 10 o'clock.
What time does the store close?	It closes at 5:30.

Teacher models each question and answer several times, having the student repeat both.

[Say: "Listen to *What time.*"]

Note: Like questions with *what, where, when,* and *which,* questions with *What time* use the question word order: *does the class start.*

Questions beginning with *What time* use a falling intonation pattern (final) similar to that used for statements.

DRILL: Producing Questions

Teacher gives the name of a place and a verb. Student uses them to form a question with *What time.*

Teacher	Student
the class, start	
What time does the class start?	What time does the class start?
the bank, open	
the store, close	
the library, open	
the party, start	
the supermarket, close	
the concert, start	
the post office, close	
the movie, start	
the department store, open	
the bank, close	

VOCABULARY: The Verb *find out*

What time does the bank open?	I don't know. I'll find out for you.
What time does the store close?	I don't know. I'll find out for you.

Teacher models each question and answer several times, having the student repeat only the answer.

[Say: "Listen to *find out*."]

Note: The verb *know* is also new here. Indicate the meaning of *don't know* by shrugging your shoulders and looking bewildered.

DRILL: Reply and Rejoinder

Teacher asks a question to which the student replies using *find out*.

Teacher	Student
What time does the bank open?	I don't know. I'll find out for you.
What time does the store close?	
What time does the supermarket close?	
What time does the class start?	
What time does the post office open?	
What time does the bank close?	
What time does the party start?	
What time does the library open?	
What time does the movie start?	
What time does the concert start?	

VOCABULARY: Frequency Adverbs

I always	drink coffee	for breakfast.
I usually	drink milk	for lunch.
I often	drink soda	for dinner.
I sometimes	drink soda	in the afternoon.
I hardly ever	drink soda	in the morning.
I never	drink beer	in the morning.

Teacher models the sentences several times, having the student repeat.

[Say: "Listen to *always*."]

Explain the meaning of the frequency adverbs by using a calendar for one month. Indicate the number of days per month that each frequency adverb stands for. Use the numbers below as a guide:

always – all days
usually – 25 days
often – 15 days
sometimes – 5 days
hardly ever – 1-2 days
never – 0 days.

Note: The frequency adverbs are generally used with the simple present tense rather than the present progressive tense.

STRUCTURE FOCUS: Position of Frequency Adverbs

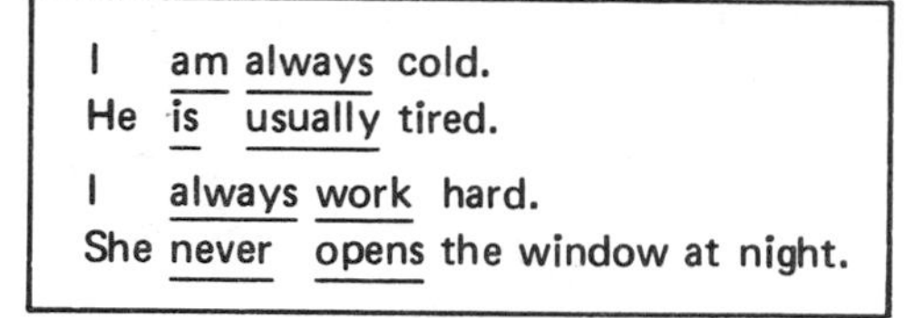
I am always cold.
He is usually tired.
I always work hard.
She never opens the window at night.

Teacher models the sentences several times, having the student repeat.

[Say: "Listen to *always*."]

Note: Frequency adverbs come after the verb *be*. They come before all other main verbs.

(Some one-word frequency adverbs may come at the beginning or end of the sentence. Do not introduce that pattern at this time.)

DRILL: Expansion Drill

Teacher makes a statement to which the student adds a frequency adverb.

Give the frequency adverb as a vocal cue.

Teacher	Student
He is tired. always	He is always tired.
Ann is hungry. usually	
Ed works hard. usually	
Jill is sick. hardly ever	
Dan drinks milk. often	
Glenn is happy. usually	
She walks fast. always	
Tom drives slowly. usually	
Ann goes to the movies. never	
Dan is thirsty. often	
Bob needs help. never	
Jill brushes her teeth in the morning. always	
John drives fast. hardly ever	

STRUCTURE FOCUS: The Use of *ever* and *never*

Do you	ever	drink beer?
No, I	never	drink beer.
Do you	ever	play ball?
No, I	never	play ball.

Teacher models each question and answer several times, having the student repeat both.

[Say: "Listen to *ever* and *never*."]

Note: Use *ever* in questions before the main verb. Use *never* in statements before the main verb.

Other frequency adverbs besides *never* can be used in answer to questions with *ever*.

DRILL: Expansion Drill

1. Teacher asks a question to which the student adds *ever*.

Teacher	Student
Do you drink beer?	
Do you ever drink beer?	Do you ever drink beer?
Do you drink coffee?	
Do you play ball?	
Do you drive fast?	
Do you work at night?	
Do you go swimming?	
Do you wear a hat?	

2. Teacher makes a statement which the student adds *never*.

Teacher	Student
I drink soda.	
I never drink soda.	I never drink soda.
I drink coffee.	
I make dinner.	
She watches television.	
Tom cuts his fingers.	
Kim plays with matches.	
Mrs. Hill hits her children.	

DRILL: Question and Answer Drill

1. **Teacher asks a question with *ever;* student replies using a frequency adverb.**

   Give the adverb as a vocal cue.

   Model three answers to the first question, as shown, to help the student understand when to use *Yes* and when to use *No.* After that, prompt him only if necessary.

   Note: In the answer, both *never* and *hardly ever* require a *No.*

Teacher	Student
Do you ever drink beer? never No, I never drink beer.	No, I never drink beer.
Do you ever drink beer? hardly ever No, I hardly ever drink beer.	No, I hardly ever drink beer.
Do you ever drink beer? sometimes Yes, I sometimes drink beer.	Yes, I sometimes drink beer.
Do you ever drink coffee at night? never	
Does the baby ever cry at night? often	
Do your children ever wash the dishes? usually	
Does Betty ever get sick? hardly ever	
Does her husband ever do the laundry? sometimes	
Does Ann ever drive to work? always	
Do the Hills ever go fishing? hardly ever	

2. **Teacher asks questions with *ever*; student gives free replies containing frequency adverbs.**

Teacher	Student
Do you ever walk to class?	[Gives free replies.]
Do you ever drink soda for breakfast?	
Do you ever watch TV in the morning?	
Do you ever speak English at home?	
Do you ever go to the movies?	
Do you ever have dinner at a restaurant?	
Do you ever eat in the kitchen?	
Do you ever get tired?	
Do you ever take aspirin for a headache?	
Do you ever work on Saturday?	
Do you ever have fish for dinner?	
Do you ever have cereal for breakfast?	
Do you ever drink coffee at night?	

VOCABULARY: *the same* and *different*

This pencil is yellow. That pencil is yellow.	The pencils are the same color.
This pen is blue. That pen is black.	The pens are different colors.

Teacher models each set of three sentences several times, having the student repeat only the sentence with *the same* or *different.*

[Say: "Listen to *the same.*"]

DRILL: Combining Sentences

Teacher makes two statements about items which are the same or different. Student replies using *the same* or *different.*

Teacher	Student
My shirt is white. Your shirt is white. The shirts are the same color.	The shirts are the same color.
Bob's shirt is blue. Ed's shirt is blue.	
Ed's shoes are black. Ann's shoes are brown.	
Sue's dress is red. Mary's dress is yellow.	
Jill's jeans are blue. Lil's jeans are blue.	
My house is green. Your house is white.	

STRUCTURE FOCUS: Comparisons with *as. . . as*

John is 25. Mary is 25.	Mary is as old as John is.
Tom is tired. Ed is tired, too.	Ed is as tired as Tom is.
The red apple was good. The yellow apple was good, too.	The red apple was as good as the yellow one was.
Ann walks slowly. Betty walks slowly, too.	Betty walks as slowly as Ann does.
I sing badly. Jill sings badly, too.	Jill sings as badly as I do.

Teacher models each set of three sentences several times, having the student repeat only the sentences with *as...as.*

[Say: "Listen to *as...as.*"]

Note: To compare two items or persons that are the same in a certain way, use *as...as* with adjectives and adverbs.

DRILL: Combining Sentences

Teacher makes statements about two persons or things that are the same in a certain way. The student combines these into one statement, using *as...as.*

Teacher	Student
Tom was tired. Ed was tired, too. Ed was as tired as Tom was.	Ed was as tired as Tom was.
I was hungry. You were hungry, too.	You were as hungry as I was.
Mary walks slowly. Sue walks slowly, too.	Sue walks as slowly as Mary does.
The red car is cheap. The blue car is cheap, too.	The blue car is as cheap as the red one is.
The bank is near. The store is near, too.	The store is as near as the bank is.
I sing badly. Bob sings badly, too.	Bob sings as badly as I do.
The green house is big. The white house is big, too.	The white house is as big as the green one is.
Ann drives carefully. Jack drives carefully, too.	Jack drives as carefully as Ann does.
Will works quickly. Ed works quickly, too.	Ed works as quickly as Will does.

DRILL: Combining Sentences

1. Teacher makes two statements indicating that two persons are the *same* in a certain way.

   Give an adjective as a vocal cue, as needed.

   Student combines the statements, using *as...as.*

Teacher	Student
John is 25. Mary is 25. old Mary is as old as John is.	Mary is as old as John is.
Tom is 30. Jack is 30. old	
Ed is 15. Dan is 15. young	
Sue weighs 100 pounds. Jill weighs 100 pounds. small	
Sam weighs 250 pounds. Cal weighs 250 pounds. big	
Ann is pretty. Sue is pretty, too.	
Bob is handsome. Jack is handsome, too.	

2. Teacher makes two statements indicating that two persons are *different* in a certain way.

   Give an adjective as a vocal cue, as needed.

   Student combines the statements, using the *-er* form of the adjective and *than.*

   (This is review.)

Teacher	Student
Mary is 25. Tom is 30. old Tom is older than Mary is.	Tom is older than Mary is.
John is 25. Jack is 30. old	
Ed weighs 150 pounds. Sam weighs 250 pounds. big	
John is 25. Ed is 15. young	
Sue weighs 100 pounds. Kim weighs 80 pounds. small	
Bob is tall. Jack is very tall.	
Ann is pretty. Mary is very pretty.	

3. Teacher makes two statements indicating that two persons are either the same or different in a certain way.

   Give an adjective as a vocal cue, as needed.

   Student must decide whether the persons are the same or different and make an appropriate comparison, using either *as...as* or *-er than.*

Teacher	Student
John is 25. Mary is 25. old Mary is as old as John is.	Mary is as old as John is.
Sue is 20. Mary is 25. old Mary is older than Sue is.	Mary is older than Sue is.
Ed is 15. Dan is 15. young	Dan is as young as Ed is.
Dan is 15. Fred is 12. young	Fred is younger than Dan is.
Sue weighs 100 pounds. Jill weighs 100 pounds. small	Jill is as small as Sue is.
Bob weighs 250 pounds. Sam weighs 250 pounds. big	Sam is as big as Bob is.
Jack weighs 200 pounds. Sam weighs 250 pounds. big	Sam is bigger than Jack is.
Ann is pretty. Sue is pretty, too.	Sue is as pretty as Ann is.
Ann is pretty. Mary is very pretty.	Mary is prettier than Ann is.
Bob is tall. Jack is very tall.	Jack is taller than Bob is.
Ed is short. Dan is short, too.	Dan is as short as Ed is.

STRUCTURE FOCUS: Verbs with No *-ing* Form in the Present Tense

I sit here every day.	I'm sitting here now.
I speak English every day.	I'm speaking English now.
I see my teacher every day.	I see my teacher now.
I hear the teacher.	I hear the teacher.
I know my neighbor's name.	I know my neighbor's name.
I want a sandwich.	I want a sandwich.
I need some money.	I need some money.
I like Jack.	I like Jack.

Teacher models both forms of the present tense several times, having the student repeat both.

[Say: "Listen to *I sit, I'm sitting.*"]

Note: Most verbs has two forms of the present tense: *I speak* and *I'm speaking.* The verbs *see, hear, know, want, need, like,* and a few others have no *-ing* form in the present tense; they can be used in only one way: *I see the car.*

The verbs in the box have already been taught. The verb *know* was introduced earlier in this lesson.

DRILL: Transformation Drill

1. Student changes statement from the simple present to the *-ing* form of the present tense.

Teacher	Student
I speak English.	I'm speaking English.
She watches television.	
Ann goes to the movies.	
Jack eats at a restaurant.	
Ann studies English.	
Jill reads the book.	

2. Student repeats the simple present tense statement, since it cannot be changed to an *-ing* form.

Teacher	Student
I hear the girl.	I hear the girl.
She sees the dog.	
We need some money.	
I like English.	
I want a glass of milk.	
He hears his name.	
I know the doctor's telephone number.	

3. Student changes the simple present tense statement to the *-ing* form when possible. Otherwise, he repeats the statement.

Teacher	Student
She speaks English.	She is speaking English.
He sees two cats.	
Ann watches television.	
I know your address.	
We need some money.	
Jill goes home.	
I like Jack.	
Ann hears Bob's car.	
Tom makes breakfast.	
I know that woman's name.	
John goes to the movies.	
I want a new coat.	

STRUCTURE FOCUS: Short Answers to Yes/No Questions (Review)

Are you cold?	Yes, I am. No, I'm not.
Was John here yesterday?	Yes, he was. No, he wasn't.
Does Ann like coffee?	Yes, she does. No, she doesn't.
Did Dan go home?	Yes, he did. No, he didn't.
Can you speak English?	Yes, I can. No, I can't.
Will you help Dan?	Yes, I will. No, I won't.

Teacher models the questions and answers, having the student repeat only the answers.

Note: This is review material so it can be gone over quickly.

[Say: "Listen to *Yes, I am; No, I'm not.*"]

DRILL: Short Answer Drill

Teacher asks a Yes/No question; student replies with a short affirmative or negative answer.

Do this drill quickly, as it is entirely review.

Teacher	**Student**
Is Dan tired?	(Yes, he is.) (No, he isn't.)

Was the room cold?
Are you tall?
Were the boys watching TV last night?
Do you watch television?
Does Sue cook dinner?
Did you buy a sweater?
Did Bob and Dan go home?
Were they going home?
Can you go to the bank?
Can Glenn go downtown?
Will Jack marry Ann?
Will you help Mr. Hunt tomorrow?
Was the telephone ringing?
Are Kim and Jill talking?
Is it windy?
Were you in class yesterday?
Do you drink coffee?
Can you speak English?
Will you read the book?
Were you sitting on the sofa?

PRONUNCIATION: Intonation Drills

1. Teacher models each sentence several times, having the student repeat. Be sure to use the contractions given.

   Next, have the student say the sentences on his own. Cue him as in a substitution drill.

   Concentrate your attention on the student's use of the correct intonation rather than on his pronunciation of any particular word.

   Note: For these simple statements of fact, the intonation rises on the last stressed word in the sentence, then falls to a final pitch. The falling intonation indicates the completion of the statement.

   A straight up-and-down line indicates a shift from one pitch to another between words or between syllables. A curved line indicates a shift from one pitch to another within a syllable.

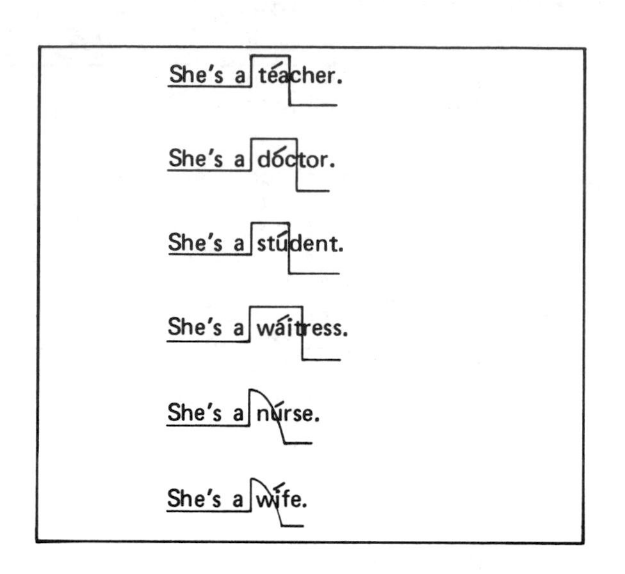

Teacher	**Student**
She's my teacher.	She's my teacher.
wife	She's my wife.
doctor	
teacher	
student	
nurse	
waitress	

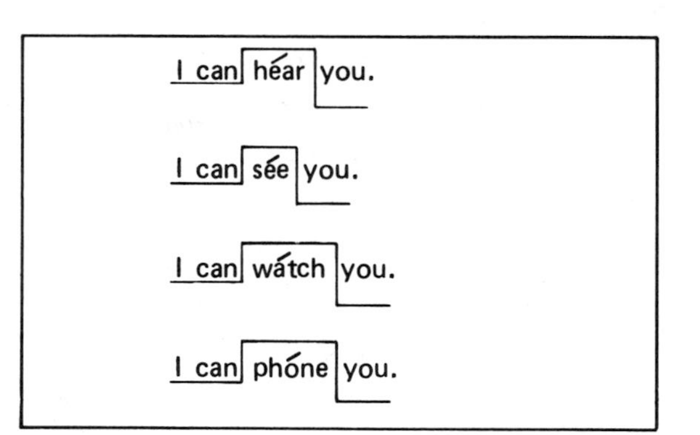

Teacher	**Student**
I can hear you.	I can hear you.
watch	I can watch you.
see	
phone	
hear	

2. Using the procedure outlined above, teacher models questions beginning with information question words.

Note: The intonation pattern for information questions is the same as that for statements.

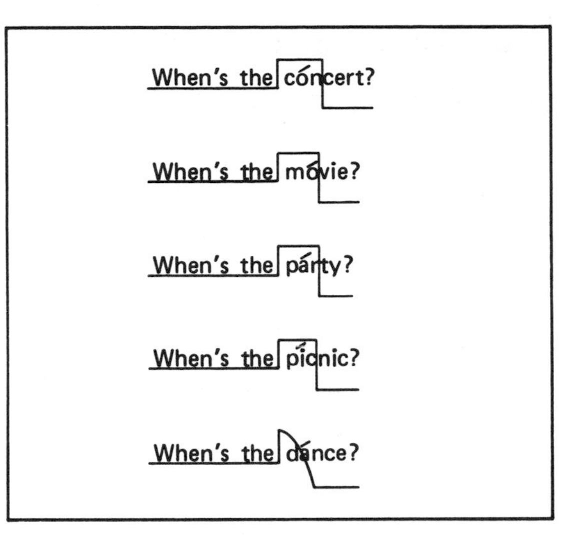

When's the cóncert?
When's the móvie?
When's the párty?
When's the pícnic?
When's the dánce?

3. Using the procedure outlined above, teacher models Yes/No questions.

Note: In Yes/No questions, the final pitch rises on the last stressed word in the sentence. The syllables after the rise are pronounced on the high note, too.

The pitch may rise slightly higher after the first rise:

Is Sue a doctor?

The second rise is not important in English, however.

If your student has difficulty with this pattern, you can practice other Yes/No questions, being sure to use only patterns already taught, as: *Was he here? Did he go?* and so on.

Is Sue a dóctor?

Is Sue a téacher?

Is Sue a stúdent?

Is Sue a wáitress?

Is Sue a núrse?

Does she speak Énglish?
write
read
like

ORAL EVALUATION

1. Review the recreation places. Student should know four of these, plus two of the replies.

   [Do the Drill on Making Replies and Requests following Vocabulary: Recreation Places.]

2. Review questions with *What time*. Student should be able to use this structure with ease.

   [Do the Producing Questions Drill following Structure Focus: Questions with *What time*.]

3. Review the verb *find out.*

   [Do the Reply and Rejoinder Drill following Vocabulary: The Verb *find out*.]

4. Review the frequency adverbs. Student should be able to use all of them in the correct word order in the sentence.

   [Do the Expansion Drill following Structure Focus: Position of Frequency Adverbs.]

5. Review the use of *ever* in questions and the use of *never* and other frequency adverbs in answers.

   [Do the Expansion Drill and part 2 (with free replies) of the Question and Answer Drill following Structure Focus: The Use of *ever* and *never*.]

6. Review *the same* and *different.*

   [Do the Combining Sentences Drill following Vocabulary: *the same* and *different*.]

7. Review comparisons with *as...as.*

   [Two Combining Sentences Drills follow Structure Focus: Comparisons with *as...as.* Do all of the first one and part 1 of the second one.]

8. Review verbs with no *-ing.* form in the present tense. Student should learn that some verbs cannot be used in the *-ing* form in the present tense.

   [Do part 3 of the Transformation Drill following Structure Focus: Verbs with No *-ing* Form in the Present Tense.]

9. Review short answers to Yes/No questions. Student should be able to answer these questions quickly, as this is all review.

   [Do the Short Answers Drill following Structure Focus: Short Answers to Yes/No Questions (Review).]

II. Reading

This review lesson does not have a chart and story. Check your student's homework from Lesson 12, both page 65 and the extra worksheet on the past tense. Then go on to the following Skills Practices, which review the sounds taught in *Skill Book 2.*

SKILLS PRACTICE: Review Short Vowels (Auditory Discrimination)

Write the five vowel letters—*a, e, i, o, u*—fairly large on separate index cards. Spread the cards in front of the student, and review the sounds and names of the letters.

Say: "I will say three words. Listen to the words.
What is the vowel sound? Pick up the vowel [indicate the cards]."

Read the following groups of words, and have the student pick up the vowel card for each group.

in, sit, brick
Ed, let, fresh.
at, can, black
us, run, truck
on, job, stop

and, match, thank
end, tent, help
up, hunt, jump
it, bring, think
odd, drop, clock

rug, duck, fun
box, shop, Tom
has, that, path
ten, them, yes
six, this, give

SKILLS PRACTICE: Review Short Vowels (Minimal Pairs in Sentences)

Before class, prepare the following exercise for the student. The student is to circle the word that is correct in the sentence and then read the sentence aloud.

Notice that the choices are minimal pairs with different vowels.

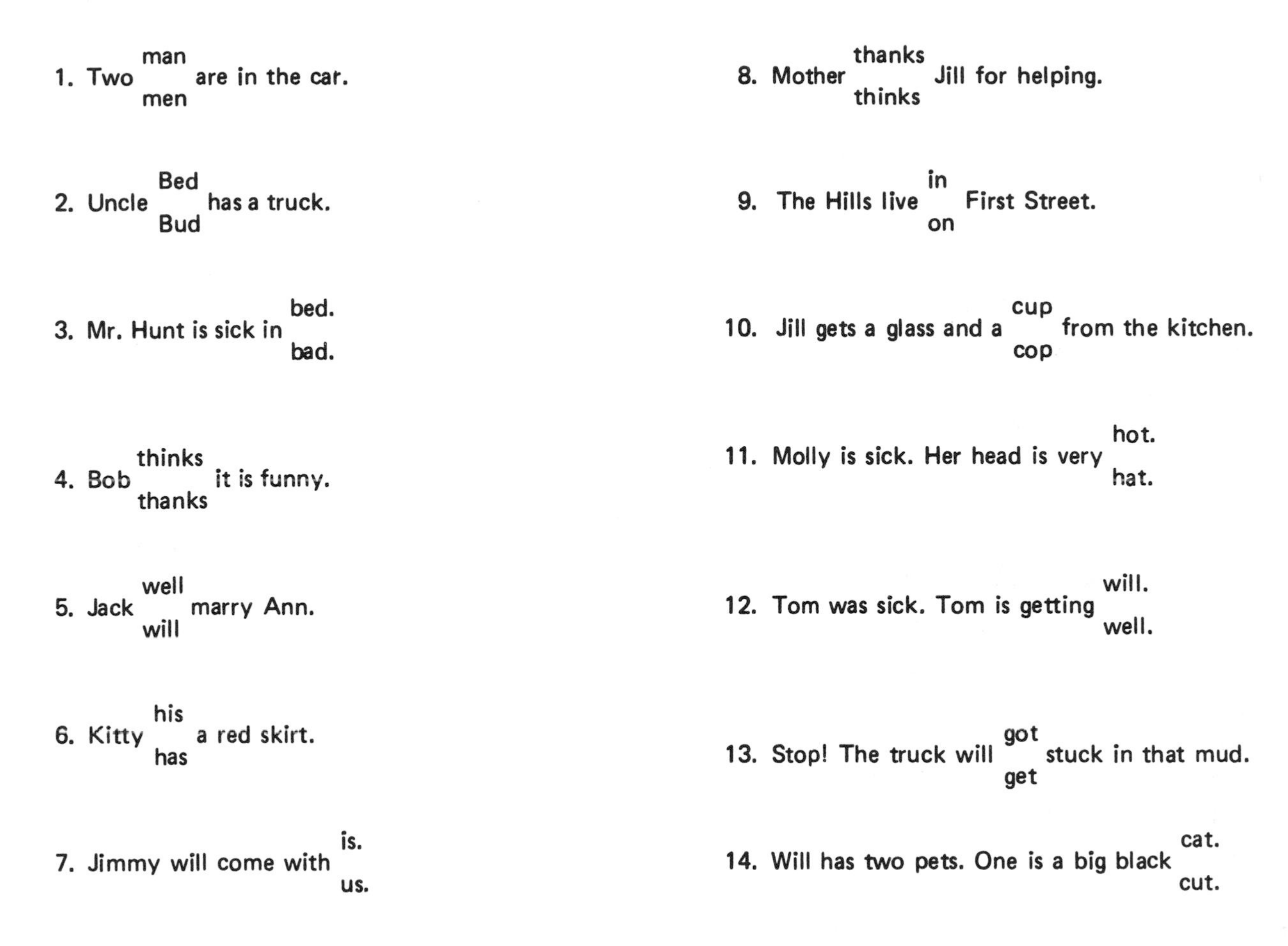

1. Two man / men are in the car.
2. Uncle Bed / Bud has a truck.
3. Mr. Hunt is sick in bed. / bad.
4. Bob thinks / thanks it is funny.
5. Jack well / will marry Ann.
6. Kitty his / has a red skirt.
7. Jimmy will come with is. / us.
8. Mother thanks / thinks Jill for helping.
9. The Hills live in / on First Street.
10. Jill gets a glass and a cup / cop from the kitchen.
11. Molly is sick. Her head is very hot. / hat.
12. Tom was sick. Tom is getting will. / well.
13. Stop! The truck will got / get stuck in that mud.
14. Will has two pets. One is a big black cat. / cut.

If the student has difficulty with the first few items, have him read both words aloud before choosing the correct one for the sentence.

If that doesn't help, read him the complete sentence, with the correct word, and then have him circle the word you said in the sentence.

SKILLS PRACTICE: Review Words Ending with Consonant + *y*

1. Write the following words as shown, with the *y*'s lined up under the *y* headings. Have the student read the words.

y	y	y	y	y	y	y
Kitty	funny	windy	carry	city	many	family
Jimmy	happy	fifty	marry	lily	very	factory
	jelly		hurry	study		
	pretty					

Then, ask: "What is the vowel sound of *y* in these words?" [Student: /y/.]

2. Write the following sentences, and have the student read them.

    1. Kitty has fifty dollars.
    2. Will Kitty marry Jimmy?
    3. Kitty's family lives in a big city.

3. Dictate the following sentences, and have the student write them.

    1. It is windy.
    2. That is funny.
    3. Jimmy is very happy.
    4. Jimmy works in a factory.

SKILLS PRACTICE: Review *wh* Contrasted with *w* and *h*

Write the letters *w* and *h* and the digraph *wh* fairly large on separate index cards. Spread the cards in front of the student, and review the sounds and names of the letters.

Say: "I will say a word. Listen to the beginning sound.
Then I will say the word in the sentence.
Pick up the beginning sound [indicate the cards.]"

Read the following items, and have the student pick up the card for the beginning sound. Repeat the word if necessary.

1. wear	She likes to wear her red dress.
2. where	Where is the bank?
3. hen	We get eggs from our hen.
4. when	When will you go?
5. weather	How's the weather today?
6. windy	It's windy today.
7. hair	She's combing her hair.
8. where	Where are you going?
9. which	Which book do you want?
10. want	I want that one.
11. with	I'm going with you.
12. why	Why are you doing that?
13. Hi	Hi, Tom. How are you?
14. what	What are you doing?
15. he	He likes ice cream.
16. help	Please help me.
17. how	How are you?
18. whistle	He can whistle loudly.

SKILLS PRACTICE: Review *ng* Contrasted with *n* and *g*

Write the letters *n* and *g* and the digraph *ng* fairly large on separate index cards. Spread the cards in front of the student, and review the sounds and names of the letters.

Say: "I will say a word. Listen to the *ending* sound.
Then I will say the word in a sentence.
Pick up the ending sound [indicate the cards]."

Read the following items, and have the student pick up the card for the ending sound. Repeat the word if necessary.

1. bag	He is carrying the bag.
2. son	My son goes to school.
3. sing	I like to sing.
4. rang	The doorbell rang.
5. run	Bob will run to the store
6. rug	There is a blue rug in the bedroom.
7. bring	Bring your sister with you.
8. King	Kitty King lives on First Street.
9. big	The Hills live in a big house.
10. thin	Kitty is getting thin.
11. thing	Put that thing down.
12. ring	Jack gave Ann a ring.

SKILLS PRACTICE: Review /er/ and /ar/

If you think the student needs to review words with /er/ and /ar/, repeat the Skills Practices on these items in Lessons 11 and 12. Add the word *work* to the irregular spellings of /er/ in Lesson 11.

III. Writing

Lesson 13 in *Skill Book 2* is a review writing lesson.

WRITING LESSON: Pages 66-67

Listen and write (words)

Dictate the following words for the student to write on page 66.

1. bed
2. run
3. it
4. tell
5. stand
6. windy
7. rock
8. first
9. arm
10. hurt
11. father
12. car
13. person
14. stop
15. ring
16. singing
17. clock
18. truck
19. bring
20. hot

Listen and write (sentences)

Dictate the following sentences for the student to write on page 67.

1. This is a big city.
2. The sun is up.
3. Ellen Bell sells eggs.
4. Is Fred very sick?
5. Fern's father ran to help her.
6. The truck is stuck.
7. The farmer parks his car.
8. Kim is Ed's sister.
9. The girl is singing.
10. Are the eggs in a box?

Check very carefully what your student has written, and have him correct any errors. Then ask him to read aloud everything he has written.

SKILLS PRACTICE: Forming *What* Questions

Before class, write the following exercise on paper. Write *what* at the top of the page. Write the statements in three sets of four statements. Write the first *What* question for each set of statements as an example for the student to follow.

Point to *what* at the top of the page, and say: "This word is *what*. Please read." [Student: *What.*]

Have the student read the first statement and the *What* question formed from it. For the remaining items in the set, have the student read the statement, say the *What* question, and then write the question. Do all three sets the same way.

Note: The second set contains two-word verbs. Both parts of the verb are used in the *What* question. The third set contains prepositional phrases. The prepositional phrase is used in the question. Notice that the last item in each set is plural.

what

1. Mr. Smith is selling his car.	What is Mr. Smith selling?
2. John is carrying the bags.	
3. Kitty is fixing the clock.	
4. The women are bringing a tent.	
5. Jill is laughing at the pup.	What is Jill laughing at?
6. Jack is looking at a picture of Ann.	
7. Mrs. Hill is putting on her black skirt.	
8. The men are picking up that large box.	
9. Don is putting the bags in the car.	What is Don putting in the car?
10. Tom is putting the bed in the truck.	
11. Mrs. Roberts is getting a doll for Molly.	
12. The girls are getting a ring for Mother.	

SKILLS PRACTICE: Forming the *-er* Comparative of Adjectives

Before class, prepare the chart below on paper for the student. (For a class, make a large wall chart and individual copies.) Also, make a copy of the writing exercise that follows the chart for each student.

			CVCC + er		
1.	dark darker	hard harder	d a r k + er ⟶ darker h a r d + er ⟶ harder	dark hard	________ ________
			CVC + C + er		
2.	hot hotter	big bigger	h o t + t + er ⟶ hotter b i g + g + er ⟶ bigger	hot big	________ ________
			-----e + r		
3.	large larger	little littler	large + r ⟶ larger little + r ⟶ littler	large little	________ ________

Row 1: 1. Point to and say first the root and then the *-er* form, having the student repeat after you.

Teacher: *Dark, darker.* [Pointing.]
Student: *Dark, darker.*

Do the same with *hard, harder.*

2. Then, pointing to the appropriate parts in the formula, give the following explanation.

Teacher: *Dark.* Consonant-vowel-consonant-consonant.
We add *e, r* to make *darker.*

3. Point to *dark* at far right.

Teacher: Please read.
Student: *Dark.*

Teacher: Write *darker.* [Point to blank at far right.]
Student: [Writes *darker.*]

4. Repeat steps 2 and 3 with *hard, harder.*

Row 2: Do this row the same way, except in step 2, give the following explanation.

Teacher: *Hot.* Consonant-vowel-consonant.
We add another consonant: *t.*
Then we add *e, r* to make *hotter.*

Row 3: Do this row the same way, except in step 2, give the following explanation.

Teacher: *Large. Large* ends with the letter *e.*
So we add *r* to make *larger.*

Now give the student the following writing exercise. Before beginning the writing, introduce the new reading word *than*: "This word is *than.* Please read."

In the exercise, the student is to write the *-er* form of the adjective at the left in the blank in the sentence and then read the completed sentence.

Let the student refer to the chart. It may also help to have him label each adjective at the left with ending *e* or *CVC* or *CVCC.*

Three of the adjectives (*fast, fat, thin*) are new reading words. The student has had a lot of oral practice with them, and he should be able to sound them out. Help him if necessary.

hard	1. That bed is hard. This bed is very hard. This bed is ________ than that bed.
hot	2. Molly's hands are hot. Molly's head is very hot. Molly's head is ________ than her hands.
large	3. That building is large. This building is very large. This building is ________ than that building.
big	4. Mrs. Hill's kitchen is big. Mrs. Hunt's kitchen is very big. Mrs. Hunt's kitchen is ________ than Mrs. Hill's kitchen.
dark	5. That street is dark. This street is very dark. This street is ________ than that street.
little	6. The cat is little. The pup is very little. The pup ________ than the cat.
fast	7. Bob has a fast car. Jack has a very fast car. Jack has a ________ car than Bob has.
fat	8. Mrs. Bird is fat. Mr. Bird is very fat. Mr. Bird is ________ than Mrs. Bird.
thin	9. Ann is thin. Kitty is very thin. Kitty is ________ than Ann.
fresh	10. The eggs from the shop are fresh. The eggs from the farm are very fresh. The eggs from the farm are ________ than the eggs from the shop.

HOMEWORK: Pages 68-69

Help your student read the new words on page 68: *copy, add, what.* Ask him to read the instructions aloud and then to do these pages at home. Also, have him study any words he wrote incorrectly on pages 66 and 67.

READING AND WRITING EVALUATION

Since the reading and writing sections of this lesson are mostly review, there is no special evaluation. You may, if you wish, review reading by having the student read any of the stories he had difficulty with. Or you may use the stories for Lesson 13 in *More Stories 2* or any of the preceding stories in this book that he hasn't already read in class. By now, the student should be able to read fairly smoothly and with good understanding of the main points of the story.

Introduction to *City Living*

In Lessons 14-16, the student's reading material is *City Living,* a small book of related stories. Reading and writing exercises based on these stories are found in *Skill Book 2,* which continues to be the student's workbook.

In Lessons 14-16 of this manual, each lesson is divided into parts that correspond to the stories in *City Living.* Each part contains conversation skills practice of the new vocabulary and structures in the related story, and then the reading of the story. The final part in each lesson contains reading and writing skills practices and exercises for the entire lesson.

Lessons 14-16 are pared down to the bare essentials. There are no Dialogs, no Oral Evaluations, and no Reading and Writing Evaluations. You should, of course, review any items that your student has great difficulty with.

The lessons related to *City Living* are an integral part of *Skill Book 2*; they should not be skipped. The student must have learned the skills in these lessons before going on to *Skill Book 3.*

The chart below shows how the lessons, the stories in *City Living,* and the exercises in *Skill Book 2* are related.

	Stories in City Living	**Pages in City Living**	**Exercise pages in Skill Book 2**
Lesson 14:	1. Jack Black Comes to the City	5 – 8	70 – top
	2. At the Dress Shop	9 – 12	70 – bottom, 71-74
Lesson 15:	3. Working in a Factory	13 – 16	75 – top
	4. City Traffic	17 – 20	75 – middle
	5. At the Market	21 – 23	75 – bottom, 76-78
Lesson 16:	6. The Puppy Got the Duck	24 – 26	There are no exercises in
	7. What Happened?	27 – 31	*Skill Book 2* for Lesson 16.

Be sure that you have a 1981 edition of *City Living* for your ESOL student.

Lesson 14

CITY LIVING: STORIES 1–2

Story 1: Jack Black Comes to the City

OBJECTIVES

When the student completes this unit, he should be able to:

1. Use the words *Mom* and *Dad.*
2. Use the verb *get* to mean *receive.*
3. Use verbs that show affection: *kiss, hug, hold hands with, pat.*
4. Use the verbs *smile at* and *laugh at.*
5. Use the word *up* in sentences like *He is coming up the street.*
6. Use the word *from* in sentences like *Dan is watching Jack from the window.*
7. Use the indirect object without *to*, as: *Ann gives Jack a gift.*
8. Use the verbs *watch, see, hear, help,* and *let* in the pattern verb + object + verb, as: *Mom lets Dan have some candy.*
9. Read the new words *coming, other, watching, dad, kiss, kisses, kissing, watches, laughing, who.*
10. Read independently the first story in *City Living,* understanding the main ideas and being able to locate details.

VISUAL AIDS

Bring to class a letter addressed to you, that you have received.

REVIEW

Review any items that your student had difficulty with when doing the Oral Evaluation in Lesson 13.

I. Conversation Skills

VOCABULARY: The Words *Mom* and *Dad*

Mrs. Smith is Dan's mother. Dan says, "Mom, I'm hungry."
Mr. Smith is Dan's father. Dan says, "Dad, I'm tired."

Teacher models the sentences several times, having the student repeat.

[Say: "Listen to *mother, Mom*."]

DRILL: Transformation Drill

Teacher gives a statement containing *Mother* or *Father*; the student changes it to a statement containing *Mom* or *Dad.*

Teacher	Student
Mother is tired.	
Mom is tired.	Mom is tired.
Father is hungry.	Dad is hungry.
Mother is sick.	Mom is sick.
Mother is tall.	Mom is tall.
Father is watching TV.	Dad is watching TV.
Mother is reading a book.	Mom is reading a book.
Father is eating breakfast.	Dad is eating breakfast.

VOCABULARY: The Verb *get (receive)*

I get a letter from my sister every week.
I got this letter yesterday.
The Smiths got Jack's letter.
Ann got a ring from Jack.

Teacher models the sentences several times, having the student repeat.

Note: In these sentences, *get* means *receive.* Explain this meaning of *get* by showing the letter you have brought in with you.

[Say: "Listen to *get*," and show the letter.]

DRILL: Question and Answer Drill

Teacher asks questions to practice *get* (meaning *receive*).

Student should answer with complete sentences for practice.

Teacher	Student
What did you get yesterday?	
I got a letter.	I got a letter.
When did you get the letter?	I got it yesterday.
Who got a ring?	Ann got a ring.
What did Ann get?	She got a ring.
Who did Ann get the ring from?	She got it from Jack.
What did the Smiths get?	They got Jack's letter.
Who did the Smiths get a letter from?	They got a letter from Jack.

VOCABULARY: Verbs That Show Affection

Ann	kisses	Jack.
Mary	hugs	her sister.
Bob	holds hands with	his girl friend.
The mother	pats	her child's head.

Teacher models the sentences several times, having the student repeat.

Pantomime the meaning of the verbs being taught.

[Say: "Listen to *kisses,*" and make a kiss in the air.]

DRILL: Question and Answer Drill

1. Teacher asks questions about Ann and Jack, eliciting answers that contain verbs of affection.

   Perform the action as a visual cue.

Teacher	Student
What's Ann doing? [Make a kiss.] She's kissing Jack.	She's kissing Jack.
What's Ann doing? [Make a hug.]	She's hugging Jack.
What's Ann doing? [Hold hands.]	She's holding hands with Jack.
What's Ann doing? [Pat your arm.]	She's patting Jack's arm.

2. Repeat the drill, with Jack as the subject of the questions and answers.

Teacher	Student
What's Jack doing? [Make a kiss.] He's kissing Ann.	He's kissing Ann.
[Continue with the rest of the verbs. Repeat *kissing* at the end of the drill.]	

VOCABULARY: The Verbs *smile at* and *laugh at*

Jack smiles at Ann.
Jack laughs at Ann's little brother.

Teacher models the sentences several times, having the student repeat.

Demonstrate the meaning of the verbs being taught.

[Indicating your mouth and smiling, say: "Listen to *smiles at*." Pause. "Jack smiles at Ann. Please repeat. Jack smiles at Ann."]

[Laugh, then say: "Listen to *laughs at*." Pause. "Jack laughs at Ann's little brother. Please repeat. Jack laughs at Ann's little brother."]

DRILL: Identifying and Performing Actions

1. Teacher performs an action (smiling or laughing) and asks the student to identify it.

Teacher	Student
[Smile.]	
What am I doing?	
You're smiling.	You're smiling.
[Laugh.]	
What am I doing?	You're laughing.
[Repeat the above.]	

2. Reverse roles, having the student perform the action.

Teacher	Student
Please smile.	[Student smiles.]
What are you doing?	I'm smiling.
Please laugh.	[Student laughs.]
What are you doing?	I'm laughing.
[Repeat the above.]	

STRUCTURE FOCUS: The Use of *up* in *coming up the street*

Jack is coming up the street.
Ann is coming up the street.
Bob is coming up the stairs.

Teacher models the sentences several times, having the student repeat.

Do not emphasize *up* as you say the sentence.

[Say: "Listen to *up*."]

DRILL: Substitution Drill with Vocal Cues

Teacher models the key sentences, then the cues.

Teacher	Student
Jack is coming up the street.	Jack is coming up the street.
path	
stairs	
street	
Bob is coming up the street.	Bob is coming up the street.
Jack	
Ann	
Dan	

STRUCTURE FOCUS: The Use of *from* in *watching (someone) from (somewhere)*

Jack is coming up the street.	Dan is watching Jack from the window.
Ann is coming up the path.	Jack is watching Ann from the kitchen window.

Teacher models each pair of sentences several times, having the student repeat only the sentences with *from.*

Do not stress the word *from* as you say the sentences.

[Say: "Listen to *watching...from*."]

DRILL: Question and Answer Drill

Teacher makes a statement about one person, such as: *Jack is coming up the street.*

Teacher then asks what a second person is doing in relation to the first person: *What is Dan doing?*

Student replies, using *watching... from...,* as: *Dan is watching Jack from the kitchen.*

The student must supply the *from* phrase by himself. If this is very difficult for him, you may give him the phrase as a vocal cue.

Teacher	Student
Jack is coming up the street. What is Dan doing?	
Dan is watching Jack from the kitchen.	Dan is watching Jack from the kitchen.
Ann is driving into the driveway. What is Jack doing?	
The children are playing in the living room. What is Mother doing?	
Sue is walking up the path. What is Betty doing?	
Jill is jumping rope. What is Mom doing?	
Dan is fixing his bicycle. What is Dad doing?	

STRUCTURE FOCUS: Indirect Object without *to*

Ann	gives		a gift	to Jack.
Ann	gives	Jack	a gift.	
Jack	sends		a letter	to Ann.
Jack	sends	Ann	a letter.	
I	hand		the English book	to you.
I	hand	you	the English book.	
Mrs. Smith	teaches		English	to the student.
Mrs. Smith	teaches	the student	English.	

Teacher models each pair of sentences several times, having the student repeat both.

Demonstrate the meaning of the new vocabulary item, *hand* used as a verb, by handing an English book to the student.

Note: Verbs like *give, send,* and *teach* can take two objects: a direct object and an indirect object. In the *ESOL Manual for Skill Book 1,* the word order taught was that of the direct object followed by the indirect object with *to*. Now, the other possible word order is taught: the indirect object without *to* before the direct object.

[Before modeling the first sentence, say: "Listen to *to Jack*."]

[Before modeling the second sentence, say: "Listen to *Jack*."]

[Continue to call attention to the indirect object in each sentence before modeling the sentence.]

Subject	Verb	Indirect Object	Direct Object
I	give	Jack	a book.
Jack	sends	Ann	a letter.

You may print the above examples on the blackboard (without the headings). Say the sentences, and have the student repeat them after you.

DRILL: Expansion Drill

Teacher says the indirect object and the sentence. Student expands the sentence by adding the indirect object without *to*.

Teacher	Student
Jack Ann gives a gift. Ann gives Jack a gift.	Ann gives Jack a gift.
Ann Bob sends a letter.	
the student Mrs. Smith teaches English.	
the boy The man sold a pen.	
him Jill reads the book.	
her friends Ann is showing the pictures.	
me The teacher is handing the book.	
the boys and girls The teacher is showing the book.	

STRUCTURE FOCUS: Verb + Object + Verb

Dan	watched	Jack	kiss	Ann.
I	heard	the boy	yell	"Help!"
I	saw	the man	run	to the boy.
He	helped	the boy	pick up	his bicycle.

Teacher models the sentences several times, having the student repeat.

[Say: "Listen to *watched Jack kiss*."]

Note: The verbs *watch, see, hear, help,* and *let* may be followed by an object and an infinitive without *to*, as: *I heard the boy yell.*

This structure was introduced in Lesson 10 with the verb *help* only. Here, it is expanded to include other verbs.

Notice how this structure differs from verbs like *want* that take an infinitive with *to*, as: *I want him to go.*

DRILL: Combining Sentences

Teacher gives two statements which the student combines into one.

Teacher	Student
Jack kissed Ann. Dan watched Jack. Dan watched Jack kiss Ann.	Dan watched Jack kiss Ann.
The boy yelled "Help!" I heard the boy.	
The man ran to the boy. I saw the man.	
Kitty fixed her car. Ann watched Kitty.	
Bob does his homework. Dad helps Bob.	
The doctor smiled at Molly. I saw the doctor.	
Molly will get well. The doctor will help Molly.	
The man drives the car. Dan watches the man.	
Jill thanked Mrs. Smith Mom heard Jill.	

VOCABULARY and STRUCTURE FOCUS: The Use of the Verb *let*

Dan wants some candy.	Mom lets Dan have two pieces of candy.
Will wants to drive the car.	Dad doesn't let Will drive the car at night.

Teacher models each pair of sentences several times, having the student repeat only the sentences with *let.*

[Say: "Listen to *lets Dan have*."]

The meaning of the new verb *let* should be clear from the context of the sentence pairs.

Note: The verb *let* is followed by an object and an infinitive without *to*. This is the same structure as in the preceding Structure Focus.

DRILL: Combining Sentences

1. Teacher gives the beginning of a sentence with *let* and a complete sentence. The student combines them into one statement, using *let*.

   Be sure that the student uses the correct pronoun form (*me, us* rather than *I, we*) in the last four items.

Teacher	Student
Mom lets Dan... Dan has two pieces of candy.	
Mom lets Dan have two pieces of candy.	Mom lets Dan have two pieces of candy.
Mother lets the boy... The boy eats two sandwiches.	
Mother lets Jill... Jill has another cookie.	
Mom and Dad let Ann... Ann goes to the party.	
The Hills let their children... Their children go to the movies.	
My brother lets me... I wear his coat.	
My sister lets me... I play with her baby.	
Our neighbor lets us... We drive his truck.	
Our neighbor lets us... We park in his driveway.	

2. Teacher gives the beginning of a sentence with *doesn't/don't let* and a complete sentence. The student combines them into one statement.

Teacher	Student
Mom doesn't let Dan... Dan drinks beer.	
Mom doesn't let Dan drink beer.	Mom doesn't let Dan drink beer.
Mom doesn't let the children... The children play ball in the house.	
Mr. Hunt doesn't let his son... His son drives the car.	
Mrs. Roberts doesn't let Molly... Molly plays with matches.	
Mr. and Mrs. Smith don't let their children... Their children watch TV.	

II. Reading

Before beginning the reading, check the student's homework from Lesson 13. Have him read both pages, 68 and 69, aloud.

Before giving your student his copy of *City Living,* number the stories in it. This will make it easier for him to understand when you refer to "the first story," "the second story," and so on.

GENERAL INSTRUCTIONS: Reading *City Living*

The purpose of the correlated reader *City Living* is to give the student an opportunity to read independently and to increase his reading speed. Accordingly, your teaching methods will focus more on continuous reading than the methods you used for the stories in *Skill Book 2.* The emphasis will be on silent reading rather than on reading aloud.

For most students

If your student has been reading the stories in *Skill Book 2* fairly well, follow the steps below to teach each of the stories in *City Living.*

Step 1: Have the student locate the beginning and the end of the story.

"Where does the (first) story start?"
"Where does the (first) story end?"

Step 2: Help the student read all of the new words in the story. (The new words are listed at the top of the page where they first appear.)

Step 3: Have the student read the story title aloud.

"Read the title of the story."

Step 4: Ask one or two guided reading comprehension questions. These serve to focus the student's attention on the main points in the story.

"What will Jack do in the city? What will Jack and Ann do?
Read the story to find out."

Step 5: Have the student read the story silently.

Step 6: Ask the student the comprehension questions given in this manual.

These questions are mostly about main points in the story. Most are literal questions, but a few are interpretive. The student should be able to answer most of these questions without looking back at the story. But, if he does need to look back, please allow him to do so.

Step 7: In *Skill Book 2,* turn to the comprehension questions for that story. Have the student read each question aloud and answer it.

These questions are about both main ideas and details in the story. *Do* allow the student to look back in the story for the answers, particularly for the details. You don't want to give the student the impression that reading must be a hunting expedition for details that he will be questioned about later.

Note: Allow the student to give short answers to comprehension questions whenever appropriate. His answers—long or short—do not have to be worded exactly like sentences in the story or like answers suggested in this manual so long as the meaning and form of his answers are correct.

Try to avoid correcting the student's pronunciation when he is expressing a thought.

For very slow students

If your student has been having a great deal of difficulty in reading the stories in *Skill Book 2,* follow the procedure outlined above, with these changes:

Step 4: End by saying: "Let's read the story to find out."

Step 5: First, *you* read the story aloud to the student. Have him follow along in his book. Be sure that he does not lose his place. You may want to have the student read aloud along with you.

Then, have the student read the story again silently.

STORY 1: Jack Black Comes to the City

Give the student his book, and point to the title on the cover.

	Teacher	Student
Introduce book	You are going to read a new book. The title of this book is *City Living.* The title is the name of the book. What's the title of this book?	 *City Living.*
	This book is about a young man and a young woman. There are seven stories in this book. Let's look at the first story.	
1. Locate story	[Open the book to p. 5.] Where does the first story start? It starts on page 5. Please repeat.	 It starts on page 5.
	[Slowly turn to end of story on p. 8.] Where does the first story end? It ends on page 8. Please repeat.	 It ends on page 8.
2. New words	[Help the student read the new words.]	
	Page 5: *coming* Page 6: *other, watching, dad* Page 8: *kiss, kisses, watches, kissing, laughing*	
3. Title	[Turn back to p. 5, and point to story title.] Please read the title of the first story.	 Jack Black Comes to the City.
4. Guided reading	[Ask these questions to guide the student's reading.]	
	What will Jack do in the city? What will Jack and Ann do? Read the story to find out.	
5. Silent reading	[Let the student read the story silently.]	
6. Comprehension	[Ask these comprehension questions.]	
	Who comes to the city? Will Jack live in the city? Who does Jack visit? Do the Smiths like Jack? What does Jack give Ann Smith? What will Jack and Ann do? Are Jack and Ann happy? Are the Smiths happy that Ann will marry Jack?	Jack (Black) does. Yes, he will. The Smiths. Yes, they do. A ring. They will marry. Yes, they are. Yes, they are.
7. Skill book	[Turn to the Study Helps in *Skill Book 2.*]	

STUDY HELPS: Page 70, *Skill Book 2*

Turn to the first set of 10 questions on page 70 of *Skill Book 2.*

Tell the student the new word *who* at the top of the page, and have him repeat it after you. (The new word *color* goes with the second set of questions. You may ignore it for now.)

Have the student read each question aloud and answer it. Let him look in the story for the answers if he needs to. If he cannot answer a question at all, help him find the place in the story where he can find the answer.

Story 2: At the Dress Shop

OBJECTIVES

When the student completes this unit, he should be able to:

1. Say prices like $2.25 and $2.50 and recognize these prices when expressed in other ways, as: *two and a half dollars, two fifty.*
2. Use the verbs *zip up, button, tie* and the nouns *zipper, buttons,* and *shoelaces.*
3. Use the preposition *without.*
4. Use the words *together* and *alone.*
5. Use some new adjectives: *slim, pink, right, wrong, long.*
6. Use the verbs *fit, match, ask, answer.*
7. Use the verb *look* + adjectives.
8. Use the verb *ask* + object + infinitive.
9. Use the passive voice in the present tense.
10. Read the new words *dress, dresses, marked, twenty, hats, six, asks, fit, but, slim, pink, matches, color, circle, or.*
11. Read independently the second story in *City Living,* understanding the main ideas and being able to locate details.
12. Read verbs and nouns ending in *-es* and write this ending on verbs and nouns ending with *-s, -x, -sh, -ch.*
13. Write the new story words from Stories 1-2 of *City Living.*

VISUAL AIDS

1. *ESOL Illustrations 2,* pp. 4-5.
2. Make a simple price tag, and mark it $30.00.
3. Bring to class the following items that you can use to demonstrate fastening clothing.
   a. A zipper, or something with a zipper.
   b. Something that can be buttoned.
   c. A pair of shoes with laces.
4. Bring to class the following items to demonstrate the verb *fit.*
   a. A box large enough to put a pencil in but too small for a book.
   b. A ring that is too small for your finger.
5. Bring some pink construction paper to class, or color the sofa pillows pink on p. 50 of *ESOL Illustrations 2.*
6. Prepare the worksheet on adding *-es* to verbs and nouns, described in this lesson.

I. Conversation Skills

VOCABULARY: Prices

Write	Model:
$2.25	Two dollars and a quarter Two twenty-five Two dollars and twenty-five cents
$2.50	Two dollars and a half Two and a half dollars Two fifty Two dollars and fifty cents
$2.75	Two seventy-five Two dollars and seventy-five cents

Teacher writes $2.25 on the board, and models the three ways to say this price. The student repeats only the last one: *two dollars and twenty-five cents.*

Teacher continues in the same way with $2.50 and $2.75, having the student repeat only the last item in each set.

Note: In this exercise, the student learns to *recognize* prices expressed in the different ways he will hear in his daily life. But he does not need to learn to *say* prices all these ways himself; it is enough for him to learn to say prices in one way at this point: _____ *dollars and* _____ *cents.*

DRILL: Recognizing and Saying Prices

1. Teacher writes four prices on the board: $6.25, $6.50, $6.75, and $6.95

   Say these prices in random order, expressing them in different ways.

   The student points to the price you are saying.

Teacher	Student
Six dollars and a half	[Points to $6.50.]
Six twenty-five	[Points to $6.25.]
Six dollars and seventy-five cents	[Points to $6.75.]
Six ninety-five	[Points to $6.95.]
[Continue in the same way.]	

2. Teacher writes a price on the board, and the student tells what it is.

   The student may express all the prices the same way: ______ *dollars and* _____ *cents.*

Teacher	Student
[Write $2.50.]	
Two dollars and fifty cents	Two dollars and fifty cents
[Write $3.50.]	
[Write $7.50.]	
[Write $10.50.]	
[Write $2.25.]	
Two dollars and twenty-five cents	Two dollars and twenty-five cents
[Write $3.75.]	
[Write $4.35.]	
[Write $2.65.]	
[Write $9.25.]	

VOCABULARY: Fastening Clothing

> This is a zipper.
> These are buttons.
> These are shoelaces.
>
> Help Bobby zip up his jacket.
> Help Bobby button his coat.
> Help Bobby tie his shoelaces.

1. Teacher models the sentences in the first set, having the student repeat. [Say: "Listen to *zipper*."]

   Use pictures on pp. 4-5 of *ESOL Illustrations 2* or the aids you have brought in to show the meaning of the nouns. (*Zipper* is a review item.)

2. Teacher models the sentences in the second set, having the student repeat. [Say: "Listen to *zip up*."]

   Demonstrate the meaning of the new verbs.

DRILL: Question and Answer Drill

Teacher, pointing to the appropriate picture on pp. 4-5 of *ESOL Illustrations 2,* asks a question to which the student responds with the correct identification.

Teacher	Student
[Point to the appropriate picture.]	
What did you help Bobby do?	I helped Bobby zip up his jacket.
	I helped Bobby button his coat.
	I helped Bobby tie his shoelaces.
What's this?	It's a zipper.
What are these?	They're buttons.
What are these?	They're shoelaces.

VOCABULARY: *without*

My wife doesn't go to class with me.	I go to class without my wife.
My children don't go to work with me.	I go to work without my children.

Teacher models each pair of sentences several times, having the student repeat only the sentence with *without*.

[Say: "Listen to *without*."]

DRILL: Producing Statements

Teacher gives the beginning of a sentence and indicates a potential companion. Student combines the two in a sentence, using *without*.

Teacher	**Student**
I go to class...	
my wife	
I go to class without my wife.	I go to class without my wife.
I go to work...	
my children	
I never go to the movies...	
my husband	
We usually go for a walk...	
the children	
I don't want to go to the concert...	
you	
I don't want to go to the party...	
you	

VOCABULARY: *together* and *alone*

I go to school	with my brother.	We go to school	<u>together</u>.
I go shopping	with my wife.	We go shopping	<u>together</u>.
I go downtown	without my friend.	I go downtown	<u>alone</u>.
I go to work	without my sister.	I go to work	<u>alone</u>.

Teacher models each pair of sentences several times, having the student repeat only the sentences with *together* and *alone.*

[Say: "Listen to *together*," and model the sentences.]

[Continue in the same way with *alone*.]

DRILL: Statement and Rejoinder (Question)

Teacher makes a statement to which the student replies with *Oh* and a question containing *together* or *alone.*

Teacher	Student
I go shopping without my husband.	
Oh, do you always go alone?	Oh, do you always go alone?
I go to school with my brother.	Oh, do you always go together?
I go to the library without my friend.	
I go fishing with my friend.	
I go to the farm without my father.	
I go camping with my brother and sister.	
I cook without my mother.	
I watch TV with my girl friend (boy friend).	

VOCABULARY: Adjectives

She isn't fat.	She's slim.
This isn't red.	It's pink.
This isn't right.	It's wrong.
This skirt isn't short.	It's long.

Teacher models the pairs of sentences several times, having the student repeat both.

The new adjectives are those underlined. Show *pink* with construction paper or with the sofa pillows colored pink on p. 50 of *ESOL Illustrations 2.* To explain *right* and *wrong,* do some simple arithmetic.

[Say: "Listen to *fat* and *slim*," and model the sentences.]

[Continue in the same way with the remaining adjectives, explaining *pink* by showing the color.]

[Explain *right* and *wrong* by adding numbers correctly and incorrectly on the board, as below.

Write: 2 + 2 = 4 Say: "This is right."
Write: 2 + 2 = 5 Say: "This isn't right. It's wrong."]

DRILL: Statement and Rejoinder

1. Teacher makes a statement containing an adjective. Student replies using a different adjective.

Teacher	Student
She isn't fat.	
She's slim.	She's slim.
This isn't red.	
This skirt isn't short.	
Mr. Hunt isn't fat.	
Those curtains aren't red.	
These pants aren't short.	

2. Teacher gives a simple addition fact. Student tells whether it is right or wrong.

   Note: The singular verb *is* is common in mathematical formulas like the ones here. If it bothers you, however, you may substitute *are*.

Teacher	Student
One and one is two.	
That's right.	That's right.
Two and two is four.	
Two and two is five.	
Four and two is nine.	
Three and three is six.	

VOCABULARY: The Verb *fit*

The pencil is small.	It fits in the box.
The book is too big.	It doesn't fit in the box.

Teacher models the sentences several times, having the student repeat.

Demonstrate the meaning of *fit* by putting the pencil in the box you have brought and by trying unsuccessfully to put the book in the box.

[Say: "Listen to *fit*," as you put the pencil in the box. "The pencil is small. It fits in the box. Please repeat."]

[Teach the negative in the same way.]

DRILL: Statement and Rejoinder

Teacher makes a statement to which the student replies with another statement, using *fit* or *doesn't/don't fit.*

Teacher	Student
These shoes are too small. They don't fit me.	They don't fit me.
These pants are too long.	
This jacket is too large.	
This ring is too small.	
This sweater is too large.	
This belt is too short.	
These shoes are not too small. They fit me.	They fit me.
These shoes are not too big.	
This sweater is not too small.	
This ring is not too small.	
This belt is not too short.	
These pants are not too long.	

VOCABULARY: The Verb *match*

The pink blouse matches my pink skirt. They are the same color.
The red blouse doesn't match my yellow skirt. They are not the same color.

Teacher models the sentences several times, having the student repeat.

[Say: "Listen to *matches.*"]

DRILL: Producing Statements

Teacher describes the colors of two articles of clothing. The student tells whether they match or do not match.

Teacher	Student
a pink blouse and a pink skirt They match.	They match.
a red blouse and a yellow skirt They don't match.	They don't match.
a green jacket and orange pants	
a black skirt and a white blouse	
a blue jacket and pink pants	
a black shirt and black pants	
a brown dress and a brown sweater	
a light blue shirt and light blue pants	

VOCABULARY: The Verb *look* + Adjectives

The black tie and the pink shirt go together.	They look good together.
The brown shoes match the brown bag.	They look pretty together.
Ann is wearing a black dress.	She looks pretty in it.
John has a new suit.	It looks good on him.

Teacher models the sentences several times, having the student repeat only the sentences with *look(s)*.

Explain to the student that "*bag* sometimes means *purse*." (Up till now, *bag* has been used to mean *suitcase*.)

[Say: "Listen to *look good.*
The black tie and the pink shirt go together.
They look good together. Please repeat.
They look good together."]

[Continue in the same way with the remaining items.]

DRILL: Question and Answer Drill

Teacher asks questions with *How* which elicit answers with *look(s) good* or *look(s) pretty.*

Teacher	Student
How does Ann look in the black dress? She looks pretty.	She looks pretty.
How does a black tie look with a pink shirt? They look good together.	They look good together.
How does Bob look in his jeans?	He looks good.
How does Sue look in her pink dress?	
How does a yellow sweater look with yellow pants?	
How does a brown jacket look with brown pants?	
How does Ann look in her green blouse and green skirt?	
How does Dan look in his new shirt and pants?	

VOCABULARY: The Verbs *ask* and *answer*

Mary asked John, "Are you going home?" John answered, "Yes, I am." She asked her mother, "Is it time for dinner?" Her mother answered, "Yes, it is."

Teacher models the sentences several times, having the student repeat.

[Say: "Listen to *asked* and *answered*."]

DRILL: Combining Sentences

Teacher gives two sentences which the student combines into one, using *asked* or *answered.*

Teacher	**Student**
Is the door open? Mary asked.	
Mary asked, "Is the door open?"	Mary asked, "Is the door open?"
The door's closed. John answered.	
Are you going home? Sue asked.	
No, I'm not. Betty answered.	
Did you see that movie? Dan asked.	
Yes, I did. Mary answered.	

STRUCTURE FOCUS: *ask* + Object + Infinitive

Bob, open the door.	I told Bob to open the door.
Bob, will you open the door?	I asked Bob to open the door.
Ann, will you help me?	I asked Ann to help me.

Teacher models the pairs of sentences several times, having the student repeat both.

[Say: "Listen to *asked Bob to open*."]

Note: Like *tell,* the verb *ask* may take an object + infinitive.

Notice the polite requests, expressed in question form with *will.*

DRILL: Making Requests and Answering Questions

Teacher tells the student to ask someone to do something. The student makes the request in question form, using *will.*

Teacher then inquires about what the student asked. The student answers, using *ask* + object + infinitive.

Be sure that the student changes the pronoun *you* to *me* in the last three items.

Teacher	Student
Ask Bob to open the door. Bob, will you open the door?	Bob, will you open the door?
What did you ask Bob? I asked Bob to open the door.	I asked Bob to open the door.
Ask Tom to close the door.	Tom, will you close the door?
What did you ask Tom?	I asked Tom to close the door.
Ask Sue to make dinner. What did you ask Sue?	
Ask Jack to go to the store. What did you ask Jack?	
Ask Betty to answer the telephone. What did you ask Betty?	
Ask Kitty to help you. What did you ask Kitty?	
Ask John to go with you. What did you ask John?	
Ask Tom to hand you the book. What did you ask Tom?	

STRUCTURE FOCUS: The Use of *but*

I like Ann. I don't like her sister.	I like Ann, <u>but</u> I don't like her sister.
Ed closed the door. He didn't close the window.	Ed closed the door, <u>but</u> he didn't close the window.
Kitty likes that dress. It doesn't fit her.	Kitty likes that dress, <u>but</u> it doesn't fit her.

Teacher models each set of three sentences several times, having the student repeat only the sentences with *but.*

Note: In this pattern, *but* is used to combine an affirmative and a negative statement.

[Say: "Listen to *but.*"]

DRILL: Combining Sentences

Teacher makes two statements—one affirmative and one negative.

The student combines them into one statement, using *but.*

Teacher	**Student**
I like dogs. I don't like cats. I like dogs, but I don't like cats.	I like dogs, but I don't like cats.
I have a fork. I don't have a knife.	
He can speak English. He can't speak Spanish.	
I like that shirt. It doesn't fit me.	
I need to send this letter. I don't have a stamp.	
Kim wants a cookie. Mother won't let her have one.	
She wants to buy a car. She doesn't have enough money.	
I want to go to the party. I don't feel well.	
Jill made dinner. She didn't do the dishes.	
Bob works quickly. He isn't very careful.	

STRUCTURE FOCUS: Passive Voice (Present Tense)

The nurse	helps	the girl.	
The girl	is helped.		
He	marks	the dress	30 dollars.
The dress	is marked		30 dollars.

Teacher models the active and passive voice of the sentences, having the student repeat both.

[Say: "Listen to *helps, is helped.*"]

The verb *mark* is new. Explain it by showing the price tag you have prepared in advance.

[Show the price tag you have made to explain *marks* and *is marked.*]

Note: The passive voice is formed with *be* + the past participle. It was first introduced in Lesson 11.

It may help the student to see the first pair of sentences written out on the board as an example.

DRILL: Transformation Drill

The teacher gives a statement in the active voice. The student changes it to a statement in the passive voice.

Teacher	Student
He marks the dress 30 dollars.	
The dress is marked 30 dollars.	The dress is marked 30 dollars.
He marks the suit 75 dollars.	
The nurse helps the girl.	
The boss helps the worker.	
She cooks the meat.	
He closes the door.	
He closes the window.	
He needs the money.	

II. Reading

STORY 2: At the Dress Shop

Teach the second story (pp. 9-12 in *City Living*), following the steps outlined for Story 1.

New words

Page 9: *dress, dresses, marked, twenty, hats, six*
Page 10: *asks*
Page 11: *fit, but*
Page 12: *slim, pink, matches*

Guided reading

"Who works at the dress shop? What does Kitty buy at the dress shop? Read the story to find out."

Comprehension

Teacher	Student
Who works at the dress shop?	Ann (Smith) does.
Who is shopping at the dress shop?	Kitty (King) is.
What does Kitty buy?	A dress, a hat, and a bag (a purse).
Does Kitty buy the first dress she puts on?	No, she doesn't.
Do you think Kitty is slim or fat?	She's slim.
Do you think Ann Smith is a good worker?	Yes, she is. *or* Yes, I do.

STUDY HELPS: Page 70, *Skill Book 2*

Turn to the second set of 10 questions on page 70 of *Skill Book 2.* Help the student read the new word *color* at the top of the page.

Have the student read each question aloud and answer it. Let him look in the story for the answers if he needs to. If he cannot answer a question at all, help him find the place in the story where he can find the answer.

CHECKUP: Page 71, *Skill Book 2*

This Checkup covers Stories 1-2 in *City Living.*

Have the student read the first new word, *circle.* Tell him the other new word, *or,* and have him repeat it after you.

Have the student read the instructions *Circle yes or no.* Then have him read the sample question, *Is Jack coming to the city?* Say: "Yes or no?" When he answers yes, say: "Circle *Yes,*" and trace the circle with your finger. Then let him complete this section by himself.

Have the student read the instructions at the bottom, *Fill in the words,* and complete this section. When he has finished, check his work on this page and help him find the answers in the stories if he missed any items.

Finally, have the student read the entire page aloud, giving the correct Yes or No answer to each question at the top.

SKILLS PRACTICE: Adding *-es* to Verbs and Nouns

Before class, prepare the following worksheet for the student to do at this time.

---s + es	--x + es	--sh + es	---ch + es
kiss kisses	fix fixes	dish dishes	watch watches
dress dresses	box boxes	fish fishes	match matches
glass glasses			

kiss	1. Jack _______ Ann.
dress	2. Kitty has two red _______.
glass	3. Mr. Smith puts on his _________.
fix	4. Jimmy _______ his car.
box	5. Mr. Arthur puts the apples in big _________.
dish	6. Bob dropped two _________.
fish	7. Mr. Hill ________ in the river.
watch	8. Mr. Hill ________ TV after dinner.
match	9. That red hat ________ Kitty's red dress.

Step 1: Say: "*Kiss* ends with the letter *s.* We add *e, s* to make *kisses.*"

Continue in the same way with the first example in each column: *fix/fixes, dish/dishes,* and *watch/watches.*

Step 2: Have the student read aloud all the words in each column.

Step 3: In the nine sentences, have the student add *-es* to the word at the left and write it in the blank. Then have him read aloud the completed sentence.

Note: Verbs and nouns ending in *z* also take *-es*, but the student has not learned any such words yet.

III. Writing

WRITING LESSON: Page 72

Study

Help your student study, and then write, these words.

1. watch
2. other
3. marked
4. twenty

Listen and write

Dictate the following words and sentences for the student to write.

1. dad
2. kiss
3. dress
4. hat
5. asks
6. fit
7. slim
8. pink

1. The dress is marked twenty dollars.
2. The pink bag matches the hat.

WRITING LESSON: Page 73

Be sure that your student understands all the instructions on page 73. Then ask him to do the writing exercises. When he has finished, check his work carefully. Then ask him to read all the words (both forms) aloud.

HOMEWORK: Page 74

Ask your student to write this page at home.

MORE READING

In the supplementary reader *More Stories 2,* the stories for Lesson 14 may be read in class or suggested for reading at home.

Lesson 15

CITY LIVING: STORIES 3–5

Story 3: Working in a Factory

OBJECTIVES

When the student completes this unit, he should be able to:
1. Use the verb *lift.*
2. Use the verb *fill* and the adjectives *empty* and *full.*
3. Use three expressions with *be + have-ing*: *having fun, having a good time, having trouble.*
4. Use noun clauses beginning with *what, when,* and *where,* as: *I know when Jack will come.*
5. Use the verbs *hurt, cut,* and *put* in the passive voice (present tense).
6. Use the present perfect tense with *just.*
7. Read the new story words *center, lot, just, boxes, started, lift, into, let, drop, any, having, fun, carry.*
8. Read independently the third story in *City Living,* understanding the main ideas and being able to locate details.

VISUAL AIDS

Bring to class an empty glass and any container of water that you can use to fill the glass with water.

I. Conversation Skills

VOCABULARY: The Verb *lift*

> Dan lifts the heavy boxes.
> He puts them into the truck.
>
> Don lifted Dan's bicycle.
> He put it into the car.

Teacher models the sentences several times, having the student repeat.

[Say: "Listen to *lifts, lifted.*"]

Demonstrate *lift* and *heavy* (also a new word here) by pretending to pick up something heavy.

DRILL: Substitution Drill with Vocal Cues

Teacher models the key sentence and gives the cues.

Teacher	Student
Don lifted the heavy boxes.	Don lifted the heavy boxes.
chair	
tables	
boxes	
bicycle	
child	

VOCABULARY: The Verb *fill* and the Adjectives *empty* and *full*

The glass	is empty.	I fill it with water.	The glass	is full.
The box	is empty.	I fill it with pencils.	The box	is full.

Teacher models the sentences several times, having the student repeat.

Demonstrate the meaning of the new words by showing an empty glass, filling it with water, then showing that the glass is full.

[Say: "Listen to *empty, fill, full.*"
As you say the sentences, demonstrate by showing an empty glass, filling it with water, then showing that the glass is full.]

DRILL: Statement and Rejoinder Drill

Teacher gives a statement with the word *empty.* Student responds with sentences containing the words *fill* and *full.*

Teacher	Student
The glass is empty. water	
He fills it with water. It's full.	He fills it with water. It's full.
The cup is empty. coffee	
The box is empty. pencils	
The glass is empty. milk	
The box is empty. cigarettes	

VOCABULARY and STRUCTURE FOCUS: Expressions with *be + have-ing*

The men are laughing.	They're having fun.
The men and women are dancing.	They're having a good time.
Jimmy's car won't always start.	He's having trouble with his car.

Teacher models the sentences several times, having the student repeat.

[Say: "Listen to *are having*."]

Demonstrate the new word *dancing*.

DRILL: Reply and Rejoinder Drill

1. Teacher asks questions to which the student gives an affirmative answer with *be + having fun* or *having a good time*.

   It doesn't matter much which expression the student uses; either one will make sense in answer to all the questions. But, if the student needs help, prompt him by giving him a cue (*fun* or *good time*).

Teacher	Student
Are the men laughing? Yes, they're having fun.	Yes, they're having fun.
Are Ann and Jack dancing? (good time)	
Is Don laughing? (fun)	
Are the men and women dancing? (good time)	
Are the children playing and laughing? (fun)	
Are your friends laughing and talking? (good time)	

2. Student replies with a negative answer, using *be + having fun* or *having a good time.*

Teacher	Student
Is Ann laughing? No, she isn't having fun.	No, she isn't having fun.
Is Sue dancing?	
Is Betty happy?	
Is Jack laughing and talking?	
Is Jimmy dancing?	
Are the children laughing and playing?	
Are the Smiths dancing?	

3. Student replies with *No* and a statement using *be + having trouble.*

   Notice that the statement is affirmative in form, even though the answer is *No.*

Teacher	Student
Will Jimmy's car start? No, he's having trouble with his car.	No, he's having trouble with his car.
Do Jimmy's brakes always stop his car?	No, he's having trouble with his car.
Do Jimmy's windshield wipers work?	
Do Jimmy's car lights work?	
Does Jimmy's car always start?	

STRUCTURE FOCUS: Noun Clauses with *what, when,* and *where*

You	know	when	Jack will come.
He	finds out	what	Jack will do.
He	knows	where	Jack will go.

Teacher models the sentences several times, having the student repeat.

[Say: "Listen to *when Jack will come.*"]

Note: In the sentences taught here, the noun clause is the object of the verb *know* or *find out.*

DRILL: Question and Answer Drill

Teacher asks a question with a noun clause. For practice, the student must give a long answer. Do not accept short answers like "Yes, I do," or "No, I don't."

Teacher	**Student**
Do you know where Ann is from?	
Yes, I know where Ann is from.	Yes, I know where Ann is from.
Do you know when the library will open?	
Do you know what they are laughing at?	
Do you know what Mary needs?	
Do you know where John is?	
Did you learn where the bus stops?	
Will you find out where Mr. Hill lives?	
Will you find out when the movie starts?	
Can you find out what Ann wants?	
Can you find out where the doctor's office is?	

DRILL: Free Reply Drill

Teacher asks a question with a noun clause. The student replies, giving the information sought in the question.

Model the first answer to indicate the form of reply that you expect here. After that, prompt the student only if he cannot think of an answer.

Teacher	Student
Do you know where Ann is from?	
Yes, she's from Italy.	Yes, she's from Italy.
Do you know where Sam is from?	
Do you know where John is?	
Do you know when the library opens?	
Do you know when the supermarket closes?	
Do you know what time it is?	
Do you know what time the movie starts?	
Did you find out what Ann wants?	
Did you find out what Mary needs?	
Did you find out where Mr. Hill lives?	

STRUCTURE FOCUS: Passive Voice (Present Tense)

Dan		hurts	his hand.	
Dan's hand	is	hurt.		
Bob		cuts	his finger.	
Bob's finger	is	cut.		
Jack		puts	the boxes	on the truck.
The boxes	are	put		on the truck.

Teacher models the active and passive voice of the sentences, having the student repeat both.

[Say: "Listen to *hurts, is hurt*."]

Note: The verbs *hurt, cut,* and *put* have a past participle that is the same as the simple form of the verb.

DRILL: Transformation Drill

Teacher gives a statement in the active voice. The student changes it to a statement in the passive voice.

Teacher	Student
Dan hurts his hand.	
Dan's hand is hurt.	Dan's hand is hurt.
Bob hurts his leg.	
Bob cuts his finger.	
Ann cuts her foot.	
Jack puts the boxes on the truck.	
Sue puts the cups in the sink.	
Mary puts the bags in the car.	

STRUCTURE FOCUS: The Present Perfect Tense with *just*

I	have	just	opened	the door.
He	has	just	closed	the door.

Teacher models the sentences several times, having the student repeat.

To demonstrate the meaning, open the door, sit down, and then say the sentence.

[Open the door, and then sit down. Say: "I have just opened the door."]

Note: The present perfect tense is introduced here only in a preliminary manner sufficient for the student to read this chapter.

The present perfect tense is formed with *have/has* + the past participle. It is presented here only with regular verbs. The present perfect tense is used to describe an event in the past which is closely related to the present time. The word *just* helps to indicate the time element.

The word *just* occurs between the auxiliary (*have/has*) and the main verb.

STRUCTURE FOCUS: Full and Contracted Forms of the Present Perfect Tense

I	have	just	opened	the door.	I've	just	opened	the door.
We	have	just	started	dinner.	We've	just	started	dinner.
You	have	just	picked up	the book.	You've	just	picked up	the book.
They	have	just	closed	the door.	They've	just	closed	the door.
He	has	just	started	dinner.	He's	just	started	dinner.
She	has	just	started	her job.	She's	just	started	her job.

Teacher models the sentences several times, having the student repeat. Practice the contracted form more often than the full form.

[Say: "Listen to *I have, I've*."]

DRILL: Substitution Drill with Vocal Cues

Teacher gives the key sentence and the cues.

Teacher	Student
I've just closed the door.	I've just closed the door.
He	
They	
She	
We	
You	
I	
I've just opened the window.	I've just opened the window.
We	
You	
They	
She	
He	
I	

II. Reading

Check your student's homework from Lesson 14. Then ask him to read aloud all of the words on the page (both forms).

STORY 3: Working in a Factory

Teach the third story (pp. 13-16 of *City Living*), following the steps outlined in Lesson 14 for Story 1.

New words

Page 14: *center, lot, just, boxes, started*
Page 15: *lift, into, let, drop*
Page 16: *any, having, fun, carry*

Guided reading

"What is Jack's job at the factory? Does Jack like his job?
Read the story to find out."

Comprehension

Teacher	Student
Where does Jack work?	He works at (in) a (glass) factory.
Does Jack drive to work?	Yes, he does.
What is Jack's job at the factory?	He puts glass in boxes. *or* He fills boxes with glass. His job is to put glass in boxes. His job is to fill boxes with glass.
Who does Jack work with?	He works with Jimmy.
Are Jack and Jimmy friends?	Yes, they are.
Do they have fun with the other workers at lunch?	Yes, they do.
Does Jack like his job at the factory?	Yes, he does.

STUDY HELPS: Page 75, *Skill Book 2*

Turn to the first set of questions on page 75 of *Skill Book 2.* (Ignore the new word, *which*; it goes with the second set of questions.)

Have the student read each question aloud and answer it. Let him look in the story for the answers if he needs to. If he cannot answer a question at all, help him find the place in the story where he can find the answer.

Story 4: City Traffic

OBJECTIVES

When the student completes this unit, he should be able to:

1. Use the nouns *ride* and *lift,* as in *I'll give you a ride (lift).*
2. Use the word *traffic* and apply the adjectives *heavy* and *light* to *traffic.*
3. Use *where* clauses with *ask,* as: *Let's ask him where the bank is.*
4. Give and understand some directions for getting around in a city.
5. Use *told* + object + information words + infinitive, as: *I told him where to go.*
6. Use the modal *must* in affirmative statements, as: *I must stop.*
7. Read the new story words *traffic, dead, battery, fast, turn, pass, passes, must, when, cop, stopping, thinking, which.*
8. Read independently the fourth story in *City Living,* understanding the main ideas and being able to locate details.

VISUAL AIDS

1. *ESOL Illustrations 2,* pp. 62-63.
2. Bring to class any small object that you can use as a "car" to trace the route on the map on p. 63 of *ESOL Illustrations 2.*

I. Conversation Skills

VOCABULARY: Giving Someone a Ride (a Lift)

Jack opens his car door.
Jimmy gets in the car.
Jack takes Jimmy to the repair shop.

Jack gives Jimmy a <u>lift</u> to the shop.
Jimmy says, "Thanks for the <u>ride</u>, Jack."

Teacher models the sentences several times, having the student repeat only the last two.

The verb *take* is new in the way it is used here. It was introduced before in *take medicine.*

[Say: "Listen," and use a Stop gesture.
Model the first three sentences. Pause
Say: "Listen to *lift.*
Jack gives Jimmy a lift to the shop. Please repeat."
Student repeats. Say: "Listen to *ride.*
Jimmy says, 'Thanks for the ride, Jack.' Please repeat."]

DRILL: Statement and Rejoinder

Teacher makes a statement. Student replies with another statement, using *a lift* or *a ride.*

Prompt the student only as long as it is necessary.

Teacher	Student
I need to go home.	
I'll give you a ride.	I'll give you a ride.
Mary wants to go to the library.	I'll give her a lift.
Jim needs to go to the repair shop.	
Mom needs to go to the supermarket.	
Dad wants to go to the library.	

VOCABULARY: *traffic* (*heavy* and *light*)

There are cars and trucks on the street.	
There is traffic on the street.	
There's a lot of traffic.	Traffic is heavy.
There's a little traffic.	Traffic is light.

Teacher models the sentences, having the student repeat.

Use p. 62 of *ESOL Illustrations 2* to illustrate heavy traffic.

[Say: "Listen to *traffic*."]

[Continue in the same way with *heavy* and *light*.]

DRILL: Statement and Rejoinder Drill

Teacher makes a statement to which the student responds with a sentence containing *heavy* or *light*.

Teacher	Student
There's a lot of traffic.	
Yes, traffic is heavy.	Yes, traffic is heavy.
There's a little traffic.	
There was a lot of traffic.	
There was a little traffic.	
There will be a lot of traffic.	
There will be a little traffic.	

VOCABULARY: Asking for Directions

Where's the bank?	There's a traffic cop.	Let's ask him where the bank is.
Where's First Street?	There's a traffic cop.	Let's ask him where First Street is.

Teacher models each set of three sentences, having the student repeat.

Use p. 62 of *ESOL Illustrations 2* to explain *traffic cop.*

Note: Notice the word order in the *where* clause in *Let's ask him where the bank is.* Be sure the student does *not* use the question word order, *where is the bank.*

[Say: "Listen." Model the entire set of three sentences, having the student repeat after you.]

DRILL: Asking for Directions

Teacher asks a question and gives as a cue the person that is to be asked for the information.

Teacher	Student
Where's the bank? traffic cop	
There's a traffic cop. Let's ask him where the bank is.	There's a traffic cop. Let's ask him where the bank is.
Where's First Street? traffic cop	There's a traffic cop. Let's ask him where First Street is.
Where's the doctor? nurse	
Where's Jack? Ann	
Where's Main Street? traffic cop	
Where's Dan? his mother	
Where are the English books? the teacher	

VOCABULARY: Giving Directions

Where's the bank?	Drive straight ahead one block. Turn left at the corner. Turn right at the next corner. Drive straight ahead two blocks. Then turn right at the traffic light. The bank is on the next corner.

Teacher models the sentences several times, having the student repeat only the directions.

Using the simple map on p. 63 of *ESOL Illustrations 2* and a small marker as a "car," trace the route as you say the sentences.

If it will help your student keep track of right and left on the map, keep turning the map so that the student is always facing the direction the "car" is moving.

[Begin by asking, "Where's the bank?"]

[Then say: "Listen. Drive straight ahead one block."
Move your marker ahead one block along the dotted line on the map. "Please repeat.
Drive straight ahead one block."]

[Continue in the same way with the remaining sentences.]

DRILL: Giving and Following Directions

1. Teacher gives the student a small marker to use as a "car" and gives him the directions in the box.

   The student moves the marker on the map on p. 63 of *ESOL Illustrations 2,* as directed.

Teacher	**Student**
Drive straight ahead one block.	[Moves marker.]
Turn left at the corner.	
Turn right at the next corner.	
Drive straight ahead two blocks.	
Turn right at the traffic light.	

2. Teacher gives the marker to the student and directs him to take the route marked on the map. Teacher asks the student to describe what he is doing.

Teacher	**Student**
[Place the marker in the starting position.]	
How do you drive from here to the bank?	I drive straight ahead one block. (And so on.)

STRUCTURE FOCUS: *told* + Object + Information Words + Infinitive

Jim, turn left now.	I	told	Jim	when	to turn.
Jim, turn left at the next corner.	I	told	Jim	where	to turn.
Sue, buy a half-gallon of milk.	I	told	Sue	how much milk	to buy.
Sue, buy three apples.	I	told	Sue	how many apples	to buy.

Teacher models the pairs of sentences several times, having the student repeat only the sentences with *told.*

[Say: "Listen to *when to turn.* Jim, turn left now.
I told Jim when to turn." Pause.
"I told Jim when to turn. Please repeat."]

DRILL: Transformation Drill

Student changes a direct command into a sentence with *told*, an information word, and an infinitive.

Prompt the student with the correct information word to use if necessary.

Teacher	Student
Jim, turn left now. I told Jim when to turn.	I told Jim when to turn.
Jim, turn left at the next corner. (where)	
Sue, buy a half-gallon of milk. (how much)	
Sue, buy three apples. (how many)	
Tom, give me the book. (what)	
Dan, go to the supermarket. (where)	
Kitty, come at six o'clock. (when)	
Jim, turn left at First Street. (where)	

STRUCTURE FOCUS: The Modal *must* in Affirmative Statements

A car	must	stop	at a red light.
We	must	eat	every day.
We	must	sleep	every night.

Teacher models the sentences several times, having the student repeat.

[Say: "Listen to *must*."]

Note: The modal *must* is followed by the simple form of the verb. It is used to indicate strong obligation.

DRILL: Substitution Drill with Vocal Cues

Teacher gives the key sentence and the cues.

Teacher	Student
I must stop at a red light. You She We He They	I must stop at a red light.
You must eat every day. sleep drink water study English have breakfast read English write English	You must eat every day.

II. Reading

STORY 4: City Traffic

Teach the fourth story (pp. 17-20 of *City Living*), following the steps outlined in Lesson 14 for Story 1.

New Words

Page 17: *traffic, dead, battery*
Page 18: *fast, turn*
Page 19: *pass, passes*
Page 20: *must, when, cop, stopping, thinking*

Guided reading

"What's wrong with Jimmy's car? How does Jack help Jimmy? Read the story to find out."

Comprehension

Teacher	Student
What's wrong with Jimmy's car?	The battery is dead.
Where does Jack take Jimmy?	He takes Jimmy to the (repair) shop.
Does Jimmy help Jack drive in city traffic?	Yes, he does

STUDY HELPS: Page 75, *Skill Book 2*

Turn to the second set of questions on page 75 of *Skill Book 2.* Help the student read the new word, *which,* at the top of the page.

Have the student read each question aloud and answer it. Let him look in the story for the answers if he needs to. If he cannot answer a question at all, help him find the place in the story where he can find the answer.

Story 5: At the Market

OBJECTIVES

When a student completes this unit, he should be able to:

1. Use *ready* and *get ready* followed by an infinitive or by *for* + a noun.
2. Use the words *person* (review), *thing,* and *animal.*
3. Use the words *list* and *shopping list.*
4. Use *single, married,* and *get married.*
5. Use the verbs *plan* and *give... back.*
6. Recognize times of day expressed with *half past, a quarter after,* and *a quarter to* (the hour).
7. Read the new story words *married, planning, past, list, things, bread, butter, another, shopping.*
8. Read independently the fifth story in *City Living,* understanding the main ideas and being able to locate details.
9. Read and write the plural form of nouns ending in consonant + *y,* changing *y* to *i* and adding *-es,* as: *city, cities.*

VISUAL AIDS

1. Print a list of names. Print clearly: *Kitty, Jimmy, Jack, Ann, Dan,* and your student's name.
2. Print a list of things: *bell, brick, truck, letter, bed, bag, doll,* and *clock.*
3. Print a shopping list: *ducks, eggs, olives, apples,* and *matches.*
4. Bring a cardboard clock to class.
5. Prepare the chart and writing exercises described in the Skills Practice.

I. Conversation Skills

VOCABULARY: *ready* and *get ready*

Dinner is on the table.	It's		ready to eat.
Jack is putting on his coat.	He's	getting	ready to go out.
Tom did his homework.	He's		ready for class.
Dan's taking off his clothes.	He's	getting	ready for bed.

Teacher models the pairs of sentences several times, having the student repeat only those with *ready*.

[Say: "Listen to *ready to*."]

Note: The word *ready* can be followed by an infinitive or by *for* + a noun.

DRILL: Statement and Rejoinder

1. Teacher makes a statement; student replies, using the word *ready*.

   Give the student a cue (in parentheses) only if he needs help.

Teacher	Student
Dinner is on the table. It's ready to eat.	It's ready to eat.
Ann has her coat on. (go out)	She's ready to go out.
The duck is cooked. (eat)	It's ready to eat.
Dan washed his hands. (eat)	He's ready to eat.
Sue did her homework. (class)	She's ready for class.
Tom took off his clothes. (bed)	He's ready for bed.
Tom studied his English book. (class)	He's ready for class.

2. Teacher asks a question to which the student replies, using *getting ready.*

   Give the student a cue if he needs help.

Teacher	Student
Why is Tom studying his book? He's getting ready for class.	He's getting ready for class.
Why is Dan taking off his clothes? (bed)	
Why is Jimmy putting on his new suit? (a party)	
Why is Dan washing his hands? (dinner)	
Why is Sue putting on her hat and coat? (church)	
Why is Ann buying cookies and soda? (her party)	
Why is Kitty putting soda and sandwiches in a basket? (a picnic)	

VOCABULARY: *person, animal, thing*

A woman	is a	person.
A cat	is an	animal.
A clock	is a	thing.

Teacher models the sentences several times, having the student repeat.

Note: The word *person* is a review item.

[Say: "Listen to *person*."]

[Continue in the same way with *animal* and *thing*.]

DRILL: Identification Drill

Teacher gives the name of a person, animal, or thing. The student identifies the item in a sentence, using the words *person, animal,* or *thing.*

The student should use the pronoun *it* to refer to an animal.

Teacher	Student
Jack	
He's a person.	He's a person.
Jack and Ann	They're persons.
clock	
cat	
clocks and watches	
Dan	
pens and pencils	
dog	
Mrs. Smith	
students	
cats and dogs	
Betty	
snakes	

VOCABULARY: *a list, a shopping list*

This is a list of names.
Is your name on the list?

This is a list of things.
Is *clock* on the list?

This is a shopping list.
Did you write *eggs* on your shopping list?

Teacher models the sentences several times, having the student repeat.

Show the student the list of names, the list of things, and the shopping list that you have prepared.

[Say: "Listen to *list*," as you show your student the list of names. See if he can pick out his name in the list.]

[Continue in the same way with the next two pairs of sentences, using the lists you have prepared in advance.]

DRILL: Question and Answer Drill

1. Teacher asks questions about the list of names. For practice, the student must give a long answer. Do not accept "Yes, it is," or "No, it isn't."

   Ask only about names that the student can read whether they are on the list or not.

Teacher	Student
[Hold up the list of names.]	
Is Ann's name on the list?	Yes, her name is on the list.
Is Jill's name on the list?	No, her name isn't on the list.
[Continue in the same way.]	

2. Teacher asks questions about the list of things. Use the same procedure as in part 1.

Teacher	Student
Is *bell* on the list?	Yes, *bell* is on the list.
Is *rug* on the list?	No, *rug* isn't on the list.
[Continue in the same way.]	

3. Teacher asks questions about the shopping list.

Teacher	Student
Are *ducks* on the list?	Yes, *ducks* are on the list.
Is *jelly* on the list?	No, *jelly* isn't on the list.
[Continue in the same way.]	

VOCABULARY: *single, married, get married*

Are you married or single?	I'm single.
Are you married or single?	I'm married. I got married last June.

Teacher models each question and answer several times, having the student repeat both.

[Say: "Listen to *married, single*."]

DRILL: Reply and Rejoinder

Teacher asks if various persons are married. Student gives a short *Yes* or *No* answer and adds a statement containing *married* or *single.*

Nod your head to indicate that persons are married; shake your head to indicate that a person is single.

Teacher	Student
Are Ann and Jack married? [Nod.]	
Yes, they are. They got married two months ago.	Yes, they are. They got married two months ago.
Is Jack married? [Shake head.]	
No, he isn't. He's single.	No, he isn't. He's single.
Is Betty married? [Shake head.]	
Are Don and Betty married? [Nod.]	
Is Tom married? [Shake head.]	
Are John and Sue married? [Nod.]	
Am I married? [Shake or nod as appropriate.]	
Are you married?	

VOCABULARY: The Verb *plan*

Ann's going to have a party for her friends.
She makes a list of friends to telephone. She makes a list of things to buy.
Ann's planning the party for her friends.

Teacher models the sentences several times, having the student repeat only the last one with *planning.*

[Say: "Listen to *planning.*"
Model the four sentences, having the student repeat only the one with *planning* more often than you say the others.]

DRILL: Multiple-Slot Substitution Drill with Vocal Cues

Teacher gives the key sentence and the cues.

Teacher	Student
Ann's planning a party for her friends.	Ann's planning a party for her friends.
for her family	
dinner	
for Jack	
a party	
for her mother and father	
a picnic	
for her friends	

VOCABULARY: The Verb *give... back*

I gave you my book yesterday. Please give it back to me.
Jack gave me his pen yesterday. I'll give it back to him today.

Teacher models the sentences several times, having the student repeat.

[Say: "Listen to *give... back.*"]

DRILL: Statement and Rejoinder

Teacher makes a statement; student makes a reply with *give... back.*

Teacher	Student
I gave you my book yesterday. I'll give it back tomorrow.	I'll give it back tomorrow.
a quarter	
my sweater	
a dollar	
my jacket	
a pencil	
my new pen	

VOCABULARY: Other Ways of Expressing Time

Write:	Model:
10:30	It's half past ten. It's ten thirty.
3:45	It's a quarter to four. It's three forty-five.
4:15	It's a quarter after four. It's four fifteen.

Teacher writes 10:30 on the board, and models the two ways to say this time. The student repeats only the last one: *It's ten thirty.*

Teacher continues in the same way with 3:45 and 4:15, having the student repeat only the last item in each set. (The last items in each set are review items.)

Use the clock faces on p. 64 of *ESOL Illustrations 2* that have the quarter- and half-hours shaded in to show the meaning of *half past, quarter to,* and *quarter after.*

Note: In this exercise, the student learns to *recognize* the time expressed in the different ways he will hear in his daily life. But he does not need to learn to *say* the time in all these ways himself; it is enough for him to learn to say the time in one way, the "digital clock" way: *ten thirty, ten fifteen, ten forty-five,* and so on.

This exercise is similar to the one on various ways of expressing prices in Lesson 14.

DRILL: Recognizing and Expressing Time

1. Teacher says time, expressing it with *half past.*

   Using a cardboard clock, the student sets the clock to the time the teacher has said and then says the time in the "digital clock" way.

Teacher	Student
[Set clock at 1:30.] It's half past one.	It's one thirty.
It's half past two.	[Sets clock at 2:30.] It's two thirty.
[Continue around the clock on the half hours.]	

2. Continue in the same way with *quarter after.*

Teacher	Student
[Set clock at 1:15.] It's a quarter after one.	It's one fifteen.
It's a quarter after two.	[Sets clock at 2:15.] It's two fifteen.
[Continue in the same way around the clock.	

3. Continue in the same way with *quarter to.*

   The student may have some difficulty because the hour is said differently in these two ways of expressing the time.

Teacher	Student
[Set the clock at 12:45.] It's a quarter to one.	It's twelve forty-five.
It's a quarter to two.	[Sets clock at 1:45.] It's one forty-five.
[Continue in the same way around the clock.]	

II. Reading

STORY 5: At the Market

Teach the fifth story (pp. 21-23 of *City Living*), following the steps outlined for Story 1 in Lesson 14.

New words

Page 21: *married, planning*
Page 22: *past, list, things, bread, butter, another, shopping*

Guided reading

"What are Ann and Jack planning? What do they do to get ready? Read the story to find out."

Comprehension

Teacher	Student
What are Ann and Jack planning?	They're planning a dinner.
Who will come to the party?	Ann's family and Jack's family.
Does Ann make a shopping list?	Yes, she does.
Do Ann and Jack buy the things on the list?	Yes, they do.

STUDY HELPS: Page 75, *Skill Book 2*

Turn to the third set of questions on page 75 of *Skill Book 2.* Have the student read each question aloud and answer it. Let him look in the story for the answers if he needs to. If he cannot answer a question at all, help him find the place in the story where he can find the answer.

You might want to have the student answer question 4 by writing a list of the persons who will come to Ann and Jack's dinner, using the first paragraph on page 22. Have him count the total. He should count eight persons who are coming. Then point to the following sentence on page 22 and say: "It says, 'Ann and Jack will have dinner for ten persons.' Who are the other two persons?" The student should be able to figure out that they are Ann and Jack (the hosts).

CHECKUP: Page 76, *Skill Book 2*

This Checkup covers Stories 3-5 in *City Living.* The student circles one of three words to complete each sentence.

Have the student read the instructions *Circle one word.* Go over the sample item with him. Then let him complete this part by himself.

Then have the student read the instructions *Fill in the words* at the bottom and complete this section. When he has finished, check his work on this page and help him find the answers in the stories if he missed any items.

Finally, have the student read the entire page aloud, reading the correctly completed sentences.

III. Writing

WRITING LESSON: Page 77

Have the student read the instructions and sample item for each part before he does that part.

The final item on the page is *name* used as a verb. Since the student has not learned *name* as a verb, help him understand the meaning by saying:

> "Mr. and Mrs. Smith are giving their baby a name.
> They are naming the baby."

When the student has finished, check his work carefully and ask him to read aloud all the words on the page—both the roots and the *-ing* forms.

SKILLS PRACTICE: Adding *-es* to Nouns that End in Consonant + *y*

Note: The final *y* is changed to *i* before endings *only* if the word ends in consonant + *y*. It is important that the student learn this principle. Early in *Skill Book 3,* the student will learn words that end in vowel + *y*, as: *day.* The plural of such words is formed merely by adding *-s*.

Before class, prepare the following small chart and the writing exercises in this Skills Practice.

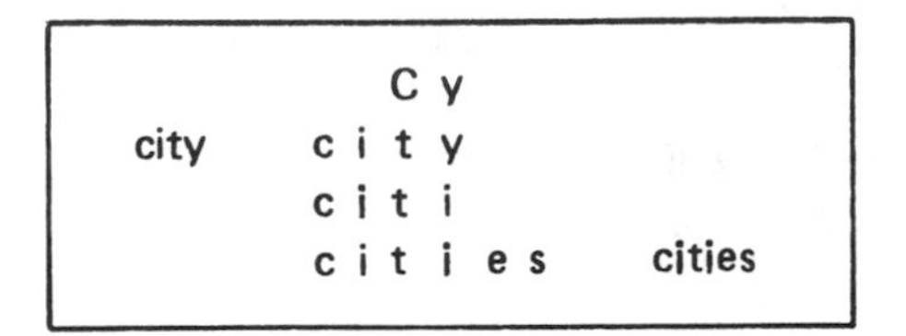

Do this	**Say this:**
Point to *city* at left.	Teacher: Please read. Student: City.
Point to *t* in *city* at center.	Teacher: Is this a consonant or a vowel? Student: It's a consonant.
Point to the label *C* over the *t*.	Teacher: That's right! It's a consonant.
	Teacher: What letter does *city* end with? Student: *y.*
Point to the label *Cy* over *city.*	Teacher: That's right! *City* ends with consonant, *y.*
	Teacher: To write *cities,*
Point to *y* in *city.*	change *y...*
Point to *i* in *citi.*	to *i...*
Point to *es* in *cities.*	and add *e, s.*
Point to *cities* at right.	Teacher: Please read. Student: Cities.

Write the following nouns. Have the student read each noun aloud. Then have him identify the last two letters in each word as "consonant, *y*," and label them *C-y.* Have him say the plural, then write it below the singular.

city	lily	family	factory	battery
________	________	________	________	________

Have the student fill in the blank with the plural form of the noun at the left and then read the completed sentence aloud.

city 1. Big ____________ have a lot of traffic.
lily 2. Mrs. Arthur has some ____________ in her garden.
factory 3. This city has many ____________.
family 4. Jack's family and Ann's family come to dinner.
The two ____________ have fun.
battery 5. That shop sells ____________.

HOMEWORK

Ask your student to do this page at home. Have him do the first item in each part in class to be sure he knows what to do.

MORE READING

In *More Stories 2,* you may use any stories for Lessons 1-14 that the student has not already read. Save the stories marked Lesson 15 until you have completed *City Living,* as they contain new words from the last two stories in *City Living.*

Lesson 16

CITY LIVING: STORIES 6–7

Story 6: The Puppy Got the Duck

OBJECTIVES

When a student completes this unit, he should be able to:
1. Use the noun *park* (*in the park*).
2. Use the verb *leave* and its past tense form *left.*
3. Use time clauses with *when.*
4. Use *but* to combine an affirmative and a negative statement.
5. Make the question *What happened?* and answer it.
6. Read the new story words *puppy, left, went, park, did, faster, laughed.*
7. Read independently the sixth story in *City Living,* understanding the main ideas and being able to locate details.

I. Conversation Skills

VOCABULARY: *in the park*

We went on a picnic	in the park.
Jack and Ann sit and talk	in the park.

Teacher models the sentences several times, having the student repeat.

Use p. 61 of *ESOL Illustrations 2* to explain the meaning of *park.*

[Say: "Listen to *the park.*" Point to the park on p. 61 of *ESOL Illustrations 2* as you say the sentences.]

DRILL: Question and Answer Drill

Teacher asks questions about what people do in the park and cues the answer expected.

For practice, the student should include the phrase *in the park* in his answer.

Teacher	Student
What do Ann and Jack do in the park?	
They go for a walk in the park.	They go for a walk in the park.
go on a picnic	
go to a concert	
sit on the grass	
What does Betty do in the park?	
reads a book	
sits on the grass	
eats lunch	
What do Jack and Jim do in the park?	
play ball	
sit and talk	
ride their bicycles	

VOCABULARY: *leave, left*

I leave my house	at 8 o'clock	every morning.	Then, I go	to work.
I left my house	at 8 o'clock	yesterday.	Then, I went	to work.
I leave work	at 5 o'clock	every day.	Then, I go	home.
I left work	at 5 o'clock	yesterday.	Then, I went	home.

Teacher models the sentences several times, having the student repeat only those with *leave* and *left.*

[Say: "Listen to *leave* and *left*."]

DRILL: Question and Answer Drill

Teacher asks questions about what time the student left an event or a place. Student answers, using *I left.*

Teacher	Student
What time did you leave your house?	
I left my house at 8 o'clock.	I left my house at 8 o'clock.
What time did you leave the party?	
What time did you leave your sister's house?	
What time did you leave the restaurant?	
What time did you leave the dance?	
What time did you leave the library?	

STRUCTURE FOCUS: Time Clauses with *when*

Time clause	Main clause
When it's cold,	Ann wears a coat.
When Ann has a headache,	she takes an aspirin.
When Bob was sick,	he went to the doctor.
When Ann left the shop,	the puppy left, too.

Teacher models the sentences several times, having the student repeat.

[Say: "Listen to *When*."]

Note: When the present tense is used in the *when* clause, the present or the future tense is used in the main clause.

When the past tense is used in the *when* clause, the past tense is used in the main clause.

DRILL: Combining Sentences

Teacher gives two statements, which the student combines into one, using a *when* clause.

Teacher	Student
It's cold. Ann wears a coat.	
When it's cold, Ann wears a coat.	When it's cold, Ann wears a coat.
He came. Ann left.	
The telephone rang. I answered it.	
The clock stops. Tom will fix it.	
The baby cries. His mother will give him some milk.	
Ann has a headache. She takes an aspirin.	
Mom needs milk. Dan goes to the store.	
The concert ended. We left.	

STRUCTURE FOCUS: The Use of *but* to Combine Parallel Sentences

She has a headache. I don't have a headache.	She has a headache, but I don't.
She isn't tired. Bob is tired.	She isn't tired, but Bob is.
Ann hurried. Jack didn't hurry.	Ann hurried, but Jack didn't.

Teacher models each set of three sentences several times, having the student repeat only the sentences with *but*.

[Say: "Listen to *but*."]

Note: In this pattern, *but* is used to combine two grammatically parallel statements—one negative, one affirmative.

DRILL: Combining Sentences

Teacher makes two similar statements—one negative, one affirmative.

The student combines them into one statement, using *but*.

Teacher	Student
She isn't tired. Bob is tired. She isn't tired, but Bob is.	She isn't tired, but Bob is.
Jack is tall. Dan isn't tall.	
Bob has a headache. Jill doesn't have a headache.	
Ann was happy. Jill wasn't happy.	
I hurried to work. Mary didn't hurry.	
Jim drives a car. Dan doesn't drive a car.	
Glenn isn't having fun. Will is having fun.	
Betty wore a coat. Ann didn't wear a coat.	

STRUCTURE FOCUS: The Question *What happened?*

What happened?	A truck hit Dan's car.
What happened?	Dan cut his head.
What happened?	Dan went to the hospital.

Teacher models the question and the answer several times, having the student repeat both.

[Say: "Listen to *What happened?*"]

DRILL: Statement and Question Drill

The teacher makes a statement, to which the student replies with the question *What happened?* The teacher answers the question.

After going through the drill this way, the student and the teacher reverse roles and repeat the drill.

Teacher: The baby's crying.
What happened?
Student: What happened?
Teacher: He hurt his hand.

Teacher: John went to the doctor.
Student: What happened?
Teacher: He cut his hand.

Teacher: Dan's head hurts.
Student: What happened?
Teacher: He hit his head.

Teacher: Kitty went to the hospital.
Student: What happened?
Teacher: She cut her leg.

[Reverse roles.]

II. Reading

STORY 6: The Puppy Got the Duck

Teach the sixth story (pp. 24-26 of *City Living*), following the steps outlined in Lesson 14 for Story 1.

New words

Page 24: *puppy, left, went, park*
Page 25: *did, faster*
Page 26: *laughed*

Guided reading

"Ann and Jack bought three ducks. What happened to one duck?
Read the story to find out."

Comprehension

These oral questions are more detailed than those for the previous stories, so allow the student to look back in the story for the answers if he needs to.

Teacher	Student
Where did Ann and Jack go when they left the market?	They went into the park.
What animal went after them?	A puppy.
Why did Ann and Jack stop in the park?	The sun (It) was very hot.
Where did they sit?	In the grass.
Where were their bags?	In back of them.
What happened to one duck?	The puppy picked it up and ran.
Who ran after the puppy?	Ann and Jack did.
Did they get the duck from the puppy?	No, they didn't.
Who went back to the market to get another duck?	Jack did.
What did Ann do?	She hurried to start dinner.

Note: There are no exercises in *Skill Book 2* for Stories 6-7 of *City Living.*

Story 7: What Happened?

OBJECTIVES

When a student completes this unit, he should be able to:

1. Use the noun *stitches* and the verb *stitched up.*
2. Use the words *early, late, on time,* and *in a hurry.*
3. Use the command *Hurry up!*
4. Read the new story words *happened, bad, stitches, badly, ready, seven, stitched.*
5. Read independently the last story in *City Living,* understanding the main ideas and being able to locate details.
6. Write the new words in Stories 3-7.
7. Read and write the *-ing, -es,* and *-ed* forms of verbs ending in consonant + *y*, changing *y* to *i* when appropriate, as: *hurry, hurrying, hurries, hurried.*

VISUAL AIDS

1. Use the picture of Fern with stitches in her leg on p. 51 of *ESOL Illustrations 2.*
2. Sew some stitches on a piece of cloth or paper to illustrate *stitches.*
3. Prepare the exercises described in the Skills Practice.

I. Conversation Skills

VOCABULARY: The Noun *stitches* and the Verb *stitched up*

> Fern cut her leg.
> Fern went to the doctor.
>
> The doctor put some stitches in Fern's leg.
> The doctor stitched up Fern's leg.

Teacher models the sentences several times, having the student repeat only the last two.

[Say: "Listen to *stitches.*" Show the picture on p. 51 of *ESOL Illustrations 2* and the stitches you have made.]

Use the picture on p. 51 of *ESOL Illustrations 2* and the cloth or paper with stitches that you have prepared in advance.

[Continue in the same way with *stitched up.*]

VOCABULARY: *early, late, on time*

The movie starts at 7:30.	It's 7 o'clock.	We're early.
The movie starts at 7:30.	It's 8 o'clock.	We're late.
The movie starts at 7:30.	It's 7:30.	We're on time.

Teacher models each set of three sentences, having the student repeat only the last sentence in the set.

[Say: "Listen to *early*."]

[Continue in the same way with *late* and *on time*.]

DRILL: Statement and Rejoinder

Teacher makes two statements about time. Student replies, using *early, late,* or *on time.*

Teacher	Student
The movie starts at 7:30. It's 7 o'clock. We're early.	We're early.
The dance starts at 9 o'clock. It's 10 o'clock.	We're late.
The movie starts at 7:30. It's 7:30.	We're on time.
The concert starts at 8 o'clock. It's 7:30.	We're early.
The bus leaves at 9 o'clock. It's 9 o'clock.	We're on time.
The supermarket closes at 5:30. It's 6 o'clock.	We're late.
The store opens at 9 o'clock. It's 8:30.	We're early.

VOCABULARY: *in a hurry*

The doctor leaves his office at 5:30.	It's 5:20.	I'm in a hurry.
The store closes at 9 o'clock.	It's 8:45.	I'm in a hurry.

Teacher models each set of three sentences several times, having the student repeat only the sentence with *in a hurry.*

[Say: "Listen to *in a hurry*."]

DRILL: Statement and Rejoinder

Teacher makes three statements about time. Student replies, using *in a hurry.*

Teacher	Student
Betty wants to take the plane. The plane leaves at 8 o'clock. It's 7:30. She's in a hurry.	She's in a hurry.
Jack wants to go to the store. The store closes at 9 o'clock. It's 8:45.	He's in a hurry.
Dan wants to go the movies. The movie starts at 7:30. It's 7:15.	He's in a hurry.
Kitty wants to take the bus. The bus leaves at 2 o'clock. It's 1:45.	She's in a hurry.
Jack and Ann want to take the train. The train leaves at 4 o'clock. It's 3:30.	They're in a hurry.

VOCABULARY: *Hurry up!*

> Jim wants Kitty to walk faster. He says, "Hurry up!"
> Ann wants Jack to get ready faster. She says, "Hurry up!"

Teacher models the pairs of sentences several times, having the student repeat only the sentences with *Hurry up!*

[Say: "Listen to *Hurry up!*"]

DRILL: Question and Answer Drill

Teacher makes a statement and asks a question, to which the student replies, using *Hurry up!*

Teacher	Student
Jim wants Kitty to walk faster. What does he say? He says, "Hurry up!"	He says, "Hurry up!"
Ann wants Jack to get ready faster. What does she say?	
Betty wants Jim to put on his coat faster. What does she say?	
Mother wants Dan to come into the house fast. What does she say?	
Tom wants the taxi driver to drive faster. What does he say?	

II. Reading

Check the student's homework from Lesson 15 on page 78 of *Skill Book 2.* Have the student read aloud both the root and the *-ing* form of all the verbs.

STORY 7: What Happened?

Teach the last story (pp. 27-31 of *City Living*), following the steps outlined in Lesson 14 for Story 1.

New words

Page 27: *happened*
Page 28: *bad, stitches*
Page 29: *badly, ready, seven*
Page 31: *stitched*

Guided reading

"Why are the Smiths late for the dinner? What happened to them?
Read the story to find out."

Comprehension

Allow the student to look back in the story for the answers if he needs to. Notice that the questions are in the past tense, although the story is written in the present tense.

Teacher	Student
Did the Smiths go to the dinner by car?	Yes, they did.
Another car stopped quickly. What did Mr. Smith do?	He stopped his car quickly.
How did Dan cut his head?	It (his head) hit the glass.
How did Sam cut his hand?	It (his hand) hit the glass.
Where did the Smiths take their children?	To a doctor's office. *or* To Dr. Chan's office.
What did the doctor do to Dan's head?	She put stitches in it.
What did the doctor do to Sam's hand?	She put stitches in it.
Were the Smiths late for dinner?	Yes, they were.
What time did the Blacks and the Smiths have dinner?	They had dinner at half past seven (7:30).

III. Writing

WRITING LESSON

There is no Writing Lesson in *Skill Book 2* for Lesson 16. Do the following work on separate (lined) paper.

1. Help the student study the spelling of the new story words in Stories 3-7 (pp. 13-31 of *City Living*) and write them.
2. Dictate the following sentences for the student to write:

    1. Jack went into the parking lot.
    2. Ann is having lunch with Jack.
    3. Ann and Jack are having fun.
    4. Bread and butter are on the shopping list.
    5. Ann left work at six.
    6. Ann got ready for dinner.
    7. What happened?
    8. Ann went into another shop.

3. Write the following exercise for the student. Have him read aloud each statement at the left. Have him say, then write, a *when* question based on each statement. Model the first question to let him know what you expect him to do.

1. Jack had lunch at twelve.	When did Jack have lunch?
2. The Smiths had dinner at six.	
3. Kitty visited her mother after work.	
4 Dinner was ready at seven.	
5. Ann and Jack got married.	

SKILLS PRACTICE: Adding Endings to Verbs That End in Consonant + *y*

Step 1: Write the following verbs, lined up as shown. In the first set, have the student read both forms of each verb aloud.

In the second set, have the student identify the last two letters of each word as "consonant, *y*," label them *C-y*, and write the *-ing* form in the blank.

	hurry	carry	marry	study
	hurrying	carrying	marrying	studying

	hurry	carry	marry	study
Add *-ing*.	________	________	________	________

Step 2: Write the following verbs, lined up as shown. In the first set, have the student read all three forms of each verb aloud.

In the second set, have the student identify the last two letters of each verb as "consonant, *y*" and label them *C-y*.

Point out to the student that: – "To write ***hurries,*** change *y* to *i* and add ***es***."
– "To write ***hurried,*** change *y* to *i* and add ***ed***."

Have the student write the *-es* and *-ed* forms in the blanks, and then read all three forms aloud.

	hurry	carry	marry	study
	hurries	carries	marries	studies
	hurried	carried	married	studied

	hurry	carry	marry	study
Add *-es*	________	________	________	________
Add *ed*	________	________	________	________

Step 3: Have the student write the *-ed* form of the word at left in the sentence and then read the completed sentence aloud.

-ed	
marry	1. Ann and Jack got ____________ .
study	2. John ____________ after dinner.
hurry	3. Kitty ____________ to work.
carry	4. Tom ____________ the bags to the car.
marry	5. Are Kitty and Jimmy ____________ ?

MORE READING

In the correlated reader *More Stories 2,* the stories for Lesson 15 may be read after *City Living* is completed.

Oral Evaluation for Skill Book 2

This Oral Evaluation covers the material introduced in the Conversation Skills sections of Lessons 1-16. The Oral Evaluation is divided into two parts. Part I is a review of 75 vocabulary items, grouped according to topic and presented in approximately the same order as they were introduced. Part II is a review of the basic structural patterns taught, grouped according to patterns.

PART I. VOCABULARY

Procedure: The 75 vocabulary items in this part appear on the Teacher's Evaluation Form which follows. To conduct this part of the Oral Evaluation, follow the directions below for each set of items.

Items 1-6
Use pp. 4-6 of *ESOL Illustrations for Skill Book 2.*
Ask the student to name the articles of clothing.
You may begin by saying: "This is __________."

Items 7-11
Use pp. 9-11 of *ESOL Illustrations 2.*
Ask the student to identify some daily activities.
You may ask: "What does (do) ________ do in the _________?"

Items 12-15
Use pp. 12-13 of *ESOL Illustrations 2.*
Ask the student to name persons one knows.
You may begin by saying: "This is my __________."

Items 16-20
Use pp. 14-15 of *ESOL Illustrations 2.*
Ask the student to name buildings in a city.
You may ask: "What's this?"

Items 21-28
Use pp. 18-19 of *ESOL Illustrations 2.*
The student should give the adjective opposite to the one in your question, as: "Is the man short?" "No, he's tall."

21. [Point to the *tall* man.] Is the man short?
22. [Point to the *big* man.] Is the man little?
23. [Point to the *low* building.] Is the building tall?
24. [Point to the *small* building.] Is the building large?
25. [Point to the *old* man.] Is the man old?
26. [Point to the *handsome* man.] Is the man ugly?
27. [Point to the *new* building.] Is the building old?
28. [Point to the *ugly* building.] Is the building pretty?

Items 29-32
Use p. 20 of *ESOL Illustrations 2.*
Ask the student to give the weather expressions.
Say: "How is the weather today?"
The student should answer: "It's _________."

Items 33-37
Use p. 22 of *ESOL Illustrations 2.*
Ask the student to identify kitchen items.
Say: "What is this?"

PART I. VOCABULARY: Teacher's Evaluation Form

Student's Name ________________________________

Student's Native Language ________________________________

Date of Enrollment ________________________________

Date Student Entered *Skill Book 2* Level ________________________________

Date Evaluation Given ________________________________

	1	2	3
1. coat			
2. jacket			
3. sweater			
4. jeans			
5. shoes			
6. dress			
7. cook			
8. eat and drink			
9. wash ... hands			
10. watch TV			
11. sleep			
12. baby			
13. friends			
14. neighbor			
15. boss			
16. city			
17. (big) building			
18. library			
19. school			
20. hospital			

	1	2	3
21. tall			
22. big			
23. low			
24. small			
25. old			
26. handsome			
27. new			
28. ugly			
29. windy			
30. sunny			
31. rainy			
32. snowy			
33. kitchen			
34. stove			
35. sink			
36. cabinet			
37. refrigerator			

	1	2	3
38. thin			
39. fat			
40. old			
41. stuck (in the mud)			
42. truck			
43. bus			
44. train			
45. bicycle			
46. carton of eggs			
47. bottle of soda			
48. six-pack of beer			
49. package of cookies			
50. pack of cigarettes			
51. purse			
52. wallet			
53. basket			
54. lunch box			
55. suitcase (bag)			

	1	2	3
56. grass			
57. bench			
58. stairs			
59. floor			
60. sofa			
61. classroom			
62. office			
63. waiting room			
64. men's room			
65. ladies' room			
66. red light (traffic light)			
67. parking lot			
68. parking meter			
69. gas station			
70. driveway			
71. to the movies			
72. to a (the) party			
73. to a (the) restaurant			
74. on a picnic			
75. for a walk			
Part I Totals			

Items 38-41 Use p. 23 of *ESOL Illustrations 2.*
Ask the student to say the adjectives.
Say: "The man (woman, taxi) is getting ________."

Items 42-45 Use pp. 25-27 of *ESOL Illustrations 2.*
Ask the student to identify means of transportation.
Say: "This is ________."

Items 46-50 Use pp. 28-29 of *ESOL Illustrations 2.*
Ask the student to identify food in containers.
Say: "This is ________."

Items 51-55 Use p. 40 of *ESOL Illustrations 2.*
Ask the student to identify containers for carrying things.
You may say: "This is ________."

Items 56-60 Use p. 41 of *ESOL Illustrations 2.*
Ask the student to identify items of seating.
You may ask: "Where is ________ sitting?"

Items 61-65 Use pp. 44-45 of *ESOL Illustrations 2.*
Ask the student to identify public rooms.
You may ask: "Where does ________ work?" and similar questions.

Items 66-70 Use pp. 56-57 of *ESOL Illustrations 2.*
Ask the student to identify places related to driving and parking.
Point to the appropriate picture as you ask the questions below.

66. Where does Bob stop his car?
67. Where does Bob park his car at work?
68. Where does Bob put his quarter?
69. Where does Bob buy gas?
70. Where does Bob park his car at home?

Items 71-75 Use pp. 59-61 of *ESOL Illustrations 2.*
Ask the student to identify recreation places.
You may ask: "Where are you going?"

Scoring: Assess your student's performance and check the appropriate column on the Teacher's Evaluation Form.

Check column 1 if the student identifies the picture fairly quickly and with fairly understandable pronunciation.

Check column 2 if the student identifies the picture with some hesitation but with fairly understandable pronunciation.

Check column 3 if the student identifies the picture incorrectly or if, after a short wait, he cannot identify it at all.

No matter how the student answers, do not tell him he is right or wrong. Do not look disappointed or disapproving if he gives you an incorrect answer or no answer at all. Go on briskly with the evaluation.

PART II. STRUCTURAL PATTERNS

Procedure: In this part, the student is asked to produce the major structural patterns that have been taught. The 75 items in this part are listed below. They are grouped in sets according to structural patterns.

In each set of items, there are two examples for you to use to show the student what is expected of him. Say both the teacher's cue and the expected student response. Have the student repeat the response after you.

For the remaining (numbered) items in the set, give only the cues. Do not prompt the student or help him. If he seems confused, simply repeat the two examples given, having him repeat the responses after you. If he cannot do one drill, proceed briskly to the next one without showing signs of disapproval or discouragement.

Set A. Questions with *Who/What* in Subject Position

Teacher's cue	Student response
Jill is the big sister.	Who is the big sister?
The milk is in the refrigerator.	What is in the refrigerator?

1. Bob is going home.
2. Kim is the little sister.
3. Glenn and Ed are working hard.
4. A pen is on the table.
5. His shoes are on the floor.

Set B. Questions with *Which*

Teacher's cue	Student response
Ann is reading the English book.	Which book is Ann reading?
Mary lives in the white house.	Which house does Mary live in?

6. Dan is in the gift shop.
7. Glenn is buying the English book.
8. Will plays with the brown ball.
9. Glenn and Liz live in the big gray house.

Set C. Prepositional Phrases as Noun Modifiers

Teacher's cue	Student response
This is a picture. This is Kitty King.	This is a picture of Kitty King.
This is a building. The building is on Main Street.	This is a building on Main Street.

10. This is a picture.
    This is my sister's baby.
11. This is a bank.
    The bank is on Beacon Street.
12. This is a woman.
    The woman is with her baby.
13. This is a lily.
    The lily is on the table.

Set D. Questions with *Is there* and *Are there*

Teacher's cue	Student response
There's a bank on Main Street.	Is there a bank on Main Street?
There are some pet shops downtown.	Are there any pet shops downtown?

14. There's an orange on the table.
15. There are some apples in the kitchen.
16. There is a post office on Main Street.
17. There are two windows in the bedroom.

Set E. Past Tense of *be* and *have*

Teacher's cue	Student response
I am cold today.	I was cold yesterday.
I have a headache.	I had a headache.

18. It is cold.
19. He has a class.
20. The buildings are new.
21. You have dinner at 6 o'clock.

Set F. Questions in the Past Tense

Teacher's cue	Student response
You had dinner last night.	Did you have dinner last night?
Ann was at home yesterday.	Was Ann at home yesterday?

22. Bob had my book.
23. Ann had class yesterday.
24. You were in class yesterday.
25. Bob was here yesterday.

Set G. The Use of *many/much* with Nouns

Teacher's cue	Student response
He has a lot of friends.	He has many friends.
He doesn't have a lot of money.	He doesn't have much money.

26. He has a lot of eggs.
27. She has a lot of neighbors.
28. He doesn't drink a lot of milk.
29. He doesn't drink a lot of beer.

Set H. Answers to Questions with *How*

Teacher's cue	Student response
How does Ed work?	Quickly.
How do you come to class?	By bus.

30. How do you work?
31. How does Glenn run?
32. How do you go downtown?
33. How do you go to your sister's house?

Set I. Questions with *can* and *will*

Teacher's cue	Student response
Ann will buy the book tomorrow.	Will Ann buy the book tomorrow?
Bob can speak English.	Can Bob speak English?

34. You will help Mr. Hunt tomorrow.
35. She will eat the apple.
36. She can swim here.
37. She can carry the bag.

Set J. Past Tense Statements with Irregular Verbs

Teacher's cue	Student response
I go shopping every day.	I went shopping yesterday.
I do my homework every day.	I did my homework yesterday.

38. We buy some milk every day.
39. She gives money to Glenn.
40. The dog runs after the cat.
41. I get thirsty every day.
42. You drink a glass of water every day.
43. I make breakfast every morning.
44. I see my neighbor every day.
45. He puts on his clothes in the morning.
46. I say, "Hello."
47. I take off my clothes at night.

(In this set and the next, if the student forgets to include the time expression, but uses the correct past tense form of the verb, mark his answer correct.)

Set K. The Use of *be + going to* to Indicate Future Time

Teacher's cue	Student response
I'm buying bread now.	I'm going to buy bread tomorrow.
She's reading the book now.	She's going to read the book tomorrow.

48. He's buying a wallet.
49. They are sitting on the bench.
50. Jack is marrying Ann.
51. You are studying English now.
52. They are playing ball.

Set L. The Use of *and...too* and *not...and...not either*

Teacher's cue	Student response
I am a teacher. Mary is a teacher.	I am a teacher, and Mary is too.
Helen wasn't sick. Mary wasn't sick.	Helen wasn't sick, and Mary wasn't either.

53. Mary is from Puerto Rico.
    John is from Puerto Rico.
54. Bob and Glenn are in the car.
    Sue is in the car.
55. I teach English.
    My husband teaches English.
56. I'm not a doctor.
    Mary isn't a doctor.

[illegible] I don't speak Chinese.
[illegible]n doesn't speak Chinese.

Set M. Comparative Form of Adjectives

Teacher's cue	Student response
Dan is young. Ed is very young.	Ed is younger than Dan is.
Sue is thin. Kim is very thin.	Kim is thinner than Sue is.

58. Ann is pretty.
    Kitty is very pretty.
59. This apple is sweet.
    This orange is very sweet.
60. I am happy.
    Ann is very happy.
61. Jack is a good student.
    Ann is a very good student.
62. These cookies are bad.
    Those cookies are very bad.

Set N. Frequency Adverbs

Teacher's cue		Student response
I am cold.	always	I am always cold.
I work hard.	usually	I usually work hard.
63. He is tired.	always	
64. Ed works hard.	usually	
65. Bob needs help.	never	
66. Jill is sick.	hardly ever	

Set O. Indirect Object without *to*

Teacher's cue	Student response
I gave the pen to Jack.	I gave Jack the pen.
Jack sends a letter to Ann.	Jack sends Ann a letter.

67. I hand the English book to you.
68. Jill reads the book to him.
69. Mrs. Smith teaches English to the students.
70. The teacher is showing the book to the children.

Set P. Short Answers to Yes/No Questions

Teacher's cue	Student response
Can you speak English?	Yes, I can.
Will Ann help us?	No, she won't.

71. Can you swim?
72. Were you in class yesterday?
73. Did Dan have dinner with you last night?
74. Are you going to buy the book tomorrow?
75. Will your sister come here tomorrow?

Scoring: Assess your student's performance and check the appropriate column on the Teacher's Evaluation Form that follows.

Evaluate the student's performance on a scale of 1 to 3, using the same criteria as for the vocabulary.

Check column 1 if the student gives the correct structure, responding fairly quickly and with fairly understandable pronunciation.

Check column 2 if the student gives the correct structure with some hesitation but with fairly understandable pronunciation.

Check column 3 if the student cannot form the structure correctly or if, after a short wait, he cannot respond at all.

Evaluate only the structure in question. For example, suppose the student is asked to transform a statement containing an indirect object with *to* to a statement containing an indirect object without *to*. After the cue "I hand the English book to you," he says: "I hand you the book," responding fairly quickly and with good pronunciation. In such a case, check column 1 even though the student has omitted the word *English*. He *has* formed a statement containing the indirect object without *to*, and that is the structure in question.

EVALUATING THE STUDENT'S PERFORMANCE

Part I. Vocabulary

If your student gets a total of 60 or more checks in columns 1 and 2, he is ready to begin *Skill Book 3.*

You should, however, look over the vocabulary items he missed and review them, a few at a time, in subsequent lessons.

If your student gets a total of 45-59 checks in columns 1 and 2, you must spend some time reviewing the vocabulary items he missed before beginning *Skill Book 3.*

Anything less than 44 checks in columns 1 and 2 indicates need for extensive review before beginning *Skill Book 3.*

Always combine review of vocabulary with review of structural patterns. For example, if a student was unable to name any of the foods in containers, combine a review of those items with a review of question and answer patterns.

Part II. Structural Patterns

If your student gets a total of 60 or more checks in columns 1 and 2, he is ready to begin *Skill Book 3.*

It is important, however, that you analyze the items he missed. If he missed most or all of the items in a section, be sure to review that structural pattern again before beginning *Skill Book 3.*

If your student gets less than 60 in columns 1 and 2, it is especially important to review any basic structures he is having difficulty with before beginning *Skill Book 3.*

Review only those structures that caused the most difficulty. If a student missed only one item in a section, review would generally not be necessary. Watch for sections in which the student missed most or all of the items, and review those structures in particular. In general, the more checks in column 3 in a particular section, the more time you will need to spend reviewing that structure.

PART II. STRUCTURAL PATTERNS: Teacher's Evaluation Form

Student's Name ____________________

Student's Native Language ____________________ Date of Enrollment ____________________

Date Student Entered *Skill Book 2* Level ____________________ Date Evaluation Given ____________________

		1	2	3
Set A:	1.			
	2.			
	3.			
	4.			
	5.			
Set B:	6.			
	7.			
	8.			
	9.			
Set C:	10.			
	11.			
	12.			
	13.			
Set D:	14.			
	15.			
	16.			
	17.			
Set E:	18.			
	19.			
	20.			
	21.			
Set F:	22.			
	23.			
	24.			
	25.			

The publisher hereby grants permission to reproduce this Teacher's Evaluation Form for the purpose of evaluating student performance.

		1	2	3
Set G:	26.			
	27.			
	28.			
	29.			
Set H:	30.			
	31.			
	32.			
	33.			
Set I:	34.			
	35.			
	36.			
	37.			
Set J:	38.			
	39.			
	40.			
	41.			
	42.			
	43.			
	44.			
	45.			
	46.			
	47.			
Set K:	48.			
	49.			
	50.			
	51.			
	52.			

		1	2	3
Set L:	53.			
	54.			
	55.			
	56.			
	57.			
Set M:	58.			
	59.			
	60.			
	61.			
	62.			
Set N:	63.			
	64.			
	65.			
	66.			
Set O:	67.			
	68.			
	69.			
	70.			
Set P:	71.			
	72.			
	73.			
	74.			
	75.			

Part II Totals			

Reading and Writing Evaluation for Skill Book 2

To evaluate the student's progress in reading and writing skills, use the separate publication *Checkups for Skill Book 2,* available from New Readers Press.

OBJECTIVES

The objectives of the evaluation are:

1. to measure the student's progress in relation to the learning objectives
2. to diagnose the student's strengths and weaknesses in phonics, reading comprehension, and writing
3. to develop the student's confidence in taking a test.

ADMINISTERING THE CHECKUPS

Checkups for Skill Book 2 consists of five parts. Simple written directions are given for each part, and most parts have one or two sample questions. Go over the directions and samples with the student before he does each part. Help him correct any errors he makes in the samples, but do *not* correct his errors in the actual test items.

Begin by having the student write his name at the top of page 1.

Checkup 1: Sound-Symbol Relationships (Pages 1-3)

The student fills in the missing letter or letters for sounds taught in *Skill Book 2:*

- the short vowel sounds /a/, /e/, /i/, /o/, /u/, /y/, represented by *a, e, i, o, u, y.*
- the sound /ar/, represented by *ar.*
- the sound /er/, represented by *er, ir, ur.*
- the double consonants *ll, nn, ss, tt,* representing a single sound.
- the sound /k/, represented by *c, k, ck.*
- the sounds /wh/, /ng/, and voiced /th/, represented by *wh, ng,* and *th.*
- the beginning consonant blends *cl, gl, br, dr, tr, st.*

Each word, with a blank for each missing letter, is printed next to the illustration for the word. There are 37 items and one sample.

What to do

Have the student read the title *Checkup 1* and the direction *Fill in the letters* and do the two sample items, *bed* and *bell.* Have him say each word aloud and then fill in the missing letter or letters.

Let the student complete Checkup 1 by himself. When he has finished page 1, however, check to be sure he has understood the directions before you let him complete pages 2-3.

Checkup 2: Adding Endings (Page 4)

There are three parts in this checkup. The student adds *-s* or *-es* to six words, *-ed* to four words, and *-ing* to four words. In the last two parts, he must sometimes double the final consonant of the root word before adding the ending. Two samples are shown for each part.

What to do

Have the student read the title *Checkup 2.*

Add *-s* or *-es* to the word. Then write the word. Have the student read these directions and the two sample items: *arm, arms* and *glass, glasses.* Then let him complete this part.

Add *-ed* to the word. Then write the word. Have the student read these directions and the two sample items: *visit, visited* and *stop, stopped.* Call attention to the *pp* in *stopped.* Then let him complete this part.

Add *-ing* to the word. Then write the word. Have the student read these directions and the two sample items: *fish, fishing* and *cut, cutting.* Call attention to the *tt* in *cutting.* Then let him complete this part.

Checkup 3: Word Recognition (Page 5)

The student circles one of three words to complete a sentence. There are 20 items and one sample.

What to do

Have the student read the title *Checkup 3* and the direction *Circle one word.* Have him read the sample sentence *(Tom went to the city in his... cat, car, can.)* to himself, circle the right word, and then read the completed sentence aloud.

Then let the student complete this page by himself. (It may help him to keep his place if he uses a strip of paper as a marker under the sentence he is working on.)

Checkup 4: Listen and Write (Page 6)

The student writes 10 words and 5 sentences from dictation. Sentences include the use of capital letters, periods, possessive endings *-'s* and *-s',* and question marks.

What to do

Have the student read the title *Checkup 4* and the direction *Listen and write.* Then say: "I will say some words. Write the words." Dictate these words for him to write.

1. black
2. clock
3. grass
4. drop
5. start
6. windy
7. plan
8. slim
9. lunch
10. which

Then dictate these sentences for him to write at the bottom of the page.

1. That is the Hills' dinner.
2. Fern's skirt is burning.
3. Is the farmers' market in the city?
4. Are the eggs fresh?
5. Bud is Mrs. Hill's brother.

Checkup 5: Reading Comprehension (Pages 7-8)

The student reads a short paragraph, then answers three to five questions by circling *Yes* or *No.* There are six paragraphs with a total of 22 questions. One sample paragraph with two questions is given.

What to do

Have the student read the title *Checkup 5* and the direction *Circle Yes or No.* Have him read the sample paragraph silently and then aloud. Have him read each question, tell whether Yes or No is the right answer, and then circle the right answer. If he doesn't give the right answer, help him find the place in the paragraph that tells the answer.

Then let the student complete Checkup 6 by himself.

CHECKUPS FOR SKILL BOOK 2: Teacher's Evaluation Form

Student's Name ______________________ Native Language ______________________

Date of Enrollment ______________________ Date Checkups Given ______________________

Section	Perfect Score	Satisfactory Score	Student's Score
1. Sound-Symbol Relationships	36	27	
2. Adding Endings	14	10	
3. Word Recognition	20	15	
4. Listen and Write	25	19	
5. Reading Comprehension	22	16	
Total Scores	**117**	**87**	

1. Sound-Symbol Relationships

Each word completed correctly counts as 1 point.
(Do not count the sample items *bed* and *bell.*)

2. Adding Endings

Each word written correctly with the ending counts 1 point.

3. Word Recognition

1. sister
2. kitchen
3. dinner
4. city
5. picture
6. stuck
7. bed
8. friends
9. office
10. dollars
11. bag
12. path
13. start
14. curtains
15. farm
16. person
17. building
18. son
19. black
20. fun

4. Listen and Write

Count 1 point for each *word* spelled correctly.

1. black
2. clock
3. glass
4. drop
5. start
6. windy
7. plan
8. slim
9. lunch
10. which

Count 3 points for each *sentence* written correctly, as follows:

— 1 point if a capital letter is used at the beginning of the sentence.
— 1 point for correct spelling of all words, including correct use of capital letters on names and correct placement of apostrophe.
— 1 point for correct end punctuation—period or question mark.

1. That is the Hills' dinner.
2. Fern's skirt is burning.
3. Is the farmers' market in the city?
4. Are the eggs fresh?
5. Bud is Mrs. Hill's brother.

5. Reading Comprehension

Each correct answer counts 1 point.

Sample	Set 1	Set 2	Set 3	Set 4	Set 5	Set 6
Do	1. No	1. No	1. Yes	1. No	1. No	1. No
not	2. Yes	2. Yes	2. No	2. No	2. Yes	2. Yes
count.	3. No	3. No	3. Yes	3. Yes	3. No	3. No
				4. Yes	4. Yes	4. Yes
						5. No

SCORING THE CHECKUPS

On the student's booklet, mark his *correct* answers rather than his wrong answers. Answer keys are included in the Teacher's Evaluation Form on the opposite page. Use this form to record his scores. Do not count the answers to sample questions.

The suggested satisfactory score is about 75% of the perfect score for each part. If you want to translate the student's score into a percentage, divide his score by the perfect score and multiply by 100.

EVALUATING THE STUDENT'S PERFORMANCE

If the student does well in comprehension, even though he may have shown some weaknesses in word attack skills, he is learning to read.

If he does poorly in comprehension, even though he scores well in word attack skills, look for reasons why he is not transferring meaning and understanding to the material he is reading.

A look at the scores of the individual parts of the *Checkups* will give an informal diagnosis of the student's strengths and weaknesses in the various skills.

If your student obviously needs strengthening in particular skills in *Skill Book 2,* do not go back to that book for review. Rather, move on to *Skill Book 3,* but supplement the lessons with special exercises to reinforce the skills which need attention. The bibliography below suggests some prepared materials and some resources for preparing your own. You may need to devise some exercises yourself.

BIBLIOGRAPHY

Avery, Bea. *Fun Learning.* Alhambra, Calif.: California Literacy, Inc., 1976. (May be ordered from California Literacy, Inc. at 317 W. Main St., Alhambra, California 91801.)

A collection of games and learning activities for reinforcement and enrichment in both reading and oral skills, with indication of their appropriateness for various skill book levels.

Eagle, Gertrude, ed. *More Stories 2.* rev. ed. Syracuse, N.Y.: New Readers Press, 1981.

This reader provides three stories correlated to the skills level of each lesson in *Skill Book 2.* In this revised edition, vocabulary and structures are also controlled to what is taught in the Laubach Way to English.

Kennedy, Katherine and Sarkisian, Ellen. *Games and Butterflies.* Syracuse, N.Y.: New Readers Press, 1979.

This teacher's resource provides listening-and-speaking, reading, and writing games and activities on different levels of difficulty. All games were developed and tested in adult basic education ESOL classes.

*McFall, Karen. *Pat King's Family.* Syracuse, N.Y.: New Readers Press, 1981.

This 64-page novel, about a young mother who learns to cope when abandoned by her husband, is based on the reading vocabulary of *Skill Books 1-2* and their correlated readers.

Pope, Lillie, et al. *Guidelines to Teaching Remedial Reading.* 2nd ed., rev. Brooklyn, N.Y.: Book-Lab, Inc., 1975. (May be ordered from New Readers Press.)

A good source of special aids for reading skills development, this revised edition includes special sections concerning ESOL students.

*Rice, Gail. *Focus on Phonics-2A: Short Vowel Sounds.* Syracuse, N.Y.: New Readers Press, 1982. Accompanying teacher's edition.

This student workbook uses a word-family approach (rhyming words) to help students learn how to read many new short vowel words. Also includes exercises on adding endings to words. Designed to be used in conjunction with *Skill Book 2* or following it.

*Rice, Gail. *Focus on Phonics-2B: Consonant Blends.* Syracuse, N.Y.: New Readers Press, 1980. Accompanying teacher's edition.

This student workbook gives practice with consonant digraphs, beginning and ending consonant blends, and the *r*-controlled vowel sounds. Designed to be used after *Skill Book 2.*

*These books, although controlled to *Skill Book 2* vocabulary, introduce additional vocabulary and grammatical structures not taught in levels 1-2 of the Laubach Way to English.

Conversation Skills Word List

Words that appear in the list below are items introduced in the Vocabulary and Structure Focus sections of this manual. Items are listed only when the student himself is asked to produce them. Items that occur only in the Dialogs are not listed.

The main entries are the normal dictionary-entry forms. Irregular forms and examples of usage and structures are listed under the main entries. An asterisk indicates that the main entry (root word) was first taught at the *Skill Book 1* level. A dash indicates that the main-entry word is taught only in the expression given below it.

The list does not include regular noun plurals nor verbs formed with *-s* or *-ing*. The student should be able to form these variants when he enters the *Skill Book 2* level.

The student learns to form the *-ed* past tense of regular verbs in Lesson 6 of this manual and the *-er* comparative of regular adjectives in Lesson 11. These variants are not included in the list, either. Irregular forms are listed, however.

Listings in boldface refer to categories of words that are introduced as a group. (The boldface words themselves are not part of the student's vocabulary, however, unless they are listed elsewhere.)

Lesson	Main Entries with Variants and Structures
7	**Aches and Pains**
12	across
11	add
7	after
10	ago
15.4	ahead
	Drive straight ahead.
5	airplane
8	alive
4	All right. (reply)
14.2	alone
13	always
15.5	animal
10	Anna
9	another
9	another one
11	answer (verb)
	answer the telephone
14.2	He answered, "Yes, I am."
11	armchair
12	Arthur (family name)
13	as
	Ed is as old as Dan is.
	He sings as badly as I do.
14.2	ask
	Ed asked, "Are you going?"
	I asked Bob to help.
7	aspirin
3	baby
	back (noun)
	My back hurts.
8	standing with his back to...
8	in back of (prep.)
12	come back, give it back, etc.
7	backache
5	bad
11	worse
7	badly
8	bag (noun)
2	ball
7	Band-Aid
3	bank
12	barn
8	basket
2	bat (noun)
2	bathroom
12	battery
—	be
	See was, were
3	Beacon Street
2	bedroom
6	beer
7	before
6	bell
	church bell
	dinner bell
	doorbell
6	Bell (family name)
1	belt
9	bench
8	beside
11	better
8	Betty
8	between
5	bicycle
8	Black (family name)
15.4	block
	Drive straight ahead one block.
1	blouse.
5	boat
14.2	Bobby
3	boots
3	boss
6	bottle of
	bottle of soda
6	box of
	box of cereal
3	boy friend
12	brakes
5	brick (noun)
5	brick (adj.)
8	briefcase
2	bring
10	broken
11	bruise
2	brush (verb)
	brush...teeth
3	building (noun)
3	**Buildings in a City**
11	burn (noun)
11	burn (verb)
5	bus (noun)
14.2	but
	I like dogs, but I don't like cats.
16.6	She isn't tired, but I am.

Lesson	Main Entries with Variants and Structures
14.2	button (noun)
14.2	button (verb)
*	buy
8	bought
5	by
	by bus
11	I helped by making lunch.
4	cabinet
8	can (modal)
	I can speak English.
	Can you speak English?
	Yes, I can.
8	can't
	No, I can't.
9	I can't carry the box.
6	can of
	can of coffee
4	candy
9	candy factory
5	car
12	**Car, Parts of**
7	careful
7	carefully
9	car factory
8	carry
6	carton of
	carton of cigarettes
	carton of eggs
	carton of ice cream
4	ceiling
6	cereal
12	cheap
10	checkup
	He's getting a checkup.
10	chest x-ray
10	Christmas Day
6	cigarettes
8	Cindy
9	circle
3	city
10	classroom
2	closet
1	clothes
1, 3	**Clothing and Jewelry**
1	coat
11	coffee table
11	cold (noun)
	I have a cold.
1	color
1	**Colors**
10	comb...hair
4	come
13	concert
8	**Containers for Carrying**
6	**Containers, Food in**
6	cookies
15.4	cop
	traffic cop
15.4	corner (noun)
11	cover (verb)
4	counter
5	cry (verb)
11	curtains
11	cut (noun)
2	cut (verb)
4	cut up (verb)
14.1	Dad
8	Dan
1	dark
	dark blue
12	The night is dark.
8	dead
12	The battery is dead.
3	department store
8	die (verb)
13	different
2	dining room
*	do (auxiliary verb)
5	did
	Did you have dinner?
	Yes, I did.
5	didn't
	No, I didn't.
7	I didn't look.
8	do (main verb)
	I do my homework every day.
	I did my homework yesterday.
10	do the dishes
	do your job
	do the laundry
	do your work
2	doll
10	Don
6	doorbell
12	down
1	dress (noun)
1	dress shop
*	drink (verb)
8	drank
12	drive (verb)
12	driver's side
12	driveway
12	**Driving**
10	drop (verb)
4	duck (noun)
7	earache
16.7	early
10	Easter
*	eat
10	ate
11	Ed
10	either
	He isn't tired,
	and I'm not either.
7	elbow
6	Ellen
15.3	empty (adj.)
3	English class
9	enough
13	ever
	Do you ever drive fast?
12	expensive
9	factory
9	**Factories**
12	far
12	farm
12	farmer
12	farmers' market
6	fast (adj.)
	He's fast.
7	fast (adv.)
	He works fast.
5	fat
11	feel
	How do you feel?
	I feel better.
	I feel tired.
	I don't feel well.
11	fern
11	Fern (woman's name)
6	few
	a few
	He has a few apples.
15.3	fill
13	find out
—	fine
11	I feel fine.
11	fire
7	first (adj.)
	the first day of the week
11	first (adv.)
	First, I closed the door.
1	fish (adj.)
	fish dinner
3	Fisher (family name)
14.2	fit (verb)
10	fix (verb)
—	flat
12	flat tire
4	floor
3	flowers
*	for
2	He's going shopping for a gift.
11	I thanked Ed for helping.
2	fork
6	Fred
13	**Frequency Adverbs**
6	fresh

Lesson	Main Entries with Variants and Structures
3	friend
*	from
11	I stopped the curtains from burning.
14.1	I watched Dan from the kitchen.
—	front
8	in front of (prep.)
15.3	full
15.3	fun
	having fun
5	funny
11	furniture
4	**Furniture, Kitchen**
11	**Furniture, Living Room**
6	gallon
12	garage
12	garden
12	gardener
12	gas
12	gas station
*	get
5	He's getting fat.
5	get in/out of a car
	get on/off a bus
10	got
1	gift
1	gift shop
3	girl friend
*	give
8	gave
15.5	give back
9	glass
1	glasses
	He's wearing glasses.
9	glass factory
*	go
8	went
9	going to (future)
	I'm going to buy a house.
1	gold
5	good
11	better
13	That's a good idea.
15.3	having a good time
9	grass
1	gray
4	gun
9	half
	half a cup of coffee
	half of my sandwich
6	half-gallon
	half-gallon of milk
3	handsome
	happen
	What happened?
8	happy
7	hard (adj.)
	He is a hard worker.
7	hard (adv.)
	He works hard.
13	hardly ever
3	hat
*	have
5	had
15.3	having fun
	having a good time
	having trouble with...
7	headache
11	hear
11	heard
15.3	heavy
	Lift the heavy box.
15.4	Traffic is heavy.
10	Helen
6	help (verb)
6	hen
4	here
4	hit (verb)
14.1	hold hands with...
10	holiday
10	**Holidays**
12	hood (of a car)
3	hospital
2	house
5	how
	How do you go to work?
8	How do you do?
11	How do you feel?
6	how many
	How many children do you have?
15.4	I told her how many apples to buy.
6	how much
	How much coffee do you drink?
	How much is this blouse?
15.4	I told her how much milk to buy.
14.1	hug (verb)
5	hungry
6	Hunt (family name)
16.7	hurry (noun)
	I'm in a hurry.
11	hurry (verb)
16.7	Hurry up!
7	hurt (verb)
6	ice cream
—	idea
13	That's a good idea.
10	Independence Day
12	into
3	it (impersonal)
	It's rainy today.
12	It's not far from my house to school.
7	it (noun substitute)
	My pen is on the table. Do you see it?
8	Jack
1	jacket
6	jar of
	jar of jelly
1	jeans
6	jelly
15.4	Jim
3	Jimmy
10	job
5	John
10	Juan
15.3	just
	She has just started her job.
8	Kathy
8	kill
3	King (family name)
14.1	kiss (verb)
2	kitchen
3	Kitty
2	knife
13	know
10	Labor Day
10	ladies' room
11	lamp
12	large
7	last (adj.)
	the last day of the week
16.7	late
5	laugh (verb)
14.1	laugh at
10	laundry
	do the laundry
16.6	leave
16.6	left
12	left (adj.)
	make a left turn
15.4	left (adv.)
	Turn left.
14.1	let (verb)
	Dad lets Sam drive the car.
12	let's
	Let's go.
	Let's not go.
3	letter
	send a letter
3	library
15.4	lift (noun)
	Thanks for the lift.

Lesson	Main Entries with Variants and Structures
15.3	lift (verb)
5	light (noun)
	The light is on the ceiling.
12	red light
15.4	traffic light
1	light (adj.)
	light blue
12	The day is light.
15.4	Traffic is light.
4	like (verb)
3	lily
8	Linda
15.5	list (noun)
15.5	shopping list
6	little (amount)
	a little
	He has a little money.
8	live (verb: be alive)
2	living room
8	Liz
10	lock
14.2	long
*	look (verb)
14.2	He looks good.
	She looks pretty.
6	lot (amount)
	a lot of
12	lot (noun)
	parking lot
7	loud
7	loudly
7	low
	The building is low.
8	lunch box
3	Main Street
1	make
	make breakfast/lunch/dinner
10	made
12	make a right/left turn
6	many
10	Maria
14.2	mark (verb)
12	market (noun)
	farmers' market
8	marry
15.5	get married
15.5	married (adj.)
11	match (noun)
14.2	match (verb)
6	**Measurements, Liquid**
7	medicine
7	**Medicines**
10	Memorial Day
10	men's room
12	mile
10	Miller (family name)
1	Miss
	Miss Hill
10	Molly
14.1	Mom
9	month
	this month
	next month
13	movie
	Let's go to the movies.
	What time does the movie start?
3	Ms.
6	much
4	mud
15.4	must (modal)
	I must study.
12	near
3	need (verb)
3	neighbor
8	nest
13	never
3	new
10	New Year's Day
12	New York
9	next
	next week
	next month
	next year
15.4	at the next corner
*	no
4	No, thank you.
7	nosedrops
10	office
13	often
14.2	Oh
4	OK. (reply)
3	old
7	one (noun substitute)
	I have a pen. Do you have one?
9	another one
	the other one
2	or
	Is this big or little?
	Is this a pen or a pencil?
	Are we going home or downtown?
1	orange (color)
10	**Ordinal Numbers**
	first — thirty-first
9	other
9	the other one
	the others
12	out of (prep.)
	He went out of the house.
8	over (prep.)
	The light is over the desk.
6	pack of
	pack of cigarettes
6	package of
	package of cookies
1	pants (noun)
9	paper factory
16.6	park (noun)
12	park (verb)
12	parking (adj.)
	parking lot
	parking meter
13	party
12	pass (verb)
	Bob passes another car.
12	passenger's side
9	path
11	person
3	**Persons One Knows**
10	Peter
13	picnic
3	picture of
	This is a picture of my baby.
7	pill
11	pillow
14.2	pink
6	pint
15.5	plan (verb)
4	please
	Please come here.
3	post office
6	pound (noun)
12	**Prepositions of Direction**
8	**Prepositions of Location**
3	pretty
14.2	**Prices**
1	purple
8	purse
1	put on (verb)
	I'm putting on my coat.
6	quart
9	quarter of
	a quarter of the circle
7	quick
7	quickly
3	rainy
8	rat
15.5	ready
15.5	get ready
13	**Recreation Places**
12	repair shop
13	restaurant
15.4	ride (noun)
	Thanks for the ride.
	He gave me a ride.

Lesson	Main Entries with Variants and Structures
14.2	right (correct)
	That's right.
12	right (direction)
	make a right turn
15.4	turn right
1	ring (noun)
	He's wearing a ring.
6	ring (verb)
9	rang
10	Roberts (family name)
3	roses
4	refrigerator
9	rock (noun)
2	room (of a house)
2	**Rooms of the House**
10	**Rooms, Public**
4	rug
*	run
9	ran
5	sad
8	Sam
13	same
6	say
	Bob says, "I'm going home."
11	said
	I said, "Hello."
3	school
9	**Seating, Places for**
11	see
11	saw
*	sell
10	sold
3	send
11	shake
	shake hands
11	shook
1	shirt
14.2	shoelaces
1	shoes
8	shopping bag
15.5	shopping list
3	short
	The boy is short.
10	shot (noun)
	The doctor gives a shot to her.
7	shoulder
6	sick
1	sign (verb)
	She's signing the paper.
1	silver
2	sing
15.5	single
	Is he married or single?
4	sink (noun)
*	sit
8	sat
6	six-pack of
	six-pack of beer
1	skirt
2	sleep (verb)
14.2	slim
6	slow
7	slowly
12	small
14.1	smile (verb)
14.1	smile at (verb)
8	Smith (family name)
6	soda
	bottle of soda
9	sofa
7	soft
7	softly
	He speaks softly.
13	sometimes
7	sore (adj.)
	sore throat
–	sorry
4	I'm sorry.
3	snowy
2	spoon
9	stairs
6	stale
3	stamp (noun)
11	start (verb)
16.7	stitch (noun)
16.7	stitch up (verb)
10	stop (verb)
3	store (noun)
4	stove
15.4	straight ahead
	Drive straight ahead one block.
5	stuck
	The taxi gets stuck.
1	Sue
1	suit (noun)
8	suitcase
4	sun
3	sunny
3	supermarket
13	Sure. (reply)
1	sweater
*	swim
9	swam
7	take
	take medicine
	take...temperature
15.4	Jim takes him to the shop.
1	take off
	I'm taking off my coat.
11	took off
2	talk (verb)
3	tall
5	taxi
*	teach
8	taught
10	tear (verb)
10	tore
7	teaspoon of
	a teaspoon of medicine
4	telephone
6	The telephone is ringing.
11	answer the telephone
5	tell
	She tells him, "Come in."
7	Ann tells her it is good.
10	told
	He told Ann, "Sit down."
11	I told Bob to go.
	I told Bob not to go.
15.5	**Telling Time, Alternate Ways**
	It's half past six.
	It's a quarter to six.
	It's a quarter after six.
7	temperature
	He takes his temperature.
11	than
	Ann is happier than I am.
	Jack makes worse coffee than Ann does.
*	thank
4	Yes, thanks.
	No, thank you.
10	Thanksgiving Day.
8	that (subordinator)
	I'm happy that he will come.
11	then
	First, I closed the door.
	Then, I walked to my desk.
	I was studying.
	Then I stopped to eat.
4	there (adv.)
	It is there.
3	there (place-filler)
	There is a pen on the table.
	There are two banks downtown.
7	thermometer
5	thin
15.5	thing
5	think
5	thirsty

Lesson	Main Entries with Variants and Structures
*	this
9	this week
	this month
	this year
7	throat
1	tie (noun: necktie)
14.2	tie (verb)
6	time (noun)
	It's time for dinner.
13	What time does the bank open?
15.3	having a good time
16.7	I'm on time.
9	**Time Expressions**
12	tire (noun)
5	tired
4	to (in infinitives)
	I want to go.
3	today
14.2	together
10	Tom
9	tomorrow
9	too
	It's too sweet.
10	He's tired, and I am too.
7	tooth
7	toothache
2	top (child's toy)
–	top
8	on top of (prep.)
2	toy
9	toy factory
5	throw away
15.4	traffic
15.4	traffic cop
15.4	traffic light
5	train
5	**Transportation, Means of**
–	trouble
15.3	having trouble with...
5	truck
12	trunk (of car)
12	turn (noun)
	make a right/left turn
15.4	turn (verb)
	turn right/left
11	TV
11	TV set
3	ugly
3	umbrella
5	Uncle Bud
8	under
12	up
	He went up the stairs.
14.1	He's coming up the street.
12	used (adj.)
13	usually
6	very
10	waiting room
13	walk (noun)
	go for a walk
4	wall
8	wallet
2	want
2	wash
1	watch (noun)
2	watch (verb)
3	was (past of be)
	He was in class.
	Was he in class?
	Yes, he was.
3	wasn't
	No, he wasn't.
11	was (auxiliary verb)
	I was studying.
1	wear (verb)
10	wore
3	**Weather Expressions**
9	week
	this week
	next week
6	weigh
6	**Weight**
6	well (adj.)
	He's well.
7	well (adv.)
	He works well.
3	were (past of be)
	You were in class.
	Were you in class?
	Yes, we were.
3	weren't
	No, we weren't.
11	were (auxiliary verb)
	You were studying.
*	what
4	What is on the stove?
15.3	I know what he will do.
15.4	I told him what to do.
16.6	What happened?
13	what time
	What time does the bank open?
*	when
15.3	I know when he will come.
15.4	I told him when to turn.
*	where
15.3	I know where he will go.
15.4	I told him where to turn.
2	which
	Which book do you want?
2	whistle (noun)
2	whistle (verb)
*	who
1	Who has a watch?
6	will (auxiliary verb)
	I will go.
	Will you go?
	Yes, I will.
6	won't
	No, I won't.
	I won't go.
12	windshield
12	windshield wipers
3	windy
2	with
	He is going with her.
	I eat olives with my fingers.
14.2	without
1	word
6	work (verb)
9	worker
11	worse
14.2	wrong
9	year
	this year
	next year
*	yes
4	Yes, thanks.
3	yesterday
3	young
14.2	zip up (verb)

Reading Word List

Skill Book 2 and its correlated reader *City Living* introduce the 262 reading words listed below, including 217 different words and 45 variants. Root words are listed as main entries. Variants with *-s* and *-'s* are not listed. Variants with *-s', -es, -ing, -ed,* and *-er* (comparative) are usually indented, but when only a variant is introduced, it is listed as a main entry. When the variant is in italics, the root word was introduced in *Skill Book 1.*

The number indicates the lesson in which the word is introduced. An asterisk indicates words introduced in titles or directions. The abbreviation *cr* stands for correlated reader.

13	*add
9	after
15.5 cr	another
15.3 cr	any
12	arm
12	Arthur
14.2 cr	ask
8	back
16.7 cr	bad
16.7 cr	badly
8	bag
12	barn
8	basket
8	bat
15.4 cr	battery
7	bed
6	bell
11	better
1	big
8	black
15.3 cr	– *boxes*
15.5 cr	bread
5	brick
4	bring
2	– bringing
5	brother
5	Buck
5	Bud
3	building
11	burn
11	– burned
11	– burning
14.2 cr	but
15.5 cr	butter
8	can
8	cannot
12	car
12	Carl
12	Carmen
15.3 cr	carry
8	– carrying
8	cat
6	cent
15.3 cr	center
10	Chan
14.2	*circle
3	city
10	clock
14.2	color
5	come
14.1 cr	– coming
15.4 cr	cop
13	*copy
11	cover
11	– covered
11	curtain
4	cut
4	– cutting
14.1 cr	dad
12	dark
15.4 cr	dead
16.6 cr	did
2	dinner
10	doctor
5	does
10	doll
10	dollar
10	Don
10	Dr.
14.2 cr	dress
14.2 cr	– dresses
15.3 cr	drop
10	– dropped
4	duck
6	Ellen
9	factory
8	family
12	far
12	farm
12	farmer
15.4 cr	fast
16.6 cr	– faster
11	father
11	fern
2	*fill
15.5	– filling
1	finger
11	first
3	Fisher
14.2 cr	fit
10	fix
6	Fred
6	fresh
7	friend
5	from
15.3 cr	fun
5	funny
12	garden
1	– *getting*
1	gift
1	– *giving*
9	glass
10	got
9	grass
5	gun
9	half
16.7 cr	happened
8	happy
12	hard
14.2 cr	hat
15.3 cr	– *having*
10	head
11	heard
6	help
11	– helping
6	hen
2	– *Hills'*
4	hit
10	hot

4	hunting
11	hurry
11	– hurried
15.3 cr	into
1	it
8	Jack
12	jar
12	jelly
3	Jimmy
10	job
10	John
15.3 cr	just
8	kill
3	King
14.1 cr	kiss
14.1 cr	– kisses
14.1 cr	– kissing
2	kitchen
3	Kitty
12	large
9	laugh
16.6 cr	– laughed
14.1 cr	– laughing
16.6 cr	left
15.3 cr	let
12	– let's
2	*letter
15.3 cr	lift
3	lily
15.5 cr	list
1	little
title cr	– *living*
10	lock
11	– *looked*
15.3 cr	lot
9	lunch
6	many
14.2 cr	marked
12	market
8	marry
15.5 cr	– married
11	match
14.2 cr	– matches
7	men
11	Miller
1	Miss
10	Molly
5	mother

3	Ms.
4	mud
15.4 cr	must
11	nurse
10	office
14.2	*or
14.1 cr	other
16.6 cr	park
12	– parking
15.4 cr	pass
15.4 cr	– passes
15.5 cr	past
9	path
11	person
11	– *picked*
3	picture
14.2 cr	pink
15.5	plan
15.5 cr	– planning
3	pretty
16.6 cr	puppy
8	quick
7	quickly
11	ran
8	rat
16.7 cr	ready
7	red
1	ring
10	rock
11	rug
11	– *running*
11	said
7	send
16.7 cr	seven
6	seventy
15.5 cr	– *shopping*
10	shot
7	sick
2	singing
1	sister
7	sit
2	– sitting
14.2 cr	six
11	skirt
14.2 cr	slim
8	Smith
5	some
4	son

8	standing
12	start
15.3 cr	– started
12	– starting
16.7 cr	stitches
16.7 cr	– stitched
10	stop
10	– stopped
15.4 cr	– stopping
5	stuck
1	*study
4	sun
8	that
7	them
11	then
15.5 cr	thing
5	think
15.4 cr	– thinking
10	Tom
10	top
15.4 cr	traffic
5	truck
15.4 cr	turn
6	twelve
14.2 cr	twenty
11	us
6	very
11	was
14.1 cr	watches
14.1 cr	– watching
7	well
16.6 cr	went
11	were
13	what
15.4 cr	when
15.4	which
2	whistle
14.1	who
6	will
3	windy
2	with
7	women
2	*word
12	work
12	– working
11	– *yelled*
11	– *yelling*